Melquíades, Alchemy and Narrative Theory: The Quest for Gold in
Cien Años de Soledad

Chester S. Halka

Holy Cross College

International Book Publishers
28021 Southfield Road • Suite 2
Lathrup Village, Michigan 48076

Library of Congress Card No.: 80-80261
ISBN: 0-936968-01-x

For Lumen and Debbie

Table of Contents

> Alchemy may be compared to the man who told his sons that he had left them gold buried somewhere in his vineyard; where they by digging found no gold; but, by turning up the ground about the roots of the vines, procured a plentiful vintage.
>
> FRANCIS BACON

Introduction

Cien años de soledad presents a narrative theory in which literature, to borrow a phrase from Antonin Artaud, is defined as "never real and always true". In the novel, the distinction between fictional events and the truths they can convey when properly understood, or deciphered, is developed through the use of a bifurcated quest, which has both literal and psychological branches. The goal of the former is material gold, while the latter seeks, ultimately, the correct understanding of a literary creation. This quest theme is a pervasive one in the narrative, beginning in the opening paragraph and culminating in the last, and directly involving twelve of the characters as it develops.

An examination of the narrative theory in García Márquez' masterpiece is facilitated by the presence of the three literary analogues: the author, Melquíades; his creation, the parchment manuscripts; and the reader, Aureliano Babilonia. A close relationship between literature and psychology emerges from the handling of these analogues, and from the related treatment of time and memory in the novel.

A basic understanding of the historical and philosophical characteristics of alchemy is pivotal in formulating the narrative theory in the work. An acquaintance with alchemy is especially helpful for interpreting the final events in the novel, where the transformative potential of literature is graphically represented in a consistently bisemic ending. Moreover, in *Cien años* alchemy is used as a metaphor for literature, and the narrator demonstrates a more than passing knowledge of this, as well as other, esoteric disciplines. The present study, therefore, begins with a brief consideration of the presence of alchemical material in the narrative, and a presentation of some background information on this often misunderstood "pseudo-science". In this exercise, and in others throughout this examination of *Cien años*, the work of two contemporary humanists who have studied alchemy, Carl Jung and the religious historian Mircea Eliade, is employed to approach alchemy and to help define its significance in the novel.

After the fundamentals of alchemy are set forth, the quest theme is identified, its pervasiveness in the narrative is demonstrated, and its dual, literal/psychological, nature is described. The characters involved in its respective branches are considered individually, in pairs of contrasting seekers, and in groups of characters who carry forward different phases of the same quest. Melquíades, who orchestrates the psychological quest, receives special attention.

In the second chapter, the dual nature of the consistent, bisemic ending is examined at length. The literal and symbolic facets of the conclusion are analyzed against the background of references, contained in the final paragraphs of the narrative, to religious and philosophical systems designed to effect psychological transformation, or "passage" to a different point of view. The presence of these references is coupled with an apparently incongruous prophecy uttered by Melquíades earlier in the work, to support an interpretation of the ending that is diametrically opposed to its literal sense. Resolving the conflict between the two readings of the narrative conclusion leads directly to an examination of the literary theory contained in *Cien años*, an exercise undertaken in chapter three. Also, in chapter two, is a discussion of the Tarot, another esoteric discipline employed in the work. An examination of the Tarot inclusions in *Cien años* complements and reinforces conclusions about the presence of alchemy in the novel.

Finally, in the third chapter, the narrative theory contained in *Cien años de soledad* is presented and scrutinized within the matrix of the literal/psychological dichotomy of the quest and the bisemic ending. The treatment of time and memory, the relation of literature and psychology, and three literary analogues—author, work and reader—are subjects addressed in this section. Literature emerges as a potential vehicle for revealing truths, assisting self-discovery, altering point of view, and setting the reader free from the prevailing cultural biases, enabling him to see "the other side of things".

❧ 1 ❧

The Quest for Gold

Melquíades and the Presence of Alchemy

in the Novel

"L<small>AS COSAS</small> tienen vida propia—pregonaba el gitano con áspero acento—, todo es cuestión de despertarles el ánima."[1] With these words, spoken by Melquíades, the characters of *Cien años de soledad* begin to speak for themselves. Melquíades is not only the first character who speaks, he is also the first one described; his importance to the novel is thus foreshadowed as the narrative begins. More has been written about Melquíades as the author of the parchment manuscripts than about his role as character in the work. These two roles are complementary, however, and his characterization can provide insights which are useful to a more complete understanding of Melquíades as an "analogue author," and also of the novel as a whole. While apparently well versed in a number of esoteric arts (astrology, demonology and prophecy are among those explicitly mentioned in the work), the gypsy wizard is primarily presented as an alchemist.

This link between Melquíades and alchemy is first established when he is introduced, in the opening paragraph of the narrative. Here he describes the magnets, "los hierros mágicos" with which he is to "awaken the soul" of the metal objects in Macondo, as "la octava maravilla de los sabios alquimistas de Macedonia (9)." Perhaps the most patent con-

nection is the alchemical laboratory this magician figure
presents to José Arcadio Buendía, "un regalo que había de
ejercer una influencia terminante en el futuro de la aldea
(12)." The brief description of this rudimentary laboratory is
interesting, for it suggests that the narrator has a more than
passing acquaintance with alchemy. Upon consulting the
several volumes Carl Jung has devoted to alchemy, which he
regards as the forerunner of depth psychology, the references given in *Cien años* are seen to be accurate. Maria the
Jewess, the distillation apparatus she invented, and the treatises by Moses and Zosimus, all mentioned in the novel, are
fundamental to alchemy. Nor is this description of the alchemical laboratory the only place where the narrator demonstrates a basic knowledge of this "pseudo-science."

It is primarily in relation to Melquíades that alchemy is
established and developed in García Márquez' work, and the
description of the gypsy, when examined in the light of
alchemical literature, indicates that the author's knowledge
of this esoteric practice may be substantial, and significant. In
the opening paragraph, Melquíades is described as:

> Un gitano corpulento, de barba montaraz y manos de
> gorrión, que se presentó con el nombre de Melquíades,
> hizo una truculenta demostración pública de lo que él
> mismo llamaba la octava maravilla de los sabios alqui-
> mistas de Macedonia (9).

Here we learn that Melquíades has "manos de gorrión" (a
characteristic referred to several times in the novel), and the
gypsy claims to possess the eighth wonder of the world, an
addition to the traditional seven. The bird association, winged and aerial, could call to mind Hermes-Mercury, the guide,
or familiar, of alchemists, and the controversy over "the
seven and the eight" is prominent in alchemical treatises.[2]
Also, he is dragging magnets, which attract metal, the alchemists' material. These are only hints, feeble by themselves perhaps, but soon after this we are told:

> Usaba un sombrero grande y negro, como las alas ex-
> tendidas de un cuervo, y un chaleco de terciopelo pati-
> nado por el verdín de los siglos (13).

Twice, then, there are "winged," "aerial" associations in the descriptions of the alchemist, to his sparrow-like hands and his raven-winged hat. It is interesting that the references are to his hands and then to his head, as true alchemy was a practice whereby manual operations in a laboratory represented, and eventually led to, a psychological transformation of the alchemist. The raven or crow figures prominently in alchemical literature. It usually refers to particular consecutive phases of the alchemical process called the *nigredo*, or *capus corvi*, and the *separatio*. As *Cien años* seems to contain two *nigredo/separatios*, we shall return to these terms below.

There are many more alchemical inclusions, and they pertain at various levels of the narrative. Some are passing references, others involve events, motifs, themes, or names of characters. Some are obvious, others less so. Examples include the name Aureliano, derived from *aureo*, gold, the goal of the alchemical *opus*, and the description of the first Aureliano Buendía as one who "había revelado desde el primer momento una rara intuición alquímica"(28). Another relates to the fusion of Úrsula's gold with a number of chemical ingredients, which results in "un chicharrón carbonizado que no pudo ser desprendido del fondo del caldero"(14). This corresponds exactly to one of the four principal phases of the medieval alchemical process, the *nigredo*. And later, in the separation of this same gold from the "jarabe espeso y pestilente" by José Arcadio Buendía and Aureliano, the succeeding phase of the alchemists' work, the *separatio*, is reflected. The role of ice in the novel, and the Colonel's golden fishes, are among other motifs, events and occurrences that can be interpreted alchemically, but the most interesting and far-reaching use of alchemy in the narrative involves the extensive quest for gold theme developed in García Márquez' saga. This, as well as the other inclusions of alchemical material, will be taken up in greater detail below. The point to be made here is that the author of *Cien años de soledad* does not seem to share the common twentieth century ignorance of alchemy. He is, at least, acquainted with its fundamental philosophy and a few of its mechanical operations, which implies that some knowledge of alchemy might contribute to a fuller appreciation of the novel. As I hope to demonstrate, this is so, for investigating the extent to which alchemy is used, and the manner in which it is employed, can be a surprisingly suggestive and provocative exercise. Ultimately, it provides a key to an understanding of ideas, contained in the novel, about narrative theory, a subject the work seems to address directly.

SOME ALCHEMICAL BACKGROUND

To begin with, a very brief synopsis of alchemy, and some of its history and philosophic underpinnings can be introduced. Alchemy represents a widespread world phenomenon. At present, extant treatises from Mesopotamia, China, India, Egypt, Greece and Western Europe have been discovered.[3] The symbols of alchemy display a remarkable variability, a trait which caused a great deal of confusion among artifexes, or alchemists, as all alchemical tracts required deciphering, and said so explicitly.[4] According to Jung, this variability of expression distinguishes alchemy from other, organized belief systems, such as Christianity, and approximates it to literary movements like surrealism. Such diversity is linked not only to a desire to protect the alchemical secrets from the abuses of the undeserving, but also to a cultivation of the imagination and richness of literary expression. Books and stories written by allegedly successful artifexes became a source of literary entertainment in the fourteenth century. The authors of these tracts were not serious practitioners of the alchemical art, but rather pseudo-alchemists who, nevertheless, "wrote with enthusiasm, in a style interesting and enticing."[5]

The fascination with alchemy common to the ancient world, and to Europe up through the sixteenth and seventeenth centuries, finds a counterpart in a contemporary Western interest in alchemical practices among several serious humanists. Foremost among these are the depth psychologist Carl Jung and the religious historian and scholar Mircea Eliade. As an historian, Eliade provides evidence to establish the widespread presence of alchemical and alchemically related thought, and its association with religious rites of initiation. True, or esoteric alchemy, is a mystical practice concerned with the psychological transformation of the artifex. Jung, who has devoted four entire volumes to alchemy, offers a theory which attempts to explain the significance of both alchemy and the religious experience, in psychological terms. As the investigations of both of these men are helpful to an understanding of the use and significance of alchemy in *Cien años*, and its importance to the narrative theory in the novel, they can be considered here, briefly.

Jung has called alchemy "the forerunner of depth psychology," which is the term for the Jungian approach to the study of the mind. All myths, according to Jung, are originally expressions of numinous experiences. (The *numinosum* is defined as "a dynamic agency or effect not caused by an arbitrary act of the will".[6] A numinous experience may be religious or secular in nature, but it is always psychological, and perceived as "revealed truth".) While for Jung the *numen* involved is the Self, the Jungian God-concept, traditionally it has been known as "Spirit" in religious systems, the almost exclusive realm of the numinous in Western society until this century. In the West, religions have been founded by individuals, based upon personal numinous experiences which are later codified into a fixed doctrine. Others can then partake of such numinous experiences "by reflection," that is, through the mediation of the religious code. There are advantages and disadvantages to such mediated encounters with the transpersonal regions, as Edward F. Edinger, an American Jungian psychologist, outlines in the following excerpt from his book *Ego and Archetype*:

> ...although collective methods [i.e., established religions] protect man from the dangers of the psychic depths, they also deprive him of the possibility of development which such experience promotes. As long as a living religion can contain members, there will be little need for the individual to have a personal encounter with the Self. He will have no need to find his individual relation to the transpersonal dimension. That task will be done for him by the Church.

This raises a serious question, i.e., whether modern Western society still has a functioning container for suprapersonal categories or archetypes. Or, as Eliot puts it, do we have no more than "a heap of broken images." The fact is that large numbers of individuals do not have living, functioning, suprapersonal categories by which they can understand life experience, supplied either by the Church or otherwise.[7]

Examining Christianity specifically, we encounter the doctrine of the Trinity, where the Father might represent the concept of numinosity, the Son the mediator through which the numinous is "made flesh", and the Holy Spirit the personal numinous experience in each individual Christian. Historically, then, the movement in Western religion has been toward an internalization of God by man: the Old Testament God is outside of man, the New Testament Christ is a God-man fusion, and the Holy Spirit represents the infusion of God into the individual. Medieval-Renaissance Church Fathers were conscious of the dangers inherent in the devotion to the Holy Spirit, which was likened to a wind which "bloweth where it listeth" [John, 3:8]. Therefore, the role of the third member of the Trinity was generally not emphasized, and movements like the *Illuminati* were discouraged. Some of the most "inspired" Christians ran the risk of imprisonment and/or being branded as heretics: Saint Theresa and Saint John in Spain, and Meister Eckhardt in Germany, are famous examples.

Introducing alchemy into this discussion, we can see how its practices fomented in individuals those inspired mystical states associated with the Holy Spirit of the Christian Church. (The identification of Mercury-Hermes, the guide and patron of alchemists, with the Holy Ghost, is not uncommon among medieval European alchemists.) The instructions for performing the *opus* tended to stimulate the individual imagination, rather than channel it into fixed rituals. And while it is true that alchemical literature does define procedures, it does so in a way which permits maximum personal interpretation and adaptation. Many alchemists evolved their own symbologies, and dreams, visions, and mystical experiences were common, and formed an integral part of the overall work.

Basically, both the Church and practices like alchemy were concerned with bringing the individual into contact with the transpersonal realm, the latter more directly, the former more indirectly, via the mediation of ridgidly fixed dogma. Many similarities between these two systems can be established, and, in the fifteenth through the seventeenth centuries this was, in fact, done.[8] Still, as alchemy was most akin to the mystical aspect of the Christian Church, there are also many differences between the two belief systems. According to Jung, its affinity with individual, non-mediated numinous experience constitutes alchemy's "compensatory relationship" to the Medieval-Renaissance Church, a Church which discouraged and even repressed such mysticism, in an attempt to maintain its ideological hold over a Europe inundated by recently discovered Classics of the ancient world. Here we come to an important stage in the history of alchemy and other Hermetical practices.

The thirst for mystical revelation seems to have been quite widespread in Renaissance Europe. Eliade observes that Cosmo de Medici, who entrusted Marsilio Ficino with the translation of the Plato and Plotinus manuscripts he had collected over the years, came upon the manuscript of what was later to be called *Corpus hermeticum*. He insisted that Ficino put all else aside and render it into Latin with all possible haste. The translation was completed in 1463, and is the first Greek text translated and published by Ficino. Eliade comments:

> This detail is important. It sheds light on an aspect of the Italian Renaissance ignored or at least neglected by the historians of a generation ago. Both Cosmo and Ficino were thrilled by the discovery of a primordial revelation, that is, the one disclosed in the Hermetical writings. And, of course, they had no reason to doubt the Egyptian, that is, the oldest revelation accessible—one which preceded that of Moses and which inspired Pythagoras and Plato as well as the Persian Magi....
>
> Such an extravagant interest in Hermeticism is highly significant. It discloses the Renaissance man's longing for a "primordial revelation"... It reveals also a profound dissatisfaction with the medieval theology and medieval conceptions of man and the universe; a reaction against what we may call "provincial," that is, purely *Western* Christianity; a longing for a universalistic, transhistorical, "mythical" religion.[9]

While the Church insisted that numinosity be identified with Christian dogma, even though it had lost much of its original vital force for many people, alchemy fostered the search for new forms of numinous contents within the "flask", the material projection of the artifex' mind.

To sum up, then, alchemy, in Europe, served to keep individual numinous experience alive, even at the expense of organized religion, and this phenomenon "compensated" for the Church's position of maintaining a unified community, even at the expense of a living religious, or psychological, experience. And it is in art, and especially in literature, that Jung, Eliade, and other humanists feel the work of alchemy and systems like it, the attempt to put the individual psychologically back into touch with the transpersonal realm, is being carried on in the modern world.[10]

Although many of the procedures associated with alchemy are extremely ancient, some dating back to the Babylonian metallurgists' trade, philosophically it is a child of the Greek Hermetic tradition. Alchemy, consistent with its Neoplatonic basis, assumes that all matter shares a common essence, though this might be manifested in very different forms. Fire and water, for instance, are theoretically interchangeable from an alchemical point of view. In fact, the union of these apparent opposites is a favorite paradigm for a successful alchemical *opus*, as it signifies the discovery of a state of existence, or of mind, wherein the *unus mundus* or cosmic identity of all forms, is manifest.

According to alchemical doctrine, Spirit is captive in Matter, and dependent upon man for its liberation. The Soul, of both the universe and the alchemist, first descends into Matter, where it is "captured," and later, after purification, it is separated and can ascend once again to Spirit. Since, for the alchemist, all matter is essentially interchangeable, the microcosm of his flask, or furnace, corresponds to the macrocosm of the universe. He attempts to hasten the process of universal purification inside his laboratory, with the guidance of a familiar, or supernatural agent, who assists his work. (In medieval Europe this familiar was Hermes-Mercury, often called Mercurius, the winged messenger of Zeus-Jupiter.) There are several phases in the alchemical dramatization of this cosmic process of purification and liberation. The alchemist begins by fusing some gold with a number of chemical compounds, thereby forming the *masa confusa*, or *prima materia.* This phase represents the descent of Spirit into Matter, and its consequent entrapment there. The rest of the *opus* addresses the task of liberating the gold, or waking the soul of all metals. If successfully performed, the result of the artifex' laboratory operations is the philosophers' stone, and a few grains of this substance was said to transmute great quantities of lead into pure gold. Before the work can be successfully completed, however, the *masa confusa* must pass through many permutations. Among these, the major ones are: the *nigredo*, a stage of dissolution and death; the *separatio*, wherein matter and the soul are separated, one from the other and the *albedo*, or dawn, the phase in which the breath that awakens the soul is liberated, and the soul is free to reascend into Spirit. Sometimes the *nigredo* and *separatio* are considered as two steps in a single phase, and in *Cien años* both a literal and a symbolic, or psychological, *nigredo/separatio* sequence can be seen. The *nigredo* phase represents chaos and putrefaction, and is often accompanied by images of death (the artifex'), desolation and total destruction. The *separatio* focuses on the separation of Spirit and Matter, and the potential for the subsequent liberation of the former. The *nigredo* and *separatio* are indispensable to the overall alchemical *opus*, for without them success, the "ascent", or *albedo*, is impossible.

The goal of the alchemical process is expressed as the transmutation of the *prima materia* or *masa confusa* into the philosophers' stone, the "true mercury," or "true gold" of the alchemists. There are literally hundreds of designations for this "stone", comparable to the numerous names for Christ, the central image of the Christian Church. (Christ was, in fact, a common cognomen for the philosophers' stone in Medieval-Renaissance Europe.)[11] Esoterically, the philosophers' stone, the alchemists' "true gold," represents spiritual enlightenment or self-discovery. The alchemical flask physically resembles, and also symbolizes, the artifex' head, the "furnace" wherein the "true", psychological, changes occur. As changes in the alchemist's mind do in fact transform the macrocosm, by altering his perception of it, alchemy, at the esoteric level, can be seen to make sense.

While the more intelligent practitioners of the alchemical art understood the *opus* symbolically, at least eventually, many did not. Stories of successful "projections" of mercury or lead into gold were widespread. Literal-minded alchemists really believed that all metals, other than gold, were imperfect gold, and would eventually be brought to perfection by Nature, in their flasks, with their alchemical assistance.

THE QUEST FOR GOLD

In the pages which follow, I hope to demonstrate that an alchemical quest for gold is developed in *Cien años de soledad*. As in alchemy, in the novel this theme is a dual one, involving both the external search for material, or literal, gold, as well as an internal search for psychological, or "true" gold. In the work, the latter motif is associated with inner peace, self-discovery and liberation, and the deciphering of the alchemist Melquíades' manuscripts. This bifurcated theme, whose branches are interwoven throughout the narrative, begins in the first paragraph and continues through to the last, involves almost all of the male characters directly, as well as most of the women, is reflected in various levels of the text (among them the linguistic, the literal and the symbolic), and is central to an appreciation of the role of alchemy and the narrative theory in the work. This theme is primarily developed in two ways, through time and in time. That is, the six Buendía men most directly involved in the two quests can be seen grouped in two ways: as three pairs of opposites, each pair "narrative contemporaries" whose quest activities are carried forth simultaneously; as two sets of three characters who develop the material and non-material aspects of the quest for gold theme in the novel through time.

THROUGH TIME
Two Groups of Three

		Three Material Seekers	Three Non-material Seekers
In Time	Three Pairs of Opposites	José Arcadio Buendía ..	Colonel Aureliano Buendía
		Aureliano Segundo	José Arcadio Segundo
		José Arcadio (3rd)	Aureliano Buendía-Babilonia

This theme will be examined from both of these perspectives, beginning with the second, those characters who are related by the nature of their quest. First, the three most involved in the quest for material gold, the founder, José Arcadio Buendía, Aureliano Segundo, and the last José Arcadio, will be considered.[12]

THE MATERIAL OR LITERAL QUEST

Gold is first mentioned in the opening paragraph of the novel, in a passage that could serve as a mental profile of the "literal-minded" alchemists mentioned above:

> José Arcadio Buendía, cuya desaforada imaginación iba siempre más lejos que el ingenio de la naturaleza, y aun más allá del milagro y la magia, pensó que era posible servirse de aquella invención inútil [Melquíades' magnets] para desentrañar el oro de la tierra (9).

This initial reference to gold is explicitly linked to alchemy. Not only does Melquíades describe his magnets as "la octava maravilla de los sabios alquimistas de Macedonia" a few sentences earlier, but his first words, "Las cosas tienen vida propia...todo es cuestión de despertarles el ánima," are also clearly alchemical, referring to "la liberación del soplo que hace vivir a los metales," a phrase found later in the novel (p. 38).

The first words uttered by José Arcadio Buendía in the narrative concern gold. They are addressed to Úrsula, after the founder has bought Melquíades' magnets: "Muy pronto ha de sobrarnos oro para empedrar la casa"(10). His enterprise fails, but the subsequent disenchantment is soon forgotten, and once again he seeks gold, this time within the flasks and retorts of the alchemical laboratory. Related to this second endeavor is another passage from the first chapter which makes the identification of the founder and the "literal alchemist" explicit:

> Además...Melquíades dejó muestras de los siete metales correspondientes a los siete planetas, las fórmulas de Moisés y Zósimo para el doblado del oro, y una serie de apuntes y dibujos sobre los procesos del *Gran Magisterio*, que permitían a quien supiera interpretarlos intentar la fabricación de la piedra filosofal. Seducido por la simplicidad de las fórmulas para doblar el oro, José Arcadio Buendía cortejó a Úrsula durante varias semanas, para que le

> permitiera desenterrar sus monedas coloniales y aumen-
> tarlas tantas veces como era posible subdividir el azogue...
> Entonces José Arcadio Buendía echó treinta doblones en
> una cazuela, y los fundió con raspadura de cobre, oropi-
> mente, azufre y plomo. Puso a hervir todo a fuego vivo en
> un caldero de aceite de ricino hasta obtener un jarabe
> espeso y pestilente más parecido al caramelo vulgar que al
> oro magnífico (14).

Obviously, at least at this point in the narrative, José Arcadio
Buendía is not one "quien supiera interpretar los apuntes y
dibujos sobre los procesos del *Gran Magisterio*". His interest is
focused exclusively upon material gold, and he initiates a
quest which is taken up by his great-grandson, Aureliano
Segundo. In the novel, several links are established between
the quests of these two characters. One involves an act by
Aureliano Segundo that recalls the founder's first words,
"Muy pronto ha de sobrarnos oro para empedrar la casa":

> un día en que Aureliano Segundo amaneció con el humor
> rebosado, apareció con un cajón de dinero, una lata de
> engrudo y una brocha, y cantando a voz en cuello las viejas
> canciones de Francisco el Hombre, empapeló la casa por
> dentro y por fuera, y de arriba abajo, con billetes de a peso
> (167-68).

A further echo of this link may be seen later in the story,
when Aureliano Segundo is searching for Úrsula's buried
gold:

> En el último año, le había mandado [Petra Cotes] recados
> apremiantes a Aureliano Segundo, y éste le había contes-
> tado que ignoraba cuando volvería a su casa, pero que en
> todo caso llevaría un cajón de monedas de oro para empe-
> drar el dormitorio (281).

Perhaps the most interesting connection between these
two characters and the material quest involves the concept
"Úrsula's gold". For his enterprises, José Arcadio Buendía
uses gold coins Úrsula received from her father, "que ella
había enterrado debajo de la cama en espera de una buena
ocasión para invertirlas" (10). Aureliano Segundo, whose animal lottery business has been ruined by the sempiternal
rains that visit Macondo after the massacre of the banana
company's workers in the plaza, begins to search for "la

fortuna enterrada en algún lugar que sólo Úrsula conocía"
(278). This is a reference to gold found in a plaster statue of
Saint Joseph left at the house by three strangers. The statue
is introduced into the saga precisely when Aureliano Segundo papers the house with money. Úrsula has workmen re-
move the pasted bills and repaint the house, and prays that
God return the family to its original poverty. Instead, the
San José complicates her situation.

> Sus súplicas fueron escuchadas en sentido contrario. En
> efecto, uno de los trabajadores que desprendía los billetes
> tropezó por descuido con un enorme San José de yeso que
> alguien había dejado en la casa en los últimos años de la
> guerra, y la imagen hueca se despedazó contra el suelo.
> Estaba atiborrada de monedas de oro... En los últimos
> tiempos, Úrsula le había puesto velas y se había postrado
> ante él, sin sospechar que en lugar de un santo estaba
> adorando casi doscientos kilogramos de oro. La tardía
> comprobación de su involuntario paganismo agravó su
> desconsuelo (168).

Úrsula buries the treasure under her bed, the same place she
had interred the dubloons José Arcadio Buendía used in his
alchemical experiments. Aureliano Segundo, despite a Tarot
card consultation with Pilar Ternera, who tells him the gold
cannot be found for at least three years, attempts to unearth
it immediately. The description of his enterprise provides
another link with José Arcadio Buendía, and also the idea of a
quest:

> Presa de un delirio exploratorio comparable apenas al del
> bisabuelo cuando buscaba la ruta de los inventos, Aure-
> liano Segundo perdió las últimas bolsas de grasa que le
> quedaban, y la antigua semejanza con el hermano gemelo
> se fue otra vez acentuando, no sólo por el escurrimiento de
> la figura, sino por el aire distante y la actitud ensimismada
> (279).

In passing, the renewed resemblance mentioned here between the twin brothers, the second "pair" of seekers we
shall consider, should be noted.

Aureliano Segundo is frustrated in his quest, but the gold
from the Saint Joseph is eventually unearthed by his son, the

last José Arcadio:

> Una noche vieron [José Arcadio and a friend] en la alcoba
> donde dormía Úrsula un resplandor amarillo a través del
> cemento cristalizado, como si un sol subterráneo hubiera
> convertido en vitral el piso del dormitorio (314).

While he is not searching for this particular gold (he is not
even aware of its existence), José Arcadio's material quest is
well established in the novel:

> José Arcadio, que abandonó el seminario tan pronto como
> llegó a Roma, siguió alimentando la leyenda de la teología
> y el derecho canónigo, para no poner en peligro la herencia
> fabulosa de que le hablaban las cartas delirantes de su
> madre, y que había de rescatarlo de la miseria y la sordidez
> que compartía con dos amigos en una buhardilla del Tras-
> tevere. Cuando recibió la última carta de Fernanda, dictada
> por el presentimiento de la muerte inminente, metió en
> una maleta los últimos desperdicios de su falso esplendor,
> y atravesó el océano en una bodega donde los emigrantes
> se apelotonaban como reses de matadero, comiendo maca-
> rrones fríos y queso agusanado (311-12).

José Arcadio, then, sails to America in search of gold ("la
herencia fabulosa"). Here, an interesting line of conjecture,
one which would bring the quest for material gold in the
novel full circle neatly, emerges. Sailing from Europe to
America in search of wealth, instead of in the name of God,
can recall fifteenth-century *conquistadores*. Besides suggesting
more universal parallels to actions in the fictional Macondo, a
motif common in *Cien años*, sailing from Europe to America is
one of several echoes, or similarities, involving the situations
of the last José Arcadio and that of a conquistador mentioned
in the opening paragraph of the work, a figure associated
with José Arcadio Buendía's initial foray for gold.

The first José Arcadio Buendía, attempting to unearth
gold with Melquíades' magnets, finds only:

> una armadura del siglo XV con todas sus partes soldadas
> por un cascote de óxido,... Cuando José Arcadio Buendía
> y los cuatro hombres de su expedición lograron desarticu-
> lar la armadura, encontraron dentro un esqueleto calcifi-
> cado que llevaba colgado en el cuello un relicario de cobre
> con un rizo de mujer (10).

In the scene describing the murder of the last José Arcadio Buendía, reflections of this *conquistador*, and of the first José Arcadio Buendía's lust for gold (and probably the conqueror's as well) can be seen:

> ...José Arcadio estaba terminando su baño diario cuando irrumpieron por entre los portillos de las tejas los cuatro niños que había expulsado de la casa. Sin darle tiempo de defenderse, se metieron vestidos en la alberca, lo agarraron por el pelo y le mantuvieron la cabeza hundida, hasta que cesó en la superficie la borboritación de la agonía, y el silencioso y pálido cuerpo de delfín se deslizó hasta el fondo de las aguas fragrantes. Después se llevaron los tres sacos de oro que sólo ellos y su víctima sabían dónde estaban escondidos. Fue una acción tan rápida, metódica y brutal, que pareció un asalto de militares. Aureliano...buscó a José Arcadio por toda la casa, y lo encontró flotando en los espejos perfumados de la alberca, enorme y tumefacto, y todavía pensando en Amaranta (317).

The remains of the military adventurer from the fifteenth century are uncovered when José Arcadio Buendía explores the region and the riverbed; José Arcadio dies by drowning, the result of an action "que pareció un asalto de militares". In both situations there are five characters present, one named José Arcadio Buendía, and four companions. the "rizo de mujer" found around the skeleton's neck, like a religious medallion, has its parallel in the description of José Arcadio's corpse, found "todavía pensando en Amaranta".

Whether or not these links between the last José Arcadio Buendía and the *conquistador* mentioned in the opening paragraph of the novel are intentional on the part of the author is, of course, moot. However, even if these echoes are purely coincidental, the presence and development of the quest for material gold in *Cien años de soledad* is left unaffected: it is a quest initiated by José Arcadio Buendía, the founder, and completed by the last character with this name, and a quest unified by the concept "Úrsula's gold".

THE NON-LITERAL OR PSYCHOLOGICAL QUEST

The quest for psychological or non-material gold, as well as the definition of its goal, are best cast into relief in a comparison with its counterpart, the search motivated by material wealth. This exercise is begun in the next section, but the salient, general interconnections among the three characters involved in this second branch of the quest can be offered now, and can serve as a useful background to the comparison which follows.

As with the first group, whose members can be called the José Arcadios, the Buendía men involved in the quest for "psychological gold", the first Aureliano Buendía, José Arcadio Segundo and Aureliano Buendía-Babilonia, can be considered the Aurelianos (see footnote 12). The name Aureliano refers to gold, and the first character to bear this name, the first character mentioned in the novel, is a metal worker who crafts little golden fishes. With these fishes, one of several associations between Colonel Aureliano Buendía and alchemy arises. The fish, because it has no eyelids and can therefore never close its eyes, is a favorite alchemical symbol for the alertness and concentration needed to complete the *opus*. In *Cien años*, both golden fishes and "ojos abiertos" are motifs linked with the "Aurelianos".[13] The first Aureliano Buendía also shares a workshop with Melquíades before the house is expanded, and he possesses "una rara intuición alquímica" (28).

Parallels and connections among the three characters involved in this branch of the quest abound. None of them has any part in perpetuating the Buendía line, something for which the "José Arcadios" alone are responsible. These characters who participate in the psychological quest form two great-uncle/great-nephew pairs, and the narrative explicitly establishes a type of confraternal atmosphere in both cases. Just as it was Úrsula who decided that José Arcadio Segundo, and not his twin, should have been named Aureliano, it is also she who realizes there is a bond between him and the Colonel:

Pero no tardó en darse cuenta de que él [José Arcadio Segundo] era tan insensible a sus súplicas como hubiera

podido serlo el coronel, y que estaban acorazados por la
misma impermeabilidad a los afectos. Aunque nunca supo,
ni lo supo nadie, de que hablaban en los prolongados
encierros del taller, entendió que fueran ellos los únicos
miembros de la familia que parecían vinculados por las
afinidades (225).

And this relationship, developed in the workshop the Colonel
previously shared with Melquíades, parallels one formed
later betweeen José Arcadio Segundo and Aureliano Buendía-
Babilonia, which evolves in "Melquíades' room":

Cuando Úrsula hizo abrir el cuarto de Melquíades, él
[Aureliano Buendía-Babilonia] se dio a rondarlo, a curio-
sear por la puerta entornada, y nadie supo en qué momento terminó vinculado a José Arcadio Segundo por un afecto
recíproco (295).

José Arcadio Segundo also teaches his great nephew Aureliano to read and write, and introduces him to Melquíades'
manuscripts, and their common efforts to decipher these
constitute the strongest, and most important, bond between
them.

Several curious parallels between Colonel Aureliano Buendía and his great nephew, José Arcadio Segundo, can be cited.
The former is born with his eyes open (20), and the latter
dies the same way (300). Both miraculously escape death,
repeatedly. The novel opens with a reference to the Colonel
facing a firing squad, suggesting a certain death, which,
however, does not occur. He also "escapó a catorce atentados,
a setenta y tres emboscados" (94), and even fails when he
attempts to take his own life (155-56). José Arcadio Segundo
miraculously escapes death on three occasions: the plaza
massacre, of which he is the sole surviving organizer; the
military search of Melquíades' room, during which he is
invisible to the young officer in charge (264); and in an
episode where he "escapó de milagro a cuatro tiros de revól-
ver que le hizo un desconocido cuando salía de una reunión
secreta" (252). His greatest fear is being buried alive, and he
makes Santa Sofía de la Piedad, his mother, promise to cut
his throat when he dies, something she does, in fact, do
(300).

Perhaps the most remarkable links to be found in this group of characters, however, are the physical similarities between the two Aurelianos, the Colonel and the eventual decipherer of Melquíades' manuscripts. At a certain point in the narrative, Úrsula asks Aureliano Buendía-Babilonia who he is. His response, "Soy Aureliano Buendía," elicits the reply: "Es verdad... Ya es hora de que empieces a aprender la platería" (289). And to Pilar Ternera as well, the characters with whom the novel opens and closes are physically identical:

la espléndida y taciturna anciana que vigilaba el ingreso... sintió que el tiempo regresaba a sus manantiales primarios, cuando entre los cinco que llegaban descubrió un hombre óseo, cetrino, de pómulos tártaros, marcado para siempre y desde el principio del mundo por la viruela de la soledad.
  —¡Ay—suspiró—, Aureliano!
Estaba viendo otra vez al coronel Aureliano Buendía, como lo vio a la luz de una lámpara mucho antes de las guerras, mucho antes de la desolación de la gloria y el exilio del desencanto... (333).

Finally, just as the novel opens with a reference to the Colonel in mortal danger, it closes with Aureliano Buendía-Babilonia, an exact look-alike of the Colonel before he went off to the wars, in a similarly threatening situation, with no apparent hope for escape. This parallel is discussed again below, in relation to the bisemic ending of the novel, the Tarot inclusions in the work, and the narrative theory contained in Cien años.

In the story, the contributions of the Colonel, José Arcadio Segundo and Aureliano Buendía-Babilonia to the quest for true gold, and their respective limitations, is reflected, interestingly, in numbers. The Colonel, when he finally returns from the war, eventually devotes himself to fashioning and melting down twenty-five golden fishes, in endless cycles. His purpose is explained in the words "la concentración implacable lo premio con la paz del espíritu" (174). His great-nephew José Arcadio Segundo, through the repeated readings of the unintelligible manuscripts, which reward him with a similar spiritual peace, eventually isolates the alphabet of the language in which the manuscripts are written: "Estaba seguro de que correspondían a un alfabeto de cuarenta y siete a cincuenta y tres caracteres,..." (296). His cyclical endeavors associate him with the number fifty [i.e., 47-53].[14] Aureliano Babilonia is also connected with a number in the novel, one hundred, as he deciphers the *pergaminos* when they reach that age:

> Melquíades...se iba tranquilo a las praderas de la muerte definitiva, porque Aureliano tenía tiempo de aprender el sánscrito en los años que faltaban para que los pergaminos cumplieran un siglo y pudieran ser descifrados (301-02).

So the concentration, the working alone, the cycles of golden fishes, the classification of the secret language and the final deciphering of the manuscripts are linked, one might say "esoterically", by the numerical progression 25-50-100.

Also, the events and descriptions associated with these three characters offer a parallel to the capture, purification and liberation of Spirit, spoken of in the section about alchemical philosophy. Although the first Aureliano Buendía is literally captured during the war, his "psychological" captivity is more significant. First through idealism, and later through despotism, his life of war is externally oriented, and he returns with a perspective irremediably transformed. This change of perception is represented in the narrative by the Colonel's inability to see either his father's phantom or Melquíades' room as the other family members do. The Colonel, who ultimately forges a pact with solitude, symbolizes a stage of psychological arrest, as if his involvement with the war definitively crippled him. His great nephew, José Arcadio Segundo, is initially identified with the Colonel, and in his role as union leader he carries on his great-uncle's involvement in external conflicts. Eventually José Arcadio Segundo, like the Colonel, retires from public involvements, and in Melquíades' room he undergoes a process of internal purification. He completely rids himself of the false ideas propagated by the historians and politicians about the Banana Company and the plaza massacre, and becomes the only person in Macondo in touch with the historical truth, and "el habitante más lúcido de la casa" (296). His purification is symbolized humorously when his twin brother Aureliano Segundo visits him after he has secluded himself in "el cuarto de las bacinillas", as Melquíades' room had been renamed, for six full months:

> Desde que abrió la puerta se sintió [Aureliano Segundo]
> agredido por la pestilencia de las bacinillas que estaban
> puestas en el suelo, y todas muchas veces ocupadas. José
> Arcadio Segundo...seguía leyendo y releyendo los perga-
> minos ininteligibles. Estaba iluminado por un resplandor
> seráfico...
>   —Eran más de tres mil—fue todo cuanto dijo José
> Arcadio Segundo—. Ahora estoy seguro que eran todos los
> que estaban en la estación (266).

In terms of the psychological quest, this purification is also
suggested in that José Arcadio Segundo dies with his eyes
open, the same way the Colonel was born, a fact which can
represent a recapturing of a lost perception. Finally, as regards liberation, Aureliano Buendía-Babilonia, who looks exactly like the Colonel before the war, is prepared by his
great-uncle José Arcadio Segundo to continue work on the
manuscripts. He is eventually successful in deciphering Melquíades' literature, and the psychological liberation he realizes in the process is discussed at length in the following
chapters.

The goal of the quest for "true gold" can be expressed in a
number of ways. An inner serenity that liberates the seekers
from the contradictions and pain of the outside world is one
such expression. Examples of this are "la paz del espíritu"
which Colonel Aureliano Buendía achieves through goldsmithing, the certainty and "el reposo" found by José Arcadio
Segundo in Melquíades' room, both harbingers of the enlightenment accompanying Aureliano Babilonia's act of deciphering the manuscripts at the close of the saga. Truth and
self-discovery are other expressions of the aim of this quest,
and ultimately, this goal is seen to be the transformation of
the point of view of a properly prepared reader (Aureliano
Babilonia), who correctly understands a literary creation (Melquíades' manuscripts). As mentioned above, however, this
psychological quest, and its goal, are most clearly seen when
juxtaposed to the literal search for material gold. And so, the
examination of the six Buendía men directly involved in the
two branches of the quest, taken as three pairs of "narrative
contemporaries", will be considered next. The pairs are: 1)

José Arcadio Buendía and his son, Aureliano; 2) the twins, Aureliano Segundo and José Arcadio Segundo; and 3) the last José Arcadio and Aureliano Buendía-Babilonia. The characters Remedios the Beauty and Fernanda del Carpio will also be examined, as they can be seen as embodiments of the two facets of the quest for gold.

JOSÉ ARCADIO BUENDÍA
AND COLONEL AURELIANO BUENDÍA

This pair begins its common labors in chapter two of the novel, when they set to work to separate the gold José Arcadio Buendía has fused with other substances to form "un jarabe espeso y pestilente más parecido al caramelo vulgar que al oro magnífico" (14):

> Si no perseveró [José Arcadio Buendía] en sus tentativas de construir una fábrica de hielo, fue porque entonces estaba positivamente entusiasmado con la educación de sus hijos, en especial la de Aureliano, que había revelado desde el primer momento una rara intuición alquímica. El laboratorio había sido desempolvado. Revisando las notas de Melquíades, ahora serenamente...en prolongadas y pacientes sesiones trataron de separar el oro de Úrsula del cascote adherido al fondo del caldero (28).

This passage introduces several motifs that are elaborated more fully as the quest for "true gold" is developed in the novel: the association of alchemy ("rara intuición alquímica"), with the "Aurelianos"; the re-reading of notes written by Melquíades; the "prolongadas y pacientes sesiones," which emphasize the time and patience characteristic of the Buendías involved in the psychological quest; and the *nigredo* and *separatio* phases of the alchemical *opus*. Soon after father and son begin on the "jarabe espeso y pestilente," which constitutes the *nigredo* stage of the alchemical process, we learn that the *separatio* has occurred, when they:

> alborotaron la casa con la noticia de que habían logrado vulnerar el cascote metálico y separar el oro de Úrsula.
>   En efecto, tras complicadas y perseverantes jornadas, lo habían conseguido. Úrsula estaba feliz, y hasta dio gracias a Dios por la invención de la alquimia...(32).

Earlier it was stated that alchemy was understood literally as well as symbolically. Literally, it is involved with the material level of the world and manipulations of physical matter, while esoterically it is related to the psychological state of the alchemist. The next chapter of this study examines how the literal *nigredo/separatio* seen here presages a second, corresponding process which occurs at the end of the work. In that final *separatio*, the character Aureliano Buendía-Babilonia is "separated" into the last Aureliano Buendía, the "animal mitológico", with the tail of a pig, and Aureliano Babilonia, liberated decipherer of Melquíades' literature.

As the tone of the quest for material gold is set by the founder, so the keynote for the second variation of this theme is set by what can be called his son Aureliano's revaluation of the precious metal. Colonel Aureliano Buendía is related to gold perhaps more than any other character in the novel. It becomes clear, however, that his initial attitude towards this metal is very different from his father's. He appreciates the artistic and aesthetic potential of gold, rather than its economic value. This is depicted early in the narrative:

> Preocupado por su ensimismamiento, José Arcadio Buendía le dio llaves de la casa y un poco de dinero, pensando que tal vez le hiciera falta una mujer. Pero Aureliano gastó el dinero en ácido muriático para preparar agua regia y embelleció las llaves con un baño de oro (41).

And, at the signing of the Treaty of Neerlandia, the Colonel again reflects a non-economic attitude towards gold, which is portrayed dramatically in the following passage:

> Con una parsimonia exasperante descargó [the treasurer of the liberal forces] los baúles, los abrió, y fue poniendo en la mesa, uno por uno, setenta y dos ladrillos de oro... El oro de la rebelión... [which] quedó fuera de todo control. El coronel Aureliano Buendía hizo incluir los setenta y dos ladrillos de oro en el inventario de la rendición, y clausuró el acto sin permitir discursos (155).

Finally, after the war, when he returns to his workshop and once more makes and sells golden fishes, why Aureliano practices goldsmithing is made explicit:

Con su terrible sentido práctico, ella [Úrsula] no podía
entender el negocio del coronel, que cambiaba los pescaditos por monedas de oro, y luego convertía las monedas de
oro en pescaditos, y así sucesivamente, de modo que tenía
que trabajar cada vez más a medida que más vendía, para
satisfacer un círculo vicioso exasperante. En verdad, lo que
le interesaba a él no era el negocio sino el trabajo...la
concentración implacable lo premió con la paz del espíritu
(173-74).

Ultimately, while Aureliano continues elaborating the golden
fishes, he stops selling them, reducing his "business" to
melting and recasting twenty-five fishes again and again, in
endless cycles.

Colonel Aureliano Buendía, then, initiates the spiritual
quest for "true", or psychological, gold in the novel. His
name reflects his association with gold, and his initial, non-
material interest in the precious metal is in striking contrast
to the desire for wealth manifested by his father early in the
novel. "Desde el primer momento" Aureliano displays "una
rara intuición alquímica," and he assists his father in the
physical *separatio* of Úrsula's gold. He also shares a workshop
with the alchemist Melquíades in the first part of the narrative, and he personifies the concentration and dedication
characteristic of the group of spiritual seekers.

Before continuing, with an examination of the twins José
Arcadio Segundo and Aureliano Segundo, a few words about
the development of individual characters versus development
of the two branches of the quest for gold theme warrant
mentioning. In this study, the primary interest is to trace
how the quests develop, rather than to consider how individual characters change in the novel. As stated before, after
he returns from war the Colonel does not see Melquíades'
room in the same way other members of the family do.
Moreover, he alone, of all the Buendías, can never see his
father's phantom underneath the chestnut tree. The episode
involving the young military officer who also sees the gypsy's
room with the Colonel's eyes (when he fails to see José
Arcadio Segundo sitting in it [pp. 264-65]), suggests that
Aureliano's perception has been irremediably transformed by
war. Whatever the significance of this "dis-association" of the

Colonel from other family members, and from Melquíades, such a change in character is completely consistent with the development the quest for gold theme receives in the novel. A complementary change in character is the state of "enlightened oblivion" ultimately reached by José Arcadio Buendía, which represents a mental condition diametrically opposed to his initial lust for gold. Although, at first, an example of a literal-minded alchemist, José Arcadio Buendía eventually arrives at a real understanding of many of Melquíades' secrets, and achieves spiritual peace. On the other hand, his son, the Colonel, begins to search for Úrsula's buried treasure when he is already old, as he decides to mount one last effort, "la guerra total," a plan which never materializes (pp. 209-10). The Colonel and his father, then, eventually exchange roles *vis à vis* the quest for gold in the novel. A parallel reversal also occurs with the second pair, José Arcadio Segundo and his twin brother Aureliano. The latter is the first to visit Melquíades' room and attempt to decipher the manuscripts, although he abandons both projects, definitively, when he meets Petra Cotes. The point to be made is that the two branches of the quest develop, and so do the individual characters, and the focus here is the development of the quests, rather than any changes which may occur in those who carry them forward.

José Arcadio Segundo and Aureliano Segundo

Whereas José Arcadio Buendía and his son Aureliano represent the initiation of the dual quest, and the final pair, Aureliano Buendía-Babilonia and the last José Arcadio represent its completion, the twin brothers signify its transitional phase. Just as Aureliano Segundo never succeeds in unearthing Úrsula's gold, but does father a successor who will, so his brother José Arcadio Segundo, while he never deciphers Melquíades' manuscripts, passes his knowledge on to his "spiritual son" and successor, who eventually does:

> Enseñó al pequeño Aureliano a leer y a escribir, lo inició en el estudio de los pergaminos, y le inculcó una interpretación tan personal de lo que significó para Macondo la compañía bananera, que muchos años después, cuando Aureliano se incorporara al mundo, había de pensarse que

contaba una versión alucinada, porque era radicalmente
contraria a la falsa que los historiadores habían admitido, y
consagrado en los textos escolares (296).

Besides the reference to the manuscripts, this passage
mentions something else germane to the quest theme, the
alternate, true, histories of the plaza massacre and the Banana Company transmitted by José Arcadio Segundo to Aureliano Buendía-Babilonia. Jung discusses how alchemy and
similar esoteric disciplines served to complement the prevailing canon of beliefs in medieval Europe. According to Jung,
practices like alchemy kept the channels to certain important
psychological truths open to individuals at a time when
official Church dogma had sealed them off. Aureliano Buendía-Babilonia knows the true history of the Banana Company, a reference to the three thousand persons massacred in
the plaza, but the majority of Macondo's inhabitants have
accepted "la verdad oficial de que no había pasado nada ... que
los historiadores habían admitido y consagrado en los textos
escolares" (295-96).

When Aureliano Buendía-Babilonia offers his alternate
explanation of the plaza massacre, the one he has absorbed
from José Arcadio Segundo, Fernanda, who believes the false
but historically consecrated "truth", is horrified. Her hus-
band, Aureliano Segundo, recognizes it as the version of his
brother, and the narrative offers a revealing and relevant
description of José Arcadio Segundo at this point:

Aureliano Segundo, en cambio, reconoció la versión de su
hermano gemelo. En realidad, a pesar de que todo el
mundo lo tenía por loco, José Arcadio Segundo era en
aquel tiempo el habitante más lúcido de la casa (296).

It is also made clear, in two related passages, that the
source of the truth about the plaza massacre engineered by
the Banana Company, which is transmitted by José Arcadio
Segundo to his great-nephew, is Melquíades' manuscripts.
After six months of reading and re-reading them, José Arcadio Segundo makes a single statement, a reference to the
plaza massacre: "Eran más de tres mil—fue todo cuanto dijo
José Arcadio Segundo—. Ahora estoy seguro que eran todos
los que estaban en la estación" (266). And the final statement

of his life, uttered as he dies, still reading Melquíades' manuscripts, is an echo of this one:

> El nueve de agosto, antes de que se recibiera la primera
> carta de Bruselas, José Arcadio Segundo conversaba con
> Aureliano en el cuarto de Melquíades, y sin que viniera a
> cuento dijo:
> —Acuérdate siempre de que eran más de tres mil y que
> los echaron al mar.
> Luego se fue de bruces sobre los pergaminos, y murió
> con los ojos abiertos (300).

Here, two points are noteworthy. First, the alchemist Melquíades' manuscripts are linked with true history, something
developed in the next chapter, when Aureliano Buendía-
Babilonia's deciphering is scrutinized. Secondly, the transmit-
ter of this esoteric, true history of the plaza massacre is
considered to be crazy by the society at large. The motif of
the truly wise man being mistaken for a fool by those who
espouse "official truths" is a common one in alchemical and
other mystical literature, and one discussed below when
Tarot inclusions in the novel are considered.

While José Arcadio Segundo is nowhere directly connected with material gold, his involvement in the quest for "true
gold" is well developed in several ways. One of these concerns the original resemblance between him and his brother,
mentioned previously, which returns precisely when Aureliano Segundo is searching for Úrsula's gold:

> la antigua semejanza con el hermano gemelo se fue otra
> vez acentuando, no sólo por el escurrimiento de la figura,
> sino por el aire distante y la actitud ensimismada (279).

In the narrative, then, José Arcadio Segundo's quest for
spiritual peace and truth, the repeated re-readings of the
parchment manuscripts in Melquíades' room, is concomitant
with his twin brother's search for gold.

The most elaborately developed link between José Arcadio
Segundo and the quest for gold theme, however, involves
several other characters and interrelated motifs. As will be
seen, two of these characters, his sister, Remedios the Beauty, and his twin brother's wife, Fernanda del Carpio, can
represent the two facets of the quest. The central event in

the series of interconnections of the two branches of this theme is the carnival which occurs in chapter ten of the novel. Before considering this specific event, however, the overall importance of chapter ten to the development of the quest for gold theme should be emphasized. In due course, how this chapter initiates a new "cycle" of the work will be examined, but here a brief enumeration of the various quest-related occurrences it contains can serve to illustrate how chapter ten develops many of the motifs under discussion in this study: 1) the twins's history is given here and the confusion surrounding their identities is prominently noted; 2) several references to material gold and to Melquíades' manuscripts are mentioned; 3) the Colonel reopens his work-shop; 4) Melquíades reappears for the first time since his death; 5) the Colonel's goldsmithing and the task of decipher-ing the manuscripts are linked by Aureliano Segundo, who tries, and definitively abandons, both endeavors, when he meets Petra Cotes; 6) the Saint Joseph statue filled with gold is discovered, and the last José Arcadio, who eventually dis-covers its contents, is born; 7) the carnival occurs. This last event, the carnival of Macondo, will now be examined.

REMEDIOS AND FERNANDA

Remedios has been proclaimed carnival queen, but in the middle of the celebration Fernanda arrives and Aureliano Segundo, to avoid discord, "sentó salamónicamente a Reme-dios, la bella, y a la reina intrusa en el mismo pedestal" (175). When a shooting fracas disrupts the festivities, the two queens are saved by the twins:

> En la confusión del pánico, José Arcadio Segundo logró poner a salvo a Remedios, la bella, y Aureliano Segundo llevó en brazos a la casa a la soberana intrusa . . . (175).

An examination of these two female characters reveals that each can be related, significantly, to the gold quest theme of the novel. Fernanda del Carpio is perhaps the least attrac-tive character we encounter in *Cien años*. Despite the pains taken by the narrator to place the blame largely upon her parents (her mother told her, when Fernanda was a child: "Somos inmensamente ricos y poderosos . . . Un día serás reina" (179), the "soberana intrusa" is nonetheless employed as a vehicle for introducing much that is negative about human nature into the novel. Among other things, she personifies formalism, both religious and social. Within the novel she is aptly symbolized by the "bacinilla de oro" that she brings with her to Macondo and into which she performs her bodily functions. To Fernanda this golden chamber pot is a treasure, but to other members of the family it serves as an object of ridicule. Its functional use, by association, already suggests a rather low opinion of what Fernanda represents, and an additional commentary is added when her son, the last José Arcadio, sells it and we learn: "...y la bacinilla heráldica que a la hora de la verdad sólo tuvo de oro las incrustaciones del escudo" (313).

Fernanda and "gold" are again linked, during the carnival, in the passage which introduces her to the world of *Cien años*:

El carnival había alcanzado su más alto nivel de locura... cuando apareció por el camino de la ciénaga una comparsa multitudinaria llevando en *andas doradas* a la mujer más fascinante que hubiera podido concebir la imaginación. Por un momento, los pacíficos habitantes de Macondo se quitaron las máscaras para ver mejor la deslumbrante criatura con corona de esmeraldas y capa de armiño, que parecía investida de una autoridad legítima, y no simplemente de una *soberanía de lentejuelas y papel crespón* [my emphasis] (174-75).

Fernanda, then, can be said to represent an apparent, external or "superficial gold", which suggests a parallel to the "literal" gold quest, one she is related to in several other ways. Not only is she rescued from the carnival by Aureliano Segundo, one of the "literal" seekers, but subsequently becomes his wife (following his successful "quest" to find her). They are parents of the last José Arcadio, the eventual discoverer of Úrsula's subterranean gold. Her relations with the "true quest" characters are, by way of contrast, consistently disjunctive: she fears the Colonel and avoids him whenever possible; she prohibits José Arcadio Segundo from entering the house after he becomes an employee of the Banana Company; and when the infant Aureliano Buendía-Babilonia is brought to the house by a nun, Fernanda "decidió ahogar a la criatura en la alberca tan pronto como se fuera la monja" (254). And while she never actually murders her grandson, she refuses to let him out of the house while she is alive, and even leaves orders for her son to continue this prohibition after her death.

Remedios the Beautiful, on the other hand, is related to the quest for "true gold" as Fernanda is to its opposite. Like her counterpart, Remedios is associated with two of the three characters who carry the related quest forward, Colonel Aureliano Buendía and José Arcadio Segundo. Moreover, one of her namesakes, *Renata* Remedios (Meme Buendía), is the mother of the third member of this group, Aureliano Buendía-Babilonia, and another namesake, Remedios (Moscote) Buendía, marries the Colonel.

Above we have seen how Remedios is rescued by José Arcadio Segundo from the carnival melee. Like him, she is perceived as mentally deficient, but again the narrative suggests that the opposite may be true:

> Parecía como si una lucidez penetrante le permitiera ver la realidad de las cosas más allá de cualquier formalismo. Ese era al menos el punto de vista del coronel Aureliano Buendía, para quien Remedios, la bella, no era en modo alguno retrasada mental, como se creía, sino todo lo contrario. "Es como si viniera de regreso de veinte años de guerra," solía decir (172).

Significantly, it is the Colonel, the initiator of the psychological quest, who identifies Remedios as extraordinarily lucid and possessed of exceptional perception. Her spontaneity and anti-conventional behavior receive more development in the following excerpts:

> Llegó a los veinte años sin aprender a leer y escribir, sin servirse de los cubiertos en la mesa, paseándose desnuda por la casa, porque su naturaleza se resistía a cualquier clase de convencionalismos (172).

> Lo asombroso de su instinto simplificador, era que mientras más se desembarazaba de la moda buscando la comodidad, y mientras más pasaba por encima de los convencionalismos en obediencia a la espontaneidad, más perturbadora resultaba su belleza increíble y más provocador su comportamiento con los hombres (199).

Remedios' manner contrasts sharply with the dogmatic and formal approach to life we find in Fernanda, an attitude well illustrated by two representative passages:

Hasta las supersticiones de Úrsula, surgidas más bien de la inspiración momentánea que de la tradición, entraron en conflicto con las que Fernanda heredó de sus padres, y que estaban perfectamente definidas y catalogadas para cada ocasión (183).

Fernanda, con muy buen tacto, se cuidó de no tropezar con él [Colonel Aureliano Buendía]. La exasperaban sus tazones de café a las cinco, el desorden de su taller, su manta deshilachada y su costumbre de sentarse en la puerta de la calle al atardecer. Pero tuvo que permitir esa pieza suelta del mecanismo familiar, porque tenía la certidumbre de que el viejo coronel era un animal apaciguado por los años y la desilusión, que en un arranque de rebeldía senil podría desarraigar los cimientos de la casa (184).[15]

Remedios and Fernanda are well integrated into the quest theme, and in a sense they serve to define its dual nature. Fernanda's gold-plated chamber pot is an apt parallel to the superficial nature of the literal quest for gold in alchemy. Remedios' "penetrating lucidity" is also an appropriate representation of the enlightened perception which the true alchemist sought. In fact, the phrase "como si una lucidez penetrante le permitiera ver la realidad de las cosas más allá de cualquier formalismo", recalls the description of the alchemist Melquíades' "mirada asiática que parecía conocer el otro lado de las cosas" (13). Fernanda's reality is mediated by religious dogma and social conventions, but Remedios, like Melquíades, José Arcadio Segundo and Aureliano Buendía-Babilonia, sees things differently, and perceives a reality at odds with the one generally accepted. And this latter, unpopular understanding is the true one, the narrative suggests. It is interesting in this context to consider a phrase from the first description of Fernanda:

la deslumbrante criatura con corona de esmeraldas y capa de armiño, que parecía investida de una autoridad legítima, y no simplemente de una soberanía de lentejuelas y papel crespón (174).

This excerpt, given Fernanda's association with religious dogma and social convention, suggests both the strong influence and the ultimate falsity of such externally imposed "truths". Remedios, by contrast, embodies a lucidity that links her to im-mediate reality, a truer perception of the world, and one "beyond formalism". Such a psychological state is precisely the goal of alchemy, the true philosophers' stone, and it was said to confer immortality. I mention this piece of alchemical esoterica here because Remedios, with her assumption into heaven, personifies immortality in the novel. That she disappears in a "viento de luz" is also suggestive, as light is the traditional symbol for true alchemical gold, and, indeed, for enlightenment in any religious or philosophic system. Immortality can also be seen as another link between Remedios and Melquíades, the guide of the spiritual quest, who announces at one point: "He alcanzado la inmortalidad" (68). Fernanda, on the other hand, is associated with death in the narrative. Her father, "un Caballero del Santo Sepulcro", has a funeral business, and she spends her early years making wreaths for the dead. When he dies, her father mails himself to the Buendía house in a coffin, and arrives as a pestilent health hazard. Finally, when Fernanda dies she is preserved by Aureliano Buendía-Babilonia according to a formula left by Melquíades. In a sense, then, Fernanda becomes "eternally dead", just as Remedios becomes immortal. This association of Fernanda with death can be seen as a judgment on her mediated reality, just as Remedios' assumption can represent her "otherworldly liberation", or enlightenment. Later, in the discussion on the narrative theory *Cien años* presents, how Fernanda and Remedios also symbolize the dual nature of literature, which corresponds to the bisemic gold of alchemy, will be developed.

MELQUÍADES

Before leaving the second phase of the quest for gold, one related to José Arcadio Segundo, Aureliano Segundo, and also to Fernanda and Remedios, it will be useful to consider Melquíades' involvement in this theme up to this point. He discourages the founder's quest for material gold in the opening paragraph of the novel, and later instigates the true quest by giving José Arcadio Buendía "un regalo que había de ejercer una influencia terminante en el futuro de la aldea: un laboratorio de alquimia" (12). The first pair, the Colonel and his father, is aided by the gypsy's notes as they perform their alchemical operations in search of the philosophers' stone. José Arcadio Buendía is more closely associated with the alchemical wizard, although their shared workshop, Aureliano's clairvoyance and "rara intuición alquímica" provide several points of contact between him and the sage. Aureliano's "rare alchemical intuition" is especially worthy of note in view of his revaluation of gold, and how this contrasts with his father's initial attitude.

Turning to the second pair of "seekers", we see Melquíades initially, but only temporarily, associated with Aureliano Segundo, who spends time in the gypsy's room before meeting Petra Cotes. Melquíades' first reappearance in his room, after his second death, is to the young Aureliano Segundo, who is the first Buendía to attempt to decipher the manuscripts (161). Eventually, however, and definitively, it is José Arcadio Segundo who becomes linked to the alchemical magus. For this family member, Melquíades' room can be seen as both womb and tomb, as here José Arcadio Segundo encounters peace and serenity, and later, death. Through the manuscripts José Arcadio Segundo also finds truth, and becomes "el habitante más lúcido de la casa", although this fact is not recognized by others.

From these two pairs a pattern begins to emerge. First, Melquíades gravitates away from the characters involved in the literal quest (he is very close to José Arcadio Buendía and originally intimate with Aureliano Segundo), towards those involved with its spiritual counterpart. (Actually, of course, it is the characters, as they change, who gravitate toward, or away from, Melquíades.) With the third pair in our series, the last José Arcadio and Aureliano Buendía-Babilonia, this pattern will be extended, as the former has nothing at all to do with the gypsy, while the latter is attracted to the manuscripts when young, and remains interested until he ultimately deciphers them. Secondly, Melquíades' influence gravitates away from the alchemical laboratory and the literal alchemical quest, to "Melquíades' room" and his manuscripts, which become the focal point of the non-literal, psychological, quest.

In terms of Remedios and Fernanda, who can be seen as embodiments of the two branches of the quest, Melquíades has no direct interactions with either, but several points of contact emerge between him and Remedios. Both are associated with immortality, Remedios by her assumption, Melquíades in several ways: his statement, "he alcanzado la inmortalidad" (68); his return from his physical death by drowning; and his room, which exists out of time for most of the narrative. Both these characters also apprehend a reality beyond mere appearances, Melquíades through his "mirada asiática que parecía conocer el otro lado de las cosas", and Remedios via her "lucidez penetrante" which puts her in touch with "la realidad de las cosas más allá de cualquier formalismo". Another link between the im-mediate realities of Remedios and Melquíades is seen in a description of how Melquíades, almost blind and deaf, nonetheless "se movía por entre las cosas con una fluidez inexplicable, como si estuviera dotado de un instinto de orientación fundado en presentimientos inmediatos" (67).

It can be said, then, that the alchemist Melquíades is first associated with goldsmithing, sharing a workshop with a character who later loses all contact with him. The contact between the Colonel and Melquíades is characterized by literal, or physical, gold, as is the gypsy's initial contact with José Arcadio Buendía. Later, Melquíades' presence is associated with the non-physical, supernatural nature of his room, which remains outside of the ravages of time, except in the eyes of the Colonel (and a young military officer). Thereafter, Melquíades is linked with the quest for truth, or psychological gold, a quest ultimately tied directly to literature and its proper apprehension.

AURELIANO BUENDÍA-BABILONIA AND THE LAST JOSE ARCADIO

With the final pair of seekers, the two quests are concluded. The last José Arcadio discovers Úrsula's gold and Aureliano Buendía-Babilonia deciphers Melquíades' manuscripts. These two characters have been associated with the respective quests already, in the sections dealing with the other seekers. Here it may be worthwhile to mention that each member of this final pair bears a remarkable likeness to a previous forebear involved in one of the quests. The resemblance between Aureliano Buendía-Babilonia and the Colonel, the initiator of the spiritual branch, has been alluded to above, and it is paralleled by one between the last José Arcadio and Fernanda, the embodiment of the literal branch: "Era imposible concebir un hombre más parecido a su madre (309)".

As stated previously, the pattern of Melquíades' gravitation away from the literal quest, and toward its spiritual counterpart, continues with this final pair. Although the last José Arcadio is never directly associated with Melquíades, the description of his discovery of "Úrsula's gold" parallels one of the gypsy's remarks concerning the future of Macondo. This remark, which is analyzed in the next chapter, is cardinal to our study and relevant to the completion of the other quest, the one for "true gold", which occurs when Aureliano Buendía-Babilonia deciphers Melquíades' manuscripts. Similarities in these two passages serve to link the conclusions of the respective quests, just as the return of physical similarities linked the quests of the twins, and as the common task, the *separatio*, linked their respective initiations:

> Una noche vieron [José Arcadio and a friend] en la alcoba donde dormía Úrsula un resplandor amarillo a través del cemento cristalizado, como si un sol subterráneo hubiera convertido en vitral el piso del dormitorio (314).

> Una noche creyó [Melquíades] encontrar una predicción sobre el futuro de Macondo. Sería una ciudad luminosa, con grandes casas de vidrio, donde no quedaba ningún rastro de la estirpe de los Buendía (52-53).

Both passages deal with "discovery", and certain parallels between the two are patent: each begins with the same words, "Una noche"; "un resplandor amarillo" and "sol", from the first excerpt, echo "luminosa" from the second; "cemento cristalizado" and "vitral" strike a correspondence with "casas de vidrio"; the idea of a refulgent, luminous cement is common to both.

There are other similarities, and these are taken up in the next chapter, when the completion of the psychological quest is examined in greater detail. Now, however, some of these parallels can be mentioned, at least. Perhaps the most striking one involves the passage describing José Arcadio's discovery of Úrsula's gold (the completion of the literal quest), and a passage depicting Aureliano Buendía-Babilonia's deciphering of Melquíades' manuscripts (the completion of the psychological quest), which is as follows:

> y no tuvo serenidad para sacarlos a la luz, sino que allí mismo, de pie, sin la menor dificultad, como si hubieran estado escritos en castellano bajo el resplandor deslumbrante del mediodía, empezó a descifrarlos en voz alta (349).

The linguistic similarity in the phrases "resplandor amarillo" (material gold), and "resplandor deslumbrante del mediodía" (light, or psychological gold), underlines another, more significant, parallel: the obstacles between José Arcadio and the gold (physical cement), and between Aureliano Buendía-Babilonia and an understanding of the manuscripts (Melquíades' code), are rendered transparent by light emitted by the goals of the respective quests. Both quests, then, end similarly, seeming to come to completion on their own.

Several contrasts between the two characters of this third and final pair of seekers can be established, and such an exercise suggests information which will be helpful when the novel's ending is investigated. I wish to consider three such contrasts, or links, which can be summarized by the following key words: 1) mothers; 2) incest; 3) el baño or la alberca.

First, considering "mothers" leads to Fernanda and Pilar Ternera. The former is literally the mother of José Arcadio, while the following excerpt suggests that the latter is a surrogate mother for the orphan Aureliano:

> Aquel burdel verdadero [El Niño de Oro] con aquella dueña maternal, era el mundo con que Aureliano había soñado en su prolongado cautiverio (333).

Soon after, in the same context, we see Pilar Ternera address him this way: "Bueno, niñito...ahora dime quién es" (334). The name of her brothel, El Niño de Oro, is significant in alchemy, a fact developed as the study proceeds. It also represents Pilar's explicit link to the quest for gold theme, which is pursued later, too.

Incest and *el baño*, or *la alberca*, are related within the narrative. Above, when we discussed the connection between the last José Arcadio's death and the quest for gold theme, we noted the site of death was "el baño", and that when found, he was still thinking of his great-great aunt Amaranta, the object of his frustrated incestuous affection. Aureliano Buendía-Babilonia consummates an incest with his aunt Amaranta Úrsula, and discovers, in the closing paragraph of the novel, "el instante de su propia concepción entre los alacranes y mariposas amarillas de un baño crepuscular" (350), the same place where José Arcadio dies. Also mentioned above was Fernanda's decision, never executed, to drown Aureliano Buendía-Babilonia "en la alberca", the same spot where her son is eventually drowned. Mediated by the concepts incest and *baño*, then, the last José Arcadio is associated with "frustration" and "death", whereas Aureliano Buendía-Babilonia is linked to "consummation" and "seed of life".

Both incest and the bath appear in alchemy as symbols. Incest is a common alchemical image for the *coniunctio oppositorum*, or union of opposites. The *coniunctio* is the means to creating the philosophers' stone, or, in other words, to completing the *opus*. Understood symbolically, incest signifies the perfect integration of similar and dissimilar elements. The result of successful "alchemical incest" is sometimes represented by the *rebus* (literally, "two things"), a hermaphrodite, or by the *homunculus*, that is, the Golden Child. The bath represents the dissolution of the bonds which subjugate Spirit to Matter, and is associated with the *nigredo* phase of the work, and sometimes with the *separatio* as well. This dissolution is often imaged as death by drowning, and it constitutes a crucial step in the liberation of the soul. Significantly, the alchemist Melquíades drowns, only to return as spirit, a presence in his room. Remedios the Beauty, who represents the spiritual quest in the novel, and is never really subject to material considerations, spends hours in the bath every day, before ultimately separating from her earthbound existence. The last José Arcadio Buendía, the character who completes the material quest, dies there, and Aureliano Buendía-Babilonia is conceived there, by someone named Renata Remedios Buendía. (The alchemical bath is explicitly mentioned in the narrative as well (p. l4). It is the "alambique de

María la judía", also called "el baño de María" in Spanish alchemical tracts. It is where the literal alchemical *opus* is carried forth.)

In terms of alchemical parallels, Aureliano Buendía-Babilonia's conception in the *baño* of the Buendía house identifies him with the *prima materia*, the alchemical material which the artifex sought to bring to perfection. Interestingly, when brought to perfection at the consummation of the *opus*, this *materia* is transformed into the philosophers' stone, also called the "golden embryo", "golden seed", or, again, "golden child". Aureliano's name (from the Latin diminutive for "golden"), his relation to the maternal Pilar Ternera (whose brothel is named *El Niño de Oro*), and especially the psychological *separatio* at the end of the novel (which consummates the quest for true gold), suggest that his conception in the *baño* can be linked consistently to the entire alchemical process. Developing this idea is an exercise undertaken in the next chapter.

CONCLUSION

Cien años de soledad, then, contains a quest for gold theme which has two branches interwoven throughout the narrative. One branch is concerned with literal gold, the metal, and its development is rather straightforward. The other branch is more complex, but nonetheless clearly developed. It begins with a revaluation of gold by a character who possesses "una rara intuición alquímica" and shares a workshop with the alchemist Melquíades, the orchestrator of this search. Inner peace, truth, and discovery of self are ideas associated with this facet of the quest, and they lend it a psychological color.

Such a bifurcated quest parallels the search of the alchemist in many ways, most significantly in its dual, "literal/true (or psychological)" nature. From the opening paragraph alchemy is used, and by someone who is apparently quite well-versed in its fundamentals, to develop the two facets of the gold quest in the novel. Alchemy, in conjunction with an extensive network of interconnections among various characters, facilitates establishing parallels between the quest for material gold and the quest to decipher Melquíades' manuscripts.

The basic alchemical dichotomy of literal versus true understanding, which is reflected in the quest for gold, emerges again in the consistent, bisemic ending of the novel, and forms the basis for the narrative theory contained in *Cien años de soledad*. A discussion of the specifics of this narrative theory forms the core of chapter three of this study, and the definition and interpretation of the bisemic ending is the central focus of chapter two, and the exercise to which we now turn.

NOTES

[1] Gabriel García Márquez, *Cien años de soledad* (Buenos Aires: Edit. Sudamérica, 1967), p. 9. All future references are to page numbers of this edition and will appear parenthetically in the body of the study.

[2] In alchemy, the "dilemma of the seven and eight" is an established controversy, whose nature need not concern us here. For details, see C. G. Jung, *Psychology and Alchemy*, trans. R. F. C. Hull, 2nd ed., Vol. XII of *The Collected Works of C. G. Jung* (Princeton: Bollingen, 1968), pp. 67, 154-55, 162 and figure 85.

[3] Other parts of the world may have developed similar practices which were either never recorded, or whose records were eventually destroyed. The myth of "El Dorado", the original Guarani Indian version and not the Spanish interpretation of it, is a case in point. To the Indians it signified a "lost paradise", and its attainment represented "eternal felicity". This true version of the myth was discovered only quite recently by the West, in 1912 (see Mircea Eliade, *The Quest: History and Meaning in Religion* (Chicago, Univ. of Chicago Press, 1969), pp. 101-02). It seems that the universal recognition of gold as something precious, coupled with an apparently ubiquitous belief in the duality of existence and man's innate spiritual aspiration, have resulted in the spontaneous generation of "alchemy", by whatever name, the world over.

[4] See Mircea Eliade, *The Forge and the Crucible* (London, Rider and Co., 1962), p. 164.
    Another aspect of multiple alchemical designations can be seen reflected in *Cien años*, in certain events which echo the multitude of names medieval artifexes gave to their societies. The image of Melquíades illuminated against a window, which forms part of the hereditary memory that is passed along from one generation of Buendía's to the next, finds an echo in "Les Chevaliers de la Fenêtre". Other associations which seem relevant to the novel are

"les Ilumines, les Invisibles, les Frères initiés de l'Asie, les Chevaliers du Bain, de la Bête morte (recalling the Wandering Jew, p. 292), de l'Amarante" [Luis Sauné, *L'influence des chercheurs de la "Médicine Universelle" sur l'Oeuvre de François Rabelais* (Paris: Librairie E. Le François, 1935), p. 21]

5 A. J. Hopkins, *Alchemy: Child of Greek Philosophy* (New York: Columbia University Press, 1934), p. 201. It seems worth noting in passing that these "true" alchemical adventure stories are similar to other imaginative literature of the time, such as the romances of chivalry. In view of the "God, Gold and Glory" motivation of the XV and XVI Century New World colonization, the influence of this kind of literature, and the role it played in settling the American continent, has interested many scholars. For Eliade's stimulating insights on the relation of eschatology to colonization see *The Quest*, especially pp. 88-97.

6 C. G. Jung, *Psychology and Religion: West and East*, 2nd ed., trans. R. F. C. Hull, Vol. XI of *The Collected Works* (Princeton, Bollingen, 1969), p. v.

7 Edward F. Edinger, *Ego and Archetype: Individuation and the Religious Function of the Psyche* (Baltimore: Penguin, 1972), p. 64.

8 The most famous, at least today, is probably a work entitled *Aurora Consurgens*, generally listed as an apocryphal work of Saint Thomas. It was discovered by Jung and translated by one of his disciples, Marie-Louise von Franz.

9 Eliade, *The Quest*, p. 108.

While alchemy was perhaps the most widespread embodiment of this "psychological compensation" of Christianity, it was not the only one. Alfred Douglas, in his *The Tarot: The Origins, Meaning and Uses of the Cards* (New York: Taplinger, 1972), has noted that Tarot cards were used in the rites of initiation of Medieval-Renaissance secret societies, and the "secret" they revealed related directly to a personal numinous experience, the discovery of an internal guide and voice.

10 See, for example, André Breton, *Manifestoes of Surrealism*, trans. R. Seaver and H. R. Lane (Ann Arbor: U. of Michigan, 1972), pp. 123-24. Also see Mircea Eliade, *Rites and Symbols of Initiation: The Mysteries of Birth and Rebirth*, trans. Willard R. Trask (New York: Harper and Row, 1958), pp. 134-35. See also Hans Meyerhoff, *Time in Literature* (Berkeley: U. of California, 1968), p. 78, and pp. 118-19.

Jung's Individuation process of psychological integration is based on the myth of the hero, and he draws upon modern, as well as ancient literature extensively in his works.

11 The following passage is from Eliade's *The Forge and the Crucible*:

A small book which appeared in London in 1652—*The Names of the Philosopher's Stone*—records more than 170 names for it, among which are: the Virgin's Milk, the Shade of the Sun, Dry Water, Saliva of the Moon, etc. Pernety, in his *Dictionnaire mytho-hermétique* (Paris, 1787), gives an incomplete alphabetical list of about 600 names (p. 164).

[12] If material gold is defined more generally, as wealth, then the first José Arcadio, who usurps all of Macondo's land (pp. 138-39) can be included in this group also. This group would then be comprised of all the José Arcadios in the work except José Arcadio Segundo (who belongs to the other, psychological, group), and it would also include his twin brother Aureliano Segundo. However, the novel refers several times to the confusion of the twins' identities, suggesting that the character called José Arcadio Segundo is really Aureliano Segundo, and *vice versa*. One exemplary passage can serve as a summary: "Tal vez fue ese entrecruzamiento de estaturas, nombres y caracteres lo que hizo sospechar a Úrsula que estaban barajados desde la infancia" (160). (For others, see pages 151, 160, 224, and 300). Because of drunken gravediggers, the twins are, in fact, buried under each other's names.

I have used this confusion surrounding the twins' identities, something that is reinforced by their statures, temperaments, and events in the novel, to regard Aureliano Segundo as another José Arcadio, which would mean that the four characters bearing the name José Arcadio Buendía are involved in the quest for material gold. Conversely, the other group would be made up of the three Aureliano Buendías who appear in the novel, including the character called José Arcadio Segundo. (Actually, there are also four Aurelianos, if the child with the tail of a pig is also included. As we shall see later, he should be.) The significance of such a division is twofold. First, it provides a consistent, and therefore an encouraging, separation of the Buendía men. More important, both names are connected with the quest for gold theme: *José* with the statue of San José that is filled with gold, and is a central object in the material quest in *Cien años*; and *Aureliano*, derived from the Latin *aureus*.

Finally, it is also worth noting that only two male Buendías are missing from the quest for gold as it is developed in this study, and, perhpas meaningfully, neither is called José Arcadio or Aureliano. These are Arcadio and Aureliano José, both of whom are killed while still adolescents.

[13] The eyes are the essential tool for implementing the ultimate deciphering of Melquíades' manuscripts, one expression of the goal of the "true", or psychological, quest. The Colonel is born with his eyes open and José Arcadio Segundo dies the same way (upon Melquíades' manuscripts). Additionally, José Arcadio Segundo is described at one point as having "los ojos árabes" (264), a phrase which echoes "la mirada asiática" (13) of Melquíades. A description

of Mauricio Babilonia, Aureliano Buendía-Babilonia's "physical" father, suggests Aureliano may be particularly equipped to penetrate
the secrets of Melquíades' writings: "Era joven, cetrino, con unos
ojos oscuros y melancólicos que no le habrían sorprendido tanto [a
Fernanda] si hubiera conocido a los gitanos..." (242). And, finally,
to buy the Sanskrit primer and the other books necessary for his
deciphering, Aureliano Buendía-Babilonia uses the Colonel's golden
fish for money.

14 The Sanskrit alphabet has, in fact, a varying number of characters, depending upon the source consulted. The *sacred* Sanskrit
alphabet, which is used to express the truths revealed by the gods in
the *smitri*, i. e., "hearing", or "revealed" literature, has exactly fifty,
invariably, and is considered perfect. (The word *sanskrit* means
"perfect".) The Sanskrit nature of Melquíades' manuscripts is discussed at greater length in chapter 3.

15 Two other examples of Fernanda's association with convention,
and Remedios' disdain for it, have been suggested by Audrey Aaron
in "The Total Innovation of García Márquez' *Cien años de soledad*", a
talk delivered at Wheaton College on February 28, 1976. She points
out how, according to Claude Levi-Strauss, silverware and clothing
can be seen as mediators, between man and food, and between the
individual and society, respectively. Applying Ms. Aaron's comments
to Fernanda and Remedios, we can observe that it is Fernanda who
has brought the multiple place settings to the house and who insists
upon their daily, formal use in the dining room. (Remedios is made
to eat in the kitchen, so as not to be seen by the *forasteros*, and there
"se sintió más cómoda porque al fin y al cabo quedaba a salvo de toda
disciplina" (201).) Also, unlike Remedios' proclivity to go naked,
"...que, según ella entendía era la única forma decente de estar en
casa" (199), Fernanda, when her religious calendar finally permits
her to consummate her marriage, receives Aureliano Segundo in:

> Un camisón blanco, largo hasta los tobillos y con mangas hasta
> los puños, y con un ojal grande y redondo primorosamente
> ribeteado a la altura del vientre. Aureliano Segundo no pudo
> reprimir una explosión de risa.
> —Esto es lo más obsceno que he visto en mi vida—grito,
> con una carcajada que resonó en toda la casa—. Me casé con
> una hermanita de la caridad (182).

Una noche creyó [Melquíades] encontrar una predicción sobre el futuro de Macondo. Sería una ciudad luminosa, con grandes casas de vidrio, donde no quedaba ningún rastro de los Buendía. "Es una equivocación", tronó José Arcadio Buendía. "No serán casas de vidrio sino de hielo, como yo lo soñé, y siempre habrá un Buendía, por los siglos de los siglos." (pp. 52-53)

The new world is not just an "inner reality" that adds itself to the "old world"—it is total reality.

—Anonymous author of
Aurora Consurgens, an alchemical treatise

❧ 2 ❧

The Completion of
the Psychological Quest

THE EXAMINATION of the quest theme culminates in a consideration of the character Aureliano Buendía-Babilonia and the closing paragraphs of the novel. It is here, with the deciphering of Melquíades' manuscripts, that the quest for "true gold" is consummated. As has been seen above, the material/ psychological division applied to the quest in the work is fundamental to alchemy, and in the present chapter this dichotomy is employed to scrutinize characters and passages which seem to have not only literal, but also symbolic import. This exercise is carried out at some length, for two purposes. First, to establish further the pervasiveness of the use of alchemy in the novel, as several events and descriptions take on greater significance only against the background of an acquaintance with alchemy, its symbols and its practices. Secondly, and more importantly, the consideration of such material provides a convenient scaffolding for the non-literal interpretation of the bisemic ending of the novel.

The first part of the discussion undertaken below concerns itself primarily with the second, psychological, *nigredo* and *separatio* of the narrative. These parallel the *nigredo* and *separatio* of Úrsula's gold which were discussed earlier, and they constitute the internal correspondences to physical laboratory operations analyzed previously. They occur in Aureliano Buendía-Babilonia's mind, and bring the quest for "true gold" to completion. The phase of the alchemical *opus* that succeeds the *separatio*, the *albedo*, is also discussed.

Subsequently, alchemy is seen as representative of a number of belief systems designed to effect a psychological "passage" from one point of view to another, and the many references to such passage, or systems of passage, which the final paragraphs of the novel contain, are identified and examined. Similarities between events and descriptions from the ending of the novel and historical initiatory scenarios are presented and evaluated, and the connection of such inclusions to the use of alchemy in the narrative is explained. One of these kindred systems, the Tarot, which had the same aims as alchemy in Medieval-Renaissance Europe, receives special scrutiny. Its presence in the novel is not limited to the final paragraphs, but rather is linked to Pilar Ternera, a character whose role in *Cien años de soledad* complements Melquíades' in several significant ways. Finally, how the alchemical, Tarot, and other related material contributes not only to identifying the symbolic ending that coexists with the literal one, but also to a proper interpretation of the bisemic ending itself, is addressed.

Earlier, it was observed that the laboratory operations of the alchemist signify parallel mental processes. The flask itself represents the artifex' head, and the changes occurring within the laboratory apparatus as the *opus* progresses reflect, at least ideally, psychological changes inside the alchemist's mind. As regards the *nigredo* phase of the work, the external chemical reaction corresponds to internal psychic suffering, the dissolution of previously held ideas into a state of chaos, what might be called the psychological death of the artifex. (The phrase "dark night of the soul" captures the sense of this stage of the alchemical process.) The literal *nigredo* in *Cien años*, the fusion of Úrsula's gold with other substances that produces "un jarabe espeso y pestilente" (14), is an apt alchemical description of the external counterpart of the internal, mental *nigredo*. In the *separatio*, which succeeds the *nigredo*, the gold and the dross are separated. This phase prepares the alchemical material, and, concomitantly, the alchemist's mind, for the final phase of the *opus*. Then, in the last step of the process, the divine breath, or Spirit, which animates the metals and gives them eternal life, is liberated. In the narrative, there are two explicit references to this final stage. The first words spoken in the story, by the alchemist Melquíades, concern the soul of the metal objects his magnets have brought to life: "Las cosas tienen vida propia... todo es cuestión de despertarles el ánima" (9). A second reference, to "la liberación del soplo que hace vivir los metales" (38), occurs, significantly, after José Arcadio Buendía and his son Aureliano have separated Úrsula's gold, and are actively pursuing the philosophers' stone. Within the novel, the wind that carries Remedios the Beauty away can be seen as a possible personification of this "soplo". As I seek to demonstrate below, the "huracán bíblico" at the end of the saga can also be seen in this light.

The psychological *nigredo* is often precipitated by severe personal shocks, and associated with images of death and the grave. Success at this stage (represented by the *separatio*), however, means that the ascent towards the great synthesis has been initiated, as the next step is the *albedo*, or dawn, regarded by some alchemists as assuring the end of the *Gran Magisterio*, and by the others as the end itself. Psychologically, then, as well as physically, the *nigredo* and *separatio* represent the turning point in the alchemical process. And, in alchemy, these internal and external events correspond, that is, they occur simultaneously outside and inside of the artifex. In what follows, I seek to show how, in the final paragraphs of the novel, a correspondence is established between events outside, and inside, of Aureliano Buendía-Babilonia's mind. Occurrences reflecting the *nigredo*, *separatio* and *albedo* stages of the alchemical *opus* can be observed, and their presence and significance can be helpful to a greater overall understanding of the novel.

NIGROMANTA

To establish the psychological parallel to the material separation of Úrsula's gold by José Arcadio Buendía, let us begin by considering Nigromanta, Aureliano Buendía-Babilonia's black mistress. This character is introduced towards the end of the narrative, and several links between her and alchemy appear. Perhaps the most obvious is contained in her name, which like Aureliano's (*aureo* - gold), can be seen to relate to the esoteric practice. In Medieval Europe alchemists were commonly called necromancers, and *Cien años* refers to one of the most famous of these explicitly, as "Arnaldo de Vilanova, el nigromante" (337). Besides *necromancer*, her name also suggest *nigredo*, the phase of the alchemical *opus* she is directly associated with in the novel. While it may be the most patent, however, her name is not the only alchemical connection involving Nigromanta. From Jung we learn that "Negroes, and especially Ethiopians, play a considerable role in alchemy as synonyms of the *caput corvi* [literally, "raven's head", a prominent alchemical symbol associated with the *nigredo* phase of the *opus*], and the *nigredo*, and the figure of the black female familiar, or assistant, appears in the texts, described as "the sacred harlot".[1] Such striking parrallels encourage a closer scrutiny of the character Nigromanta, and this uncovers other, possible references to alchemy, and especially to the *nigredo* stage of the *opus*. This additional material is offered not only to suggest further possible links between Nigromanta and alchemy, but also to provide more insight into the use of alchemy at the end of the novel.

Turning to the text, our introduction to the black prostitute, when seen against an alchemical background, supports the idea that there is more to Nigromanta than a strictly literal reading would indicate:

> Aureliano conversaba con él ["el más antiguo de los negros antillanos," and the only person he meets who remembers the Buendías] en el enrevesado papiamento que aprendió en pocas semanas, y a veces compartía el caldo de cabezas de gallo que preparaba la bisnieta, una negra grande, de huesos sólidos, caderas de yegua y tetas de melones vivos, y una cabeza redonda, perfecta, acorazada por un duro capacete de pelos de alambre, que parecía el almófar de un guerrero medieval. Se llamaba Nigromanta (325).

Two points in this, and proximate passages in the novel, deserve mention, especially in the context of related excerpts: 1) the textual proximity of the words *Nigromanta* and *medieval*; 2) references to the "cabezas de gallo", and to the head of Nigromanta, which is "redonda, perfecta". The first of these two points highlights what the name Nigromanta suggests, necromancy, and also serves to focus attention upon European necromancy, as opposed to African, West Indian, or other types that might seem plausible given this character's description. At the same time, the proximity of *Nigromanta* and *medieval* recalls the opening sentence of chapter eighteen, the first description we receive of Aureliano Buendía-Babilonia after the twins José Arcadio Segundo and Aureliano Segundo die, and he gravitates to the center of the narrative:

> Aureliano no abandonó en mucho tiempo el cuarto de Melquíades. Se aprendió de memoria las leyendas fantásticas del libro desencuadernado, la síntesis de los estudios de Hermann, el tullido; los apuntes sobre la ciencia demonológica, las claves de la piedra filosofal, las centurias de Nostradamus y sus investigaciones sobre la peste, *de modo que llegó a la adolescencia sin saber nada de su tiempo, pero con los conocimientos básicos del hombre medieval* [my emphasis] (301).

The second point of interest in the passage on Nigromanta, the two references to heads, is, alchemically, more significant. Nigromanta's "cabeza redonda, perfecta" will be considered first, followed by a discussion of the "cabezas de gallo". The importance of the vessel in alchemy cannot be overstated, and the fact that the flask represents the alchemist's head has been mentioned already. In the alchemical literature, the flask is often "perfectly round", a description which matches Nigromanta's head. This apparently insignificant detail links this character, within the narrative, to Remedios the Beauty, whose head is described earlier, after she cuts all her hair:

> La molestaron tanto para que se cortara el cabello de lluvia que ya le daba a las pantorillas...que simplemente se rapó la cabeza y les hizo pelucas a los santos (199).

The result is a "cráneo pelado y perfecto" (200), a description that alchemically links Remedios, who embodies the quest for "true gold", and Nigromanta, consort of Aureliano Buendía-Babilonia, the character who eventually completes this quest.

Turning to the mention of "cabezas de gallo", we come to perhaps the most relevant reference to alchemy suggested in the original passage on Nigromanta. Besides the linguistic similarity of "cabezas de gallo" to *caput corvi*, the chicken heads, and the chicken head broth, receive further elaboration germane to our study. The phrase "cabezas de gallo", in a passage following the one originally cited, unites Aureliano and Nigromanta in a common task and, at the same time, echoes an important alchemical tenet, the universal rejection of the alchemist's basic material by the unenlightened:

> Cuando andaba [Aureliano] sin un céntimo, que era los más frecuente, conseguía que en los fondos del mercado le regalaran las cabezas de gallo que iban a tirar en la basura, y se las llevaba a Nigromanta para que le hiciera sus sopas (325).

Jung, in *Psychology and Alchemy*, writes:

> but that is precisely why it is so hard to find the *lapis* [i.e., the philosophers' stone]: it is *exilis*, uncomely, it is thrown out into the street or on the dunghill, it is the commonest thing to be picked up anywhere... [2]

This "cabezas de gallo" motif reappears later, precisely when the *nigredo* phase of the opus is culminating (something discussed more fully below): "Nigromanta lo rescató [Aureliano] de un charco de vómito y de lágrimas. Lo llevó a su cuarto, lo limpió, y le hizo tomar una taza de caldo" (348).

THE SECOND NIGREDO AND SEPARATIO

Having suggested that Nigromanta, because of her name, her color, the passage introducing her into the novel and the nature of her relationship with Aureliano, might be seen as his "alchemical helpmate", the *nigredo* and *separatio* at the end of work can be traced. The death of his aunt and lover, Amaranta Úrsula, provides the "psychological shock" which initiates Aureliano's anguish. Seeking to drown his sorrow in alcohol, he suffers a loss of consciousness, something that integrates well with descriptions of alchemical *nigredos*. He is rescued by Nigromanta, the last character (other than Aure-

liano and his son "el animal mitológico") to appear in the
novel, in a paragraph which constitutes the second *nigredo* of
the narrative:

> Nigromanta lo rescató de un charco de vómito y lágrimas.
> Lo llevó a su cuarto, lo limpió, le hizo tomar una taza de
> caldo. Creyendo que eso lo consolaba, tachó con una raya
> de carbón los incontables amores que él seguía debiéndole,
> y evocó voluntariamente sus tristezas más solitarias para
> no dejarlo solo en el llanto. Al amanecer, después de un
> sueño torpe y breve, Aureliano recobró la conciencia de su
> dolor de cabeza. Abrió los ojos y se acordó del niño (348).

In this passage, the overall tone of mental anguish is obvious,
as is its physical reflection in the vomit and tears. Also patent
is the succor and assistance offered by Nigromanta, who also
joins Aureliano in his "llanto" by recalling her most private
sadnesses. The relevance of the phrase "le hizo tomar una
taza de caldo" to the *nigredo* has been alluded to above, and
here this stage of the *opus* is underscored by the blackness of
Nigromanta, as well as by the charcoal she uses to cancel
Aureliano's past debts. The idea of canceling debts is itself an
apt metaphor for the purification prerequisite to the alchemical *separatio*.

In the next paragraph, the penultimate of the novel, the
separatio occurs. This event actually culminates a longer process of separation. After Amaranta Úrsula dies, the dissolution of Aureliano's ties with the past are explicitly traced: he
first searches for his four friends, then for Mercedes, next
for the *sabio catalán*, a Melquíades-father figure, and lastly for
the maternal Pilar Ternera (347).[3] Finally, after leaving Nigromanta, the physical *separatio* takes place when Aureliano
Buendía-Babilonia is "separated" into two characters: Aureliano Babilonia, the decipherer of the manuscripts, and the
last Aureliano Buendía, the "animal mitológico", who is described as a "pellejo hinchado y reseco" (349).

With this image of the last Aureliano Buendía as a skin
which Aureliano Babilonia sloughs off, the first of a series of
initiatory elements is introduced into the closing paragraphs
of the novel, and the correspondences between external,
physical events, and internal, psychological occurrences, begins to crystallize. Skin-sloughing is an ancient religious

motif, modeled after snake molting, and it is found in numerous primitive initiation scenarios. It is associated with rebirth and immortality, as snakes were believed to be immortal, constantly rejuvenating themselves through a change of skin. This motif, in initiation rites, represents the ritual death and spiritual rebirth of the initiand, ("an ontological mutation of the existential condition", in the words of Eliade), and it constitutes the fundamental theme of all primitive initiations.[4] In *Cien años*, this "skin sloughing" is joined by a number of other elements identified by religious historians as common to initiatory ceremonies. These will be explained and examined in more detail later, but for now they can be noted: Aureliano Buendía-Babilonia becomes "another", Aureliano Babilonia; he undergoes an experience of the "mystic light" which illuminates the manuscripts; he receives a different name; he uses another language as if it were his native tongue; he assumes a new role, becoming simultaneously a character within the novel and its reader; he experiences a reordering of time, as a mythic temporal ordering supersedes the historical, or chronological, one. As alchemy is one of several esoteric systems designed to effect the psychological transformation of an individual (initiate), a consideration of the initiatory material included in the final pages of García Márquez' story can contribute to this study in two ways. First, it will help to evaluate the closing events of the narrative, and it will also assist in the forging of a more thorough understanding of why, and how, alchemy is used in *Cien años de soledad*.

Before turning to an explication of general initiatory material in the closing paragraphs of the work, however, the presence of the specific, alchemical inclusions will be traced through. First, a few words can be said about the identification of the two Aurelianos, father and son, the central figures in the physical facet of the second *separatio*. At this point in the narrative they have the same name, Aureliano Buendía, as Aureliano Buendía-Babilonia does not become aware of his true name until the final paragraph. Both are abandoned. The child is literally left alone, and Aureliano, his father, feels abandoned by the deaths of Amaranta Úrsula, the *sabio catalán*, Pilar Ternera, and by the absence of his friends and Mercedes. Also, both Aurelianos are left motherless. Amaranta Úrsula, the child's mother dies, and this final chapter opens with the death of Aureliano-Babilonia's surrogate mother, Pilar Ternera: "Pilar Ternera murió, en su mecedor de bejuco, una noche de fiesta, vigilando la entrada de su paraíso" (336). One other association between Aureliano and "niño" can be cited, and it involves the name of Pilar's "paradise", *El Niño de Oro*. It is here that Aureliano's search for the links to his past ends: "Se rompió los puños contra los muros de argamasa de *El Niño de Oro*, clamando por Pilar Ternera [italics are the author's] (348). His connection with this curiously named brothel, his filial relationship to its matron, and the significance of the child of gold to alchemy, associate Aureliano not only with his son, the child, but also with the alchemical child of gold, the goal of the *opus*.

Another important identification, the one between Aureliano Buendía-Babilonia and Amaranta Úrsula, is also germane in this context. Two excerpts suggest that these characters merge to represent a single entity as Amaranta Úrsula's pregnancy progresses:

Aureliano y Amaranta Úrsula abrieron los ojos, sondearon sus almas, se miraron a la cara con la mano en el corazón, y comprendieron que estaban tan identificados que preferían la muerte a la separación (342).

A medida que avanzaba el embarazo se iban convirtiendo en un ser único, se integraban cada vez más en la soledad de una casa a la que sólo le hacía falta un último soplo para derrumbarse (345).

These two also embody characteristics of all previous Buendía men and women. Amaranta Úrsula, in her name, recalls the mother and sister of the first Aureliano Buendía, who Aureliano Buendía-Babilonia so resembles. She is also described as "activa, menuda, indomable, como Úrsula, y casi tan bella y provocativa como Remedios, la bella", and she sews her clothes "en la rudimentaria máquina de manivela de Amaranta" (319). Along with his physical resemblance to the Colonel, Aureliano Buendía-Babilonia also incorporates the most famous characteristic of the Colonel's brother, José Arcadio, which is described variously as "su masculinidad inconcebible" (328), and "la portentosa criatura de Aureliano"

(341). Other references, such as "andaban por la casa como siempre quiso estar Remedios, la bella", "una tarde estuvieron a punto de ahogarse cuando se amaban en la alberca", and "rasgaron con sus locuras la hamaca que había resistido a los tristes amores de campamento del coronel Aureliano Buendía" (341), also recall specific characters and events from the Buendía past: making love in the *alberca* recollects Meme Buendía and Mauricio Babilonia, and almost drowning there calls forth a reference to the last José Arcadio Buendía, and also to his frustrated incestuous desires toward Amaranta. The reference to the hammock, besides the Colonel's sad love affairs, also calls to mind the seduction of Rebeca by the first José Arcadio, the first incest mentioned in the novel. Other references could be cited, but the point has been made: whatever else the events and descriptions involving these two characters may suggest, they clearly serve to recapitulate the family's past. And a logical conclusion of such a reliving of the Buendía history is that their offspring, "el animal mitológico que había de poner término a la estirpe", can be seen, not only as the culmination, but also as the embodiment of the entire Buendía past.

The motif of incest in alchemy has been introduced already, and associated with the Hermetic androgyne, a symbol of the perfect integration of opposites, and a representation of the successful completion of the *opus*. The psychological fusion of Amaranta Úrsula and her nephew into a single, "androgynous" being, can be seen as a parallel to the identification of Aureliano Buendía-Babilonia and his son. Indeed, on one level, both identifications eventually yield the same result: the death of the Buendía aspect (Amaranta Úrsula and Aureliano Buendía), and the birth of Aureliano Babilonia, *El Niño de Oro*, which represents the completion of the quest for "true gold". (In alchemical literature, too, the Hermetic androgyne and the golden child, as two symbols for the same object, the philosophers' stone, are equivalents.) The union of Aureliano Buendía Babilonia and his aunt, in alchemical terms, signifies the reintegration of the Primal Man, a reabsorption of Eve by Adam. The *separatio* of Aureliano Buendía-Babilonia into Aureliano Babilonia and Aureliano Buendía takes this scenario back one step beyond Adam and Eve. It represents the liberation of the divine breath which infused

Spirit into Matter when Adam was created. The individual soul, thus freed, is then able to reascend to Spirit. What the meaning of such religious images may be in the context of a twentieth century novel is addressed in the next chapter, when narrative theory is considered; for now, the presence of images like this one, and related "initiatory material", will only be identified.

At this time, against the backdrop of Aureliano Buendía-Babilonia's identification with Amaranta Úrsula on the one hand, and with his son and namesake on the other, the passage describing the *nigredo* and *separatio* can be introduced and examined:

> Se derrumbó en el mecedor, el mismo en que se sentó Rebeca en los tiempos originales de la casa para dictar lecciones de bordado, y en el que Amaranta jugaba damas chinas con el coronel Gerineldo Márquez, y en el que Amaranta Úrsula cosía la ropita del niño, y en aquel relámpago de lucidez tuvo conciencia de que era incapaz de resistir sobre su alma el peso abrumador de tanto pasado. Herido por las lanzas mortales de las nostalgias propias y ajenas, admiró la impavidez de la telaraña en los rosales muertos, la perseverancia de la cizaña, la paciencia del aire en el radiante amanecer de febrero. Y entonces vio al niño. Era un pellejo hinchado y reseco, que todas las hormigas del mundo iban arrastrando trabajosamente hacia sus madrigueras por el sendero de piedras del jardín. Aureliano no pudo moverse. No porque lo hubiera paralizado el estupor, sino porque en aquel instante prodigioso se le revelaron las claves definitivas de Melquíades, y vio el epígrafe de los pergaminos perfectamente ordenado en el tiempo y el espacio de los hombres: *El primero de la estirpe está amarrado en un árbol y al último se lo están comiendo las hormigas* [italics are the author's] (349).

With Aureliano's conscious realization that he can no longer endure "el peso abrumador de tanto pasado", the *nigredo* reaches its nadir, the lowest point in the descent, or dark night, of the soul. Above, how this phase of the *opus* is often described, metaphorically, as the death of the artifex, has been noted. Significantly, it is precisely at this point in the story that Aureliano sees the dead infant: "Y entonces vio al niño". The dead infant represents the physical *nigredo* which corresponds to Aureliano's psychological dissolution and death. The sentence immediately preceding "Y entonces vio al niño", contains the phrase "herido por las lanzas mortales", and these words can serve as a marker for Aureliano Buendía's death, for moments later, in "aquel instante prodigioso", when he sees the child, Aureliano *Babilonia* is born. (One could say also that Aureliano Buendía-Babilonia is reborn, or, to use Eliade's phrase once again, that Aureliano suffers "an ontological mutation of the existential condition.")

Two other points are noteworthy here. First, Aureliano's symbolic death occurs while he is sitting in the old family rocker, and this links him to another death, recounted in the opening words of this final chapter: "Pilar Ternera murió en el mecedor de bejuco, una noche de fiesta, vigilando la entrada de su paraíso" (336). Secondly, *mecedor* is explicitly identified with women throughout the narrative, and this reinforces Aureliano's "psychological androgyny". Besides Pilar Ternera's rocker, the one Aureliano is sitting in has been described exclusively in terms of Buendía women:

> el mismo [rocker] en que se sentó Rebeca en los tiempos originales de la casa para dictar lecciones de bordado, y en el que Amaranta jugaba damas chinas con el coronel Gerineldo Máquez, y en el que Amaranta Úrsula cosía la ropita del niño...(349).

In alchemy, the feminine aspect of the mind represents receptivity, and Aureliano's sitting posture and the phrase "se le revelaron las claves definitivas" reflect this feminine attitude. Later, when he deciphers the manuscripts it is his masculine mental facet that is engaged, as he actively penetrates "la lengua materna de Melquíades", an action he performs "en voz alta" and "de pie" (349).

Aureliano's "conciencia de que era incapaz de resistir sobre su alma el peso abrumador de tanto pasado", a phrase which marks the psychological *nigredo*, would seem to suggest suicide as a likely development. The macabre tone of the previous paragraphs, and the abundance of death images, also make this eventuality seem probable. However, an unforeseen turn of events, the revelation of the final keys to Melquíades' parchment manuscripts, brings a radically different resolution to his situation. And in this resolution the next stage of the alchemical *opus*, the *albedo*, can be seen.

THE ALBEDO

As a result of the revelation of Melquíades' final keys, Aureliano's state of mind changes abruptly. The consequences of the psychological *separatio*, in which he separates himself from his painful past, is described in the first sentence of the final paragraph:

> Aureliano no había sido mas lúcido en ningún acto de su vida que cuando olvidó sus muertos y el dolor de sus muertos, y volvió a clavar las puertas y las ventanas con las crucetas de Fernanda para no dejarse perturbar por ninguna tentación del mundo, porque entonces sabía que en los pergaminos de Melquíades estaba escrito su destino (349).

In the next sentence, this "extraordinary lucidity" of Aureliano's seems to strike a corresponding, external resonance in Melquíades' manuscripts:

> Los encontró intactos entre las plantas prehistóricas y los charcos humeantes y los insectos luminosos que habían desterrado del cuarto todo vestigio del paso de los hombres por la tierra, y no tuvo serenidad para sacarlos a la luz, sino que allí mismo, de pie, sin la menor dificultad, como si hubieran estado escritos en castellano bajo el resplandor deslumbrante del mediodía, empezó a descifrarlos en voz alta (349).

Other excerpts from this final paragraph reveal that this alchemical pattern of internal/external reflections continues. A connection is established between Aureliano's deciphering and discovery of his true identity in Melquíades' manuscripts on the one hand, and the destruction of the Buendía house and Macondo by the tempestuous wind, on the other. Ultimately, a complete, explicit identification of events inside Aureliano's mind with those occurring outside of it is established. This final association is developed by degrees, and in several ways.

First, in the following passage, Aureliano's deciphering and the destruction of the Buendía house are linked:

impaciente por conocer su propio origen, *Aureliano dio un salto. Entonces empezó el viento*, tibio, incipiente, lleno de voces del pasado, de murmullos de geranios antiguos, de suspiros de desengaños anteriores a las nostalgias más tenaces. No lo advirtió porque *en aquel momento estaba descubriendo los primeros indicios de su ser*, en un abuelo concupiscente que se dejaba arrastrar por la frivolidad a través de un páramo alucinado, en busca de una mujer hermosa a quien no haría feliz. Aureliano lo reconoció, persiguió los caminos ocultos de su descendencia, y *encontró el instante de su propia concepción* entre los alacranes y las mariposas amarillas de un baño crepuscular, donde un menestral saciaba su lujuria con una mujer que se le entregaba por rebeldía. Estaba tan absorto, que no sintió tampoco *la segunda arremetida del viento, cuya potencia ciclónica arrancó de los quicios las puertas y las ventanas, descuajó el techo de la galería oriental y desarraigó los cimientos. Sólo entonces* descubrió que Amaranta Úrsula no era su hermana, sino su tía, y que Francis Drake había asaltado a Riohacha solamente para que ellos pudieran buscarse por los laberintos más intrincados de la sangre, hasta engendrar el animal mitológico que había de poner término a la estirpe [my emphasis] (350).

The description of the wind, as "lleno de voces del pasado, de murmullos de geranios antiguos, de suspiros de engaños anteriores a las nostalgias más tenaces", recalls the description of the manuscripts, earlier in this paragraph, as "la historia de la familia". Another link between the deciphering and the destruction is forged by the alternating presentation of the narrative, which switches its focus back and forth from Aureliano to the wind. Finally, the transitional words and phrases which connect these changes of focus, serve to identify, more than to distinguish, these alternating descriptions.

The first of these narrative shifts occurs when Aureliano jumps ahead in search of his origins. It is here that the wind begins, and this latter event, introduced by the phrase "entonces empezó el viento", contains the hint of a causal relationship, as if in some way it might have resulted from Aureliano's "salto". In the succeeding sentence this possibility receives support, as Aureliano's search for his beginnings and the wind's starting are synchronized: "no lo advirtió [the wind's commencing] porque en aquel momento estaba descubriendo los primeros indicios de su ser". The following sentence sees Aureliano succeed in uncovering "el instante de su propia concepción," an occurrence which is also synchronized with an external event, the uprooting of the foundations of the Buendía house. (When the birth/rebirth initiation symbolism is discussed, the significance of this reference to Aureliano's "concepción entre los alacranes y mariposas" (insects traditionally symbolic of death and rebirth, respectively) will be fully developed.) Finally, in this passage the words *Sólo entonces* directly connect the house's destruction, the unhinging of its doors, windows and roof, with Aureliano's discovery of his role in the inevitable Buendía family chronicle. And the mutual *interaction* of these two levels (the internal, or microcosmic, and the external or macrocosmic), which *sólo entonces* seems to establish, approaches a mutual identification in the next sentence of the novel:

> ...Aureliano saltó once páginas para no perder el tiempo en hechos demadiado conocidos, y empezó a descifrar el instante que estaba viviendo, descifrando a medida que lo vivía, profetizándose a sí mismo en el acto de descifrar la última página de los pergaminos, como si se estuviera viendo en un espejo hablado (350).

However, I do not think this identity is fully realized until the next sentence, the last of the narrative. This final sentence begins with the phrase "Entonces dio otro salto", and it contains another echo of the internal/external synchronization we have been tracing:

> estaba previsto que la ciudad de los espejos (o los espejismos) sería arrasada por el viento y desterrada de la memoria de los hombres en el instante en que Aureliano Babilonia acabara de descifrar los pergaminos (351).

This attempt to determine exactly where the internal/external correspondences culminate may seem to be a minor point, but it is significant to our discussion. The idea of a "mirror image" still retains vestiges of separateness and duality. The end of *Cien años* can be seen to develop an alchemical concept, the *unus mundus*, a "non-dual" universe, a step beyond identical reflection to complete identity (the Hermetic androgyne), where "inside" and "outside" (along with other pairs of apparent opposites) are joined in the *coniunctio oppositorum*. Aureliano's "otro salto" would seem to cover this final step to the *unus mundus*, the successful completion of the alchemical *opus*, and the perspective from which Melquíades (or anyone who shares it), can see "the other side of things".

How such a positive interpretation of an ending which is so apparently negative can be justified requires substantial explanation, and the possible presence of an alchemical progression from *nigredo*, through *separatio* to *albedo*, forms only the first part of such an exercise. I would next like to turn to a discussion of the presence and significance of the considerable amount of initiation-related material contained in the final paragraphs of the narrative. Before beginning, however, another germane reference can be introduced. This involves a prediction Melquíades makes about the future of Macondo earlier in the story:

> Una noche creyó encontrar una predicción sobre el futuro de Macondo. Sería una ciudad luminosa, con grandes casas de vidrio, donde no quedaba ningún rastro de la estirpe de los Buendía (52-53).

This prediction by Melquíades, the character who foresees the Buendías' future with one hundred years of anticipation, "hasta en sus detalles más triviales" (349), at least justifies some questions. Is the prediction meaningless, or does it have some significance? Can the description of Macondo as "una ciudad luminosa, con grandes casas de vidrio" possibly be reconciled with the town's apparent terminal destruction as the narrative ends? This prediction is significant, I believe, and I think the second question can be answered affirmatively. Furthermore, its answer is very helpful in explaining the use of alchemy in *Cien años de soledad*, and it also provides a key to the definition of literature that is contained in the novel.

RITES OF PASSAGE

Mircea Eliade, the religious historian, provides evidence to establish the widespread presence of alchemical and alchemically related thought, and its association with religious rites of initiation. For Eliade, alchemy is one of a family of belief systems which have been used, historically, to induce "passage" of an individual from the "mundane" world to a "sacred" one. This sacred world, however, is not to be confused with a literal understanding of the Christian heaven, that is, as something awaiting man after his physical death. It is immanent, always present, but apprehensible only to the initiate. The sacred world, then, is a point of view, a special, mystical way of penetrating the appearances of things. And the representative role of alchemy, as one belief system which can induce such a passage, is noted as follows:

> The alchemist's emergence on another spiritual plane...
> may be compared with the experience of the *homo religiosus*
> who assists in the transmutation of the cosmos by the
> revelation of the sacred. [5]

In alchemy, the passage to another, spiritual plane, is said to confer immortality upon the artifex, a freedom from historical time which many other initiatory systems also claimed. Rites of passage are associated with initiations, and Eliade's studies establish the presence of strikingly similar initiatory rites and rituals in myth systems the world over. And it is interesting that, according to Eliade, these universal similarities were preserved in Europe by alchemy.U Significantly, a remarkably close agreement can be established between the final events in *Cien años* and the symbols and meaning associated with these universal initiatory patterns.

The basic theme of all forms of initiation is, according to Eliade, the ritual death and spiritual resurrection of the initiate. This fundamental motif undergoes various degrees of elaboration, but is usually accompanied by at least some of the following: ritual return to the primordial mother's womb (often symbolized by a sacred pot, cave or hut); loss of consciousness; tortures and suffering; ritual killing and/or dismemberment by a mythical agent, usually chthonic in nature; forgetting the past; learning a new language; being given a new name; learning the mythical history of the tribe; the initiate's discovery that he himself is actually the hero, or protagonist, of the ancient myths just related to him; the resolution of apparent paradoxes (such as the initate being identical to the hero of the myths), which symbolizes the "impossibility" of the quest or passage; the presence of what has been called the "mystic light".[7] In every case the purpose of the ceremony is for the initiate to be transformed into a different person, *to become another*. In the process, he is transported from the world of historical or conventional time to a sacred time, wherein he is coeternal with the mythical ancestors. (The significance of the temporal transmutations associated with initiation is a question dealt with in more depth in chapter three, when Melquíades' unconventional temporal ordering in the manuscripts is considered.)

Eliade defines three types of initiations: those designed to effect the transition from childhood to adulthood (called "puberty rites" or "tribal initiation"); those involving entrance into a confraternity or secret society; those involved with a mystical vocation. Differences exist among the three types of initiations, but he hastens to add that there are a great many fundamental similarities among them, with the result that, according to Eliade, "from a certain point of view, all initiations are much alike".[8] I mention the three kinds here, because there are a considerable number of parallels between the final events and descriptions in the novel and motifs connected with the rites of passage, and using these three types of initiations can provide a convenient division of this material, as well as a logical approach to it. Also, these three initiatory variants can be correlated with the three stages in the quest for true gold, associated, respectively, with Colonel Aureliano Buendía, José Arcadio Segundo, and Aureliano Buendía-Babilonia.

PUBERTY RITES OR RITES OF TRIBAL INITIATION

Eliade's conclusions concerning the content of initiatory revelations associated with "puberty rites" is reflected in the central event occurring at the close of *Cien años*:

> What is communicated to the novices is, then, a quite eventful mythical history—and less and less the revelation of the creative acts of the Supreme Beings. The doctrine transmitted through initiation is increasingly confined to the history of the Ancestor's doings, that is, to a series of dramatic events that took place in the dream times. To be

initiated is equivalent to learning what *happened* in the primordial Time—and not what the Gods are and how the world and man were created.[9]

Aureliano Babilonia's deciphering of Melquíades' manuscripts, which are described as "la historia de la familia" precisely when Aureliano "empezó a descifrarlos en voz alta" (349), exactly echoes this motif of the revelation of mythical history: he learns what happened. Even the adjective *mythical*, used by Eliade, is apropos, as the family history ends with "el animal mitológico". This history also reveals to Aureliano who he really is and how he fits into the universal plan. He learns that his role in the history has been explicitly established since the beginning, and that what has happened before has been designed to set the stage for what he will do. In short, he finds out that he has always been a protagonist in this "history", another fundamental motif in tribal initiations:

> Sólo entonces descubrió que Amaranta Úrsula no era su hermana, sino su tía, y que Francis Drake había asaltado a Riohacha *solamente para que* ellos pudieran buscarse por los laberintos más intrincados de la sangre, hasta engendrar el animal mitológico que había de poner término a la estirpe [my emphasis] (350).

There are other echoes of specific ceremonies in the final paragraphs. The killing of the baby by "todas las hormigas del mundo", which drag the skin to their "madrigueras", recalls the ritual killing and/or dismemberment of the initiand by an agent, one who is usually chthonic in nature. This motif dramatizes the fact that the initiate will have died to material, earth-bound existence, and will have passed over to the heaven realm. Another reflection involves Aureliano's brief loss of consciousness, which serves as a prelude to the penultimate paragraph of the novel: "Al amanecer, después de un sueño torpe y breve, Aureliano recobró la conciencia de su dolor de cabeza. Abrió los ojos y se acordó del niño" (348).

Also, in puberty initiations, the novices are physically separated from their mothers, taught by priests and members of secret societies, and, often, "pretend to have forgotten their past lives, their family relations, their names and their language, and must learn everything again".[10] Aureliano Buendía-Babilonia is literally separated from his mother, Meme Buendía, while still an infant, and until he deciphers the manuscripts he is ignorant of his name, his past life, and his family relations. Considering his experiences in the final paragraphs of the novel, how they also parallel this initiatory framework can be seen: the paths to his past, and ultimately to the maternal Pilar Ternera, are closed off to him (pp. 347-48); eventually he forgets his past ("olvidó sus muertos y el dolor de sus muertos"); he reads Sanskrit as if it were his native tongue; he discovers his true identity, and receives a new name (his true one, Babilonia).

The separation of the initiands from their mothers is very often accompanied by a ritual return to the womb of the primordial mother. This is commonly symbolized by a sacred pot, cave or hut, which becomes the new center of the world. In *Cien años*, Melquíades' room is patently such a place. Curiously, this room is referred to as a cave at one point in the narrative, when Amaranta Úrsula greets Aureliano with the words: "Hola, antropófago... Otra vez en la cueva" (330). And Melquíades' room is truly a womb to José Arcadio Segundo, who finds repose and complete contentment there (where he is fed by his mother, Santa Sofía de la Piedad), and he refuses to leave it once he discovers the manuscripts.

There are two other references from the final paragraphs which are relevant to the initiatory motif of returning the initiand to the womb of the primordial mother. First, this return is reflected in the case of the baby, who is taken away by the ants to their underground burrow. The Earth has traditionally been personified as the primordial mother. Secondly, this penultimate paragraph contains graphic obstetrical imagery which begins with mention of a pot:

> Aureliano atravesó el corredor saturado por los suspiros matinales del orégano, y se asomó al comedor, donde estaban todavía los escombros del parto: la olla grande, las sábanas ensangrentadas, los tiestos de ceniza , y el retorcido ombligo del niño en un pañal abierto sobre la mesa, junto a las tijeras y el sedal (348).

As stated above, Eliade identifies the pot, along with the cave and the hut, as representative of the primordial mother in initiation scenarios of the puberty type. Here, an interesting fact emerges. In the novel, there are two other references to "olla", and both of them link Colonel Aureliano Buendía and his mother, Úrsula. The first of these involves the initial manifestation of Aureliano's clairvoyance:

> el pequeño Aureliano, a la edad de tres años, entró en la cocina en el momento en que ella [Úrsula] retiraba del fogón y ponía en la mesa una olla de caldo hirviendo. El niño, perplejo en la puerta, dijo: "Se va a caer." La olla estaba bien puesta en el centro de la mesa, pero tan pronto como el niño hizo el anuncio, inició un movimiento irrevocable hacia el borde, como impulsada por un dinamismo interior, y se despedazó en el suelo (20-21).

Later we learn that this experience constitutes the earliest memory Aureliano has of his mother (pp. 151-52). The second reference to "olla" occurs when Aureliano has decided to commit suicide:

> Allí se quitó la camisa, se sentó en el borde del catre, y a las tres y cuarto de la tarde se disparó un tiro de pistola en el círculo de yodo que su médico personal le había pintado en el pecho. A esa hora, en Macondo, Úrsula destapó la olla de la leche en el fogón, extrañada de que se demorara tanto para hervir, y la encontró llena de gusanos.
> —¡Han matado a Aureliano!—exclamó (155-56).

"Olla", then, is associated, in significant circumstances, with the character who has been linked to the initiation of the psychological quest (and whose physical resemblance to Aureliano Buendía-Babilonia is so remarkable), and his relationship to his mother, Úrsula, who may be called the primordial, or original mother of the entire Buendía family.

THE RITES OF CONFRATERNITY

According to Eliade, the rites of entrance into a secret society correspond very closely in every respect to those of "tribal" initiation but there exist differences in the emphasis that each type places upon the same rituals. For example, while obstetrical imagery is accented in puberty rites, learning a new language and actively furthering a quest (elements which may be present in "tribal" initiations), are usually more important in confraternal ceremonies. In the novel, the threads of confraternal initiation are easily traced. When Aureliano Babilonia deciphers Melquíades' manuscripts, he consummates a quest several characters before him have attempted, and, significantly, he is explicitly initiated into this enterprise by José Arcadio Segundo:

> En realidad, a pesar de que todo el mundo lo tenía por loco, José Arcadio Segundo era en aquel tiempo el habitante más lúcido de la casa. Enseñó al pequeño Aureliano a leer y a escribir, *lo inició en el estudio de los pergaminos*, y le inculcó una interpretación tan personal de lo que significó para Macondo la compañía bananera, que muchos años después, cuando Aureliano se incorporara al mundo, había de pensarse que contaba una versión alucinada, porque era radicalmente contraria a la falsa que los historiadores habían admitido, y consagrado en los textos escolares [my emphasis] (296).

Moreover, José Arcadio Segundo classifies the language of the manuscripts, and passes it on to his great nephew, who identifies it as Sanskrit (p. 296). In their private, "confraternal" meetings, then, José Arcadio Segundo literally initiates Aureliano Buendía-Babilonia into a quest, and transmits a new language to him, two events directly linked to the manuscript deciphering in the final paragraph of the novel.

Colonel Aureliano Buendía, whose "confraternal links" to José Arcadio Segundo were mentioned in the first chapter of this study, is also involved with the transmission of language skills in the novel. Just as José Arcadio Segundo teaches his great nephew Aureliano to read and write (p. 296), the Colonel teaches José Arcadio Segundo's father, Arcadio, the same basic skills: "Se había dedicado [Arcadio] a aprender el arte de la platería con Aureliano, quien además lo había enseñado a leer y escribir" (53). And so, in terms of learning language, a progression can be established among the three characters involved in the spiritual, or psychological, branch of the quest. The Colonel teaches Arcadio to read and write Spanish, thereby transmitting what might be called the "tribal", or general group language. This, like his links to "la olla", would associate Colonel Aureliano Buendía with the first type of initiation. José Arcadio Segundo not only teaches

Aurelino Buendía-Babilonia how to read and write Spanish, but he also passes on a classification of a new language to him, and this transmission of Sanskrit links him to the confraternal rites of passage. Finally, Aureliano Buendía-Babilonia, using one of the golden fishes the Colonel has left behind, buys a Sanskrit primer and learns the new language, which eventually enables him to complete the quest: he diciphers the manuscripts "como si hubieran estado escritos en castellano" (349).

THE MYSTIC LIGHT

The ending of *Cien años* also contains parallels to the shamanistic initiation ceremonies. This category, as previously mentioned, is very much akin to the other two types, as regards rites. Once more, as with the distinction between tribal and confraternal initiations, it is only in the emphases where ceremonial differences emerge. The purpose of this third level initiation is to establish the initiate as a wise man, one of the elect. A distinguishing feature in such rituals is an experience of the "mystic light", which is normally of central importance in these rites of passage. The final paragraph of the novel offers several descriptions that can be seen in terms of such initiations.

In the following passage, a mystic light, simultaneously illuminating Aureliano Babilonia and the manuscripts, permits him to begin deciphering them:

> no tuvo [Aureliano] serenidad para sacarlos a la luz, sino que allí mismo, de pie, sin la menor dificultad, como si hubieran estado escritos en castellano bajo el resplandor deslumbrante del mediodía, empezó a descifrarlos en voz alta (349).

Again, as with the events and descriptions in the final pages of the novel discussed in the sections on tribal and confraternal initiation, the mystic light motif of the final paragraph has its resonances throughout the narrative, its inter-connections with the psychological quest. This mystic light emanating from the manuscripts has a correspondent illumination inside of Aureliano which is described in the opening words of this final paragraph: "Aureliano no había sido *más lúcido* en ningún acto de su vida..."(349). And, in *Cien años*, this lucidity is linked with the other characters associated with the spiritual quest: José Arcadio Segundo, Remedios the Beauty, the Colonel and Melquíades.

The words "más lúcido", used to describe Aureliano Babilonia as he is about to decipher the manuscripts, are also employed in a description of his great-uncle, which has been cited before: "En realidad, a pesar de que todo el mundo lo tenía por loco, José Arcadio Segundo era en aquel tiempo el habitante más lúcido de la casa" (296). The link forged by the repetition of "más lúcido" is strengthened by the context of this passage describing José Arcadio Segundo, as it occurs when the reunions in Melquíades' room between these two characters, and the classification and identification of Sanskrit, are mentioned (p. 296). Another excerpt links Remedios the Beauty and Colonel Aureliano Buendía with lucidness:

> Parecía como si una lucidez penetrante le permitiera ver la realidad de las cosas más allá de cualquier formalismo. Ese era al menos el punto de vista del coronel Aureliano Buendía, para quien Remedios, la bella, no era en modo alguno retrasada mental, como se creía, sino todo lo contrario. "Es como si viniera de regreso de veinte años de guerra", solía decir (172).

Here the Colonel recognizes in his great-niece a natural lucidity comparable to one he feels he has glimpsed after two decades of war.

But it is the familiar, or guide, of this quest who, perhaps more than any other character, is associated with light and brightness in the novel. There are many examples: "alumbrando con su profunda voz de órgano los territorios más oscuros de la imaginación" (13) is one, and "Un mediodía ardiente," related to Melquíades at least four times in the narrative (pp. 13, 161, 301, 302) is another. Both these phrases form part of the description of "un recuerdo hereditario" that passes from one Buendía generation to another (p. 13). The sun-like brilliance associated with his manuscripts as they are deciphered is another instance of light images linked to the gypsy wizard, and ultimately, when he disappears, Melquíades seems to become light, "esfumándose en la claridad radiante del mediodía" (302). Finally, an excerpt establishing him as one who can transmit, or resurrect, lucidity appears when he saves Macondo from the plague of forgetfulness: "Le dio a beber a José Arcadio Buendía una sustancia de color apacible, y la luz se hizo en su memoria" (49).

The significance of Melquíades' links with light and lucidity can be appreciated in this context of the mystic light type of initiation. These rites are designed to effect passage to an enlightened state, they herald the transformation of the initiate into a "wise man". In *Cien años*, it is only after "se le revelaron las claves definitivas de Melquíades" (349) that Aureliano Buendía-Babilonia's passage occurs, and he comes to share Melquíades' shamanistic point of view completely. And the "protección final", revealed to us in the final paragraph, offers one more parallel between events in the novel and rites of passage, the transportation of the initiate from the world of historical, or conventional, time, to a sacred time:

> Melquíades no había ordenado los hechos en el tiempo convencional de los hombres, sino que concentró un siglo de episodios cotidianos, de modo que todos coexistieran en un instante (350).

One final image, Melquíades' reference to the future Macondo as "una ciudad luminosa, con grandes casas de vidrio", is also related to the mystic light, and this point is taken up again below.

TWO OTHER SPECIFIC RITES OF PASSAGE

In the closing paragraphs of the novel, then, a considerable amount of material related to traditional rites of passage can be identified: loss of consciousness, suffering, obstetrical imagery, death of the initiate, "skin sloughing"; forgetting the past, learning a new language, receiving a new name, discovering the history of the tribe; an experience of a mystic light, a transformation of time consciousness and the discovery, by the initiate, that he is actually a central figure in the myth. The material can be seen to reflect three stages of initiation, a fundamental or tribal type, which might be associated with Colonel Aureliano Buendía; a more specific, confraternal induction, where transmission of esoteric understanding and initiation into a quest are central, a stage one could associate with José Arcadio Segundo; and a very specific, shamanistic kind of passage, involving a direct penetration or understanding of the mysteries, a type linked, in the novel, with Aureliano Buendía-Babilonia.

One more very important initiatory motif has not yet been discussed fully. This is the Symplegades motif, which symbolizes the impossibility of the quest or passage, and often involves the resolution of apparent paradoxes. It is so named for two rocks, the Smyplegades, that clashed together intermittently, making safe passage for ships impossible. However, they parted long enough to allow the hero Jason to pass through with his argonauts. In *Cien años*, one typical paradox, the discovery by the initiate that he is identical to the hero or protagonist of the myths, has been mentioned. Aureliano Buendía-Babilonia is physically identical to the first Aureliano Buendía, but more significant is his discovery that Sir Francis Drake attacked Riohacha solely to allow him and Amaranta Úrsula to engender the "animal mitológico que había de poner término a la estirpe"(350). Later, this motif will be developed further when the depiction of the destruction of Macondo, and Melquíades' apparently paradoxical reference to the town as "una ciudad luminosa, con grandes casas de vidrio" (53), are addressed. Before turning to this exercise, however, other descriptions and events from the final paragraphs of the novel related to the rites of passage will be presented. These references are treated in a separate section because their importance does not relate, initially, to general initiatory scenarios, nor the specific ones of alchemy, as much as it does to two other specific belief systems, one associated with the initiations at Eleusis, in ancient Greece, and Christianity.

The ceremonies at Eleusis were symbolized by the pig, and in the characters Aureliano Buendía-Babilonia and his son, the child with a pig's tail, echoes of these rites of passage can be observed. J. E. Harrison, in her *Prolegomena to the Study of Greek Religion*, explains how each initiate had a "mystic pig", with which he was identified. The two bathed together, an act of ritual purification. Then the pig was sacrificed, the initiate was declared reborn, and the mysteries were revealed to him.[11]

Two other references from the penultimate paragraph of the narrative can be related to a different set of death and resurrection rites, those of Christianity. In the discussion on alchemy, the following passage was examined when the *separatio* was developed:

> Herido por las lanzas mortales de las nostalgias propias y ajenas, admiró la impavidez de la telaraña en los rosales muertos, la perseverancia de la cizaña, la paciencia del aire en el radiante amanecer de febrero. Y entonces vio al niño. Era un pellejo hinchado y reseco, que todas las hormigas del mundo iban arrastrando trabajosamente hacia sus madrigueras por el sendero de piedras del jardín. Aureliano no pudo moverse. No porque lo hubiera paralizado el estupor, sino porque en aquel instante prodigioso se le revelaron las claves difinitivas de Melquíades, y vio el epígrafe de los pergaminos perfectamente ordenado en el tiempo y el espacio de los hombres: *El primero de la estirpe está amarrado en un árbol y al último se lo están comiendo las hormigas* [italics are the author's] (349)

In that previous discussion, it was stated that "lanzas mortales" could serve as a marker for Aureliano *Buendía*'s death, for in "aquel instante prodigioso", when he sees the child, Aureliano *Babilonia* is born. With the sloughing off of the dead skin, embodied by the child, a separation of matter and spirit, of the profane and the sacred, takes place. "Lanzas mortales" also recalls the death of Christ on Golgotha, when he is pierced by a lance so that he will die before sundown, and separate flows of blood and water issue forth from his side. The blood and water symbolize the two facets of his dual man-god nature, and their separation also represents the liberation of Spirit from Matter. Reinforcing this link between Christ's crucifixion and this paragraph of the novel, a link suggested by "lanzas mortales", is the image of José Arcadio Buendía from the epigraph of Melquíades' manuscripts, which occurs a few sentences further on: *"El primero de la estirpe está amarrado en un árbol, y al último lo están comiendo las hormigas"* (349). The description of the founder reflects a very popular universal folk motif, the hanging of a deity in the "World Tree", of which Christ's crucifixion is one example. (It is interesting that José Arcadio Buendía, according to

Melquíades' epigraph, "está amarrado *en* un árbol", and not "*a* un árbol", as *a* would be the normal preposition to describe someone who is tied *to* a tree. The former construction, which suggests "*in* a tree", reinforces the interpretation based on the rites of passage which is offered here. Moreover, earlier in the narrative, when the founder is subdued and the tying actually occurs, he is described as "atado de pies y manos al castaño" (p. 74), a phrase that lends further support to the crucifixion image.) Interestingly, Jung associates such "suspension" with the alchemical *nigredo*, and identifies it as a reflection of psychological doubt or chaos, and suffering.[12]

A further connection also emerges in this context, this one between the image of José Arcadio Buendía "amarrado en un árbol" and the other image in Melquíades' epigraph, "y al último lo están comiendo las hormigas". The aim of initiations, whether they pertain to mystery cults (like the festivals at Eleusis), established religions (like Christianity), or esoteric practices (like alchemy), is to place the initiate into direct contact with the transpersonal realm, a contact which has somehow been lost. Sacrifices (like the pig at Eleusis, Christ on the cross, or the psychological death of the artifex in the *nigredo*), are the price of atonement, literally a recapturing of "at-one-ment", the end of solitude caused by the separation of man from cosmic oneness, or the entrapment of Spirit in Matter. In the two images from Melquíades' epigraph, then, parallels to Christ's suffering and death can be traced. José Arcadio Buendía's being "amarrado en un árbol" would correspond to Christ on the cross; the death of the last Aureliano Buendía, "que todas las hormigas del mundo iban arrastrando trabajosamente hacia sus madrigueras," would correspond to Christ in the tomb. Aureliano Buendía-Babilonia, through his *nigredo* and *separatio*, would correspond to both of these situations, and, with the *albedo*, to the resurrected Christ as well, a symbol sometimes used in alchemy to represent successful psychological transformation and passage to reintegration and perfect understanding. The significance of the use of such religious imagery is addressed later, when narrative theory is considered.

THE CORRESPONDING TRANSFORMATION OF THE WORLD

While up to this point initiation has been examined from the perspective of the initiate, the basic motif of death and resurrection also applies to his world. In alchemy, for example, the transformation of the artifex' point of view necessarily involves a concomitant transmutation of the world, as everything is perceived differently, colored by the enlightened perspective. In Christianity this phenomenon is described as a "New Heaven and a New Earth". Earlier, how the destruction of Macondo, and Aureliano Buendía-Babilonia's internal mental processes are interrelated was analyzed, when the concept of the *unus mundus,* or internal/exteral correspondences was presented. Now, against the background of the discussion on initiation, and with the help of some of its images, these internal/external reflections at the end of the novel can be examined as they relate to the world's (i.e., Macondo's) passage from the literal, or "profane", to the symbolic, or "sacred", level. The images of primary importance from the narrative are the house, the village and Melquíades' room, which parallel the house, village and initiatory hut of rites of passage ceremonies.

Employing general initiatory motifs and their specific alchemical and Christian, or Biblical, manifestations, the closing paragraphs of the novel will be scrutinized. The destruction of the Buendía house, and the apparently terminal devastation of Macondo will be considered in the context of their correspondence to Aureliano Babilonia's internal thought processes. Finally, the possibility that Macondo is ultimately transformed into a "Celestial City", one matching Melquíades' description ("una ciudad luminosa, con grandes casas de vidrio"), and that Aureliano Babilonia symbolically achieves immortality, is examined.

In ceremonies involving the rites of passage the initiatory hut represents a new orientation, a change in the way the world is perceived. This is called the *axis mundi* motif, and it signifies a new center of the world, or organizing principle of reality. During initiation the novice's home and/or village is very often symbolically destroyed and replaced by the initiatory hut. This destruction indicates the abolition of the profane, pre-initiatory world, while the hut corresponds to the spiritual recreation of the world, and the sacred history revealed during the ceremony. Such a "world-change" reflects, and complements, the alteration of the perception, or "world-view" of the initiate. The *axis mundi* motif finds expression in the narrative:

> Macondo era ya un pavoroso remolino de polvo y escombros centrifugado por la cólera del huracán bíblico, cuando Aureliano saltó once páginas para no perder el tiempo en hechos demasiado conocidos, y empezó a descifrar el instante que estaba viviendo, descifrándolo a medida que lo vivía, profetizándose a sí mismo en el acto de descifrar la última página de los pergaminos, como si estuviera viendo en un espejo hablado (350).

This passage can suggest that the physical Macondo has been destroyed already, while Aureliano, inside of Melquíades' room, continues to decipher the manuscripts. Read this way, the initiatory hut (Melquíades' perspective, represented by his room and manuscripts) has replaced the house and village as the new organizing principle and "center of the world".

To continue this reading, two other excerpts relevant to the *axis mundi* motif should be introduced, and these are the final lines of the narrative, and Melquíades' prediction concerning the future of Macondo:

> Entonces dio otro salto para anticipar a las predicciones y averiguar la fecha y las circunstancias de su muerte. Sin embargo, antes de llegar al verso final ya había comprendido que no saldría jamás de ese cuarto, pues estaba previsto que la ciudad de los espejos (o los espejismos) sería arrasada por el viento y desterrada de la memoria de los hombres en el instante en que Aureliano Babilonia acabara de descifrar los pergaminos, y que todo lo escrito en ellos era irrepetible desde siempre y para siempre, porque las estirpes condenadas a cien años de soledad no tenían una segunda oportunidad sobre la tierra (351).

> Una noche creyó [Melquíades] encontrar una predicción sobre el futuro de Macondo. Sería una ciudad luminosa, con grandes casas de vidrio, donde no quedaba ningún rastro de la estirpe de los Buendía (52-53).

The "pre-initiation Macondo" would be "la ciudad de los espejos (o espejismos)" (351), referred to as the narrative closes, while the "post-initiation Macondo" is "una ciudad luminosa, con grandes casas de vidrio" (53), the Celestial City mentioned in Melquíades' prediction.

In the last sentence of the novel, we learn that "la ciudad de los espejos (o los espejismos)" is wiped out of man's memory by the wind, and that Aureliano Babilonia is never again to leave "ese cuarto" (Melquíades' room). It is possible, I believe, to see these two statements as facets of a single phenomenon if, first, Melquíades' room is regarded as the symbol of the gypsy's "enlightened perspective", and, second, it is recalled that the *unus mundus* is a "non-dual" world, devoid of mirrors and reflections. This line of reasoning leads to two hypothetical conclusions, one concerning Aureliano and the other concerning Macondo: 1) Aureliano Babilonia does not die as the novel ends, or does not merely die, but also attains "immortality", the alchemist's goal, or is suspended forever in Melquíades' room; 2) Macondo is not destroyed (or not merely destroyed) at the end of the work, but also transformed into a city where there are no reflections or mirages, the material embodiment of Aureliano Babilonia's enlightened mind.

MACONDO: BABYLON OR "LA CIUDAD LUMINOSA"?

The destruction of a house or village has been cited above as a manifestation of the *axis mundi* motif common to initiatory rites of passage. It is replaced by another, "heavenly village", a reflection of the initiate's psychological transformation. In *Cien años*, the devastation of the Buendía house and Macondo have been identified with this *axis mundi* motif, and it has been suggested that they are transformed, becoming, like Aureliano Babilonia, "another". Just as he is changed, transmuted by the mystic light, the old Macondo and the Buendía house are reordered around the *axis mundi* of Melquíades' room.

The *axis mundi* motif can be seen at the end of another work, and its development there is relevant to *Cien años*, as the two books, and especially their endings, invite comparison. I refer to the Bible, which ends with *Revelation*. Besides the destruction common to *Revelation* and the ending of *Cien años*, other obvious parallels can be cited: the name Babilonia (which can mean Babylon in Spanish); the "revelation" of "las claves definitivas" of Melquíades manuscripts to Aureliano Babilonia; and the description of the wind which desolates Macondo as "un huracán bíblico". Macondo has been seen, by critics, as a Babylon, a city destroyed for its wickedness. I am aware of no critical references to the Celestial City with which *Revelation* concludes, however, nor to the words with which is opens:

> Then I saw a new heaven and a new earth; for the first heaven and the first earth had passed away, and the sea was no more. And I saw the holy city, New Jerusalem, coming down out of heaven; and I heard a great voice from the throne saying, "Behold, the dwelling of God is with men. He will dwell with them, and they shall be his people, and God himself will be with them; he will wipe away every tear from their eyes, and death shall be no more, neither shall there be mourning nor crying nor pain any more, for the former things have passed away (verses 1-4).

Yet these opening verses seem germane, as do descriptions of the New Jerusalem presented in *Revelation*, which correspond remarkably well to phrases in Melquíades prediction about Macondo's future, that "sería una ciudad luminosa, con grandes casas de vidrio".

> and her light was like unto a stone most precious, even like a jasper stone, clear as crystal (Ch. 21, v. 11)

> And the building of the wall of it was of jasper; and the city was *pure gold, like unto clear glass* [emphasis is mine] (Ch. 21, v. 18)

> and the street of the city was *pure gold, as it were transparent glass* [emphasis is mine] (Ch. 21, v. 21)

I have underlined phrases likning pure gold to clear glass because it is an association germane to *Cien años* for several reasons. This connection first arose in the discussion of the narrative passage describing the last José Arcadio Buendía's discovery of Úrsula's gold:

> Une noche vieron [José Arcadio and a friend] en la alcoba donde dormía Úrsula un resplendor amarillo a través del

> *cemento cristalizado*, como si un *sol* subterráneo hubiera con-
> vertido en *vitral* el piso del dormitorio [emphasis mine]
> (314)

Certain phrases from José Arcadio's discovery of Úrsula's
gold, "el cemento cristalizado" and the floor transformed into
a "golden glass", like it to the passages from *Revelation*.

Also during that earlier discussion, the similarities between this passage and others were cited. First, it was
compared to excerpts describing the completion of the other
branch of the quest theme, that for true, or psychological,
gold. The links to the revelation of "las claves definitivas de
Melquíades" to Aureliano Buendía-Babilobia, and the light
emanating from the manuscripts which permits their deciphering, both paralleled the description of Úrsula's luminous
gold as it reveals itself to José Arcadio. This passage was also
compared to the following excerpt, which can now be seen as
another expression of the successful completion of the quest
for true gold, the material embodiment of Aureliano Babilonia's enlightened mind:

> Una noche creyó [Melquíades] encontrar una predicción
> sobre el futuro de Macondo. Sería una *ciudad luminosa* con
> grandes *casas de vidrio*,... [emphasis mine] (52-53).

Moreover, these associations linking gold, transparency
and revelation have been cited explicitly by Jung in his
Alchemical Studies as descriptions of the philosophers' stone:
"the 'spiritual' or 'ethereal' (*aethereus*) philosophers' stone is a
precious *vitrum*... which was often equated with the gold
glass (*aurem vitrum*) of the heavenly Jerusalem".[13] This information further serves to identify the Macondo of Melquíades' prediction with the completion of the quest for "true
alchemical gold". It also lends support to the idea that Aureliano Babilonia's lucidity, the light emanating from the manuscripts as he deciphers them, and the luminous city of Melquíades' prognostication, can be seen as three expressions of
the same "mystic light" phenomenon.

The parallel between *Revelation* and the ending of *Cien años*
that critics have suggested is, I feel, a good one. I think it can
be extended, however. The union of Christ with the New
Jerusalem, described as his bride, corresponds to Aureliano

Babilonia's mystical transformation and its reflection in the luminous, transparent Macondo, the symbolic embodiment of his enlightened state. Both are variations of the same initiatory motif: the *axis mundi*. In terms of alchemy, Aureliano Babilonia has successfully completed the quest for true gold, and the corresponding spiritualization of matter is represented by the transformed Macondo, the "golden glass", or "true gold".

"EL HURACÁN BÍBLICO"

Another biblical reference, the phrase "huracán bíblico", which describes the wind that destroys Macondo, occurs in the final paragraph of the narrative (p. 350). This wind has been seen by critics as reminiscent of the fire that destroys Babylon in *Revelation*, and Aureliano Babilonia's last name has been invoked to reinforce this parallel. However, other interpretations are possible. *Babilonia* not only means Babylon, but also Babylonia, which is popularly recognized as the cradle of civilization. It is also the place where alchemy originated. And Macondo is not laid waste by fire, but by wind, an image which has a very different interpretation both in the Bible and in the novel. Wind is used as a simile for the spirit in Christian symbology:

> The wind blows where it wills, and you hear the sound of it, but you do not know whence it comes or whither it goes; so it is with every one who is born of the Spirit (*John*, 3:3-8).[14]

Furthermore, as a symbol of spirit, wind is not exclusively Christian, but rather universal: one example which has left remnants in the English language is the Greek word *pneuma*, meaning both *wind*, *air*, *breath*, and also *soul*, *spirit*. In the Old Testament, in Eden, God breathes Spirit into Adam. The destruction of Macondo by wind, an "huracán bíblico", and not by fire, or flood, or plague, may be significant, especially when Aureliano Babilonia's "rites of passage" are considered. Certainly the destruction of the Buendía house, and the "exile" of "pre-initiation" Macondo (and its ultimate transformation) by the Spirit, would be consistent with the rest of our initiatory interpretation of the final pages of the novel.

Moreover, the "huracán bíblico" is not the first wind associated with religion in the narrative. Another, earlier wind in Macondo carries off Remedios the Beauty, the character whose perspective symbolizes spiritual gold within the work. The description of this zephyr as "un delicado viento de luz," and the miraculous assumption it effects, bestow a spirituality upon this wind. It is also referred to as "aquel viento irreparable", and it carries Remedios "donde no podían alcanzarla ni los más altos pájaros de la memoria" (205). These two points recall, respectively, the apparently irreparable damage the "huracán bíblico" wreaks upon Macondo, and the fact that this ultimate wind erases Macondo from man's memory:

> estaba previsto que la ciudad de los espejos (o los espejismos) sería arrasada por el viento y desterrada de la memoria de los hombres en el instante en que Aureliano Babilonia acabara de descifrar los pergaminos (351).

Remedios' physical ascension in a wind of light reflects Aureliano's psychological ascent (the *albedo*) at the end of the novel, when he is bathed in the light of the manuscripts and an extraordinary internal lucidness, and surrounded by the "huracán bíblico". Memory is treated more extensively in the next chapter, but a few words are warranted here, in the context of Remedios' ascension and the internal/external metamorphoses associated with the rites of passage. Remedios' miraculous ascension carries her "más allá de los pájaros de la memoria", and in the last sentence of the novel we learn that Macondo "sería arrasada por el viento y desterrada de la memoria de los hombres". These two references to memory are of cardinal interest to this study, as both involve the true quest and its successful completion. Macondo is "desterrada de la memoria de los hombres" because its existence symbolizes a mental state which has been transformed, and of course this "exile" occurs, as the novel explicitly states, precisely "en el instante en que Aureliano Babilonia acabara de descifrar los pergaminos" (351), that is, at the completion of his psychological "passage", whereupon the old Macondo is replaced by the luminous, transfigured city. Remedios the Beauty, as embodiment of "true gold", the psychological transformation finally experienced by Aureliano Babilonia, passes on to a completely symbolic level of existence (from Earth to Heaven), one which excludes the literal Macondo. As the next chapter demonstrates, she, and the metamorphosed Macondo, represent the truth behind the words of literature.

Although I believe that the ending of *Cien años* can be interpreted in a positive, consistent way, I would not insist that the literal destruction of Macondo does not take place. I think the ending of the novel is bisemic, and consistent at both literal and symbolic levels. The parallel between Macondo and Babylon, the home of false gods, the city destroyed for its sins, is valid at one level, but not at another. As I seek to show in the next chapter, when narrative theory is discussed, Macondo, as a fictitious place, is destroyed, but the truth behind the fictitious events which occur there is not. On the contrary, the truth is thereby cast into relief. Put another way, the literal, fictional events are destroyed forever, having been transformed into the psychological truths they embody. The bisemic ending of the narrative ultimately reflects the dual nature of art that Antonin Artaud has captured so cogently in the statement: "Art is never real and always true". I would suggest that what we are witnessing in the ending of *Cien años de soledad* is an attempt to express this apparent paradox.

THE SYMPLEGADES

The reconciliation of the apparently final destruction at the end of the novel with Melquíades' earlier prediction concerning Macondo's future, and the concomitant death and immortality of Aureliano Babilonia, would integrate very well into the overall initiatory scenario that pervades the final paragraphs of the narrative: it would reflect the Symplegades motif of rites of passage. Mentioned earlier, this motif forms an important aspect of such rituals, representing the "impossibility" of the quest or passage, or a paradox which must be resolved before success can be assured. In literature, this motif is commonly associated with heroes (e.g., David's slaying of Goliath, King Arthur removing Excalibur from the stone, Moses convincing Pharaoh to let the Hebrews go), and in many initiations one apparent paradox involves the initiate's being told that he is the victim and the hero of the tribal myth. According to Eliade, this motif serves to evoke the real, non-literal or psychological nature of the initiate's passage, as the paradoxes and evident impossibilities pertain only at non-symbolic levels, when the apparent conflicts are still not properly understood. At the same time, the Symplegades motif establishes the great worth of the prize to be attained if the quest or passage is successful. In alchemy and Christianity this goal is represented by immortality, although first one must die and be reborn, an apparent paradox. And in almost all initiations, one goal is participation in the original or primordial time, before history or the conventional world of men has come into being. Interestingly, in the novel Aureliano Babilonia "goes back to the origins", both his own personal genesis (his conception in the baño), and the beginnings of the tale, Francis Drake's assault on Riohacha. In fact, his deciphering takes place "entre las plantas prehistóricas y los charcos humeantes y los insectos luminosos que habían desterrado del cuarto todo vestigio del paso de los hombres por la tierra" (349), and, with his last "salto" in the deciphering process, Aureliano perhaps goes back beyond these origins, as his name, Babilonia, implies.

In terms of this character's "immortality", several comments can be framed. First, the successful completion of the alchemical quest was said to confer immortality upon the artifex. The alchemist Melquíades, whose manuscripts Aureliano deciphers and whose point of view he assumes at the end of the novel, says at one point in the novel: "Cuando me muera, quemen mercurio durante tres días en mi cuarto.... He alcanzado la inmortalidad" (68). Aureliano Babilonia's mystic light experience during his deciphering of the manuscripts, corresponds to the successful completion of the true alchemical quest in the narrative, the search for intangible gold. His state of mind correlates with alchemical immortality. He comes to share the gypsy magus' enlightened perspective and, like Melquíades, he becomes one with the universe and has access to its secrets. In the novel, this point of view Aureliano attains is associated with Melquíades and Remedios the Beauty, two characters who do not die, but rather disappear into light. Aureliano, at the story's conclusion, may likewise dissolve into light: his experience can be seen as representative of the transformation of the characters, e-vents and descriptions of the narrative into the intangible truths they embody. Such transmutation can occur if the reader, like Aureliano Buendía-Babilonia, is properly prepared, an idea developed in the next chapter.

Aureliano's possible survival and "passage to immortality" is also reinforced by another set of narrative links, those involving Colonel Aureliano Buendía and José Arcadio Segundo. Each escapes death miraculously on numerous occasions, something discussed before [*supra.* pp.16-18]. All the other characters associated with the true quest then, the Colonel, José Arcadio Segundo, Remedios the Beauty, and Melquíades, miraculously escape death on at least one occasion, and none of them dies violently. (In the narrative, in fact, Melquíades, the Colonel and José Arcadio Segundo each escapes a violent death: the Colonel fails in his attempt at suicide (pp. 155-56); José Arcadio Segundo escapes death in the plaza massacre, and then escapes being buried alive by leaping from the railroad car of dead citizens (p. 260); Melquíades drowns (p. 69), only to be resurrected.) Aureliano Babilonia's escaping death at the end of the novel would not be uncharacteristic of the group of persons he has been associated with, and perhaps he survives. Especially significant in this context, in view of the many passages devoted to establishing the extraordinary physical likeness which exists between the Colonel and Aureliano Babilonia, is the fact that the novel opens with a reference to one facing an apparently certain death and closes with the other in a comparably hopeless situation:

Muchos años después, frente al pelotón de fusilamiento, el coronel Aureliano Buendía había de recordar aquella tarde remota en que su padre lo llevó a conocer el hielo (9).

Sin embargo, antes de llegar al verso final ya había comprendido que no saldría jamás de ese cuarto, pues estaba previsto que la ciudad de los espejos (o los espejismos) sería arrasada por el viento y desterrada de la memoria de los hombres en el instante en que Aureliano Babilonia acabara de descifrar los pergaminos, y que todo lo escrito en ellos era irrepetible desde siempre y para siempre, porque las estirpes condenadas a cien años de soledad no tenían una segunda oportunidad sobre la tierra (351).

As a result of the consistent, bisemic ending, in fact, Aureliano Babilonia both survives and dies "para siempre": as character he dies; as symbol for the transformed reader of the novel he lives on in every external reader whose point of view has been changed by literature.

THE TAROT

This discussion of the initiatory material contained in *Cien años de soledad* has been undertaken to establish a background for evaluating the significance of the use of alchemy in the novel, and will serve as scaffolding in that examination. Before entering into that exercise, however, another esoteric practice included in the narrative should be considered. This is the Tarot, an esoteric discipline which uses a special deck of cards to pursue its mystical designs. Contemporary with alchemy, it served a similar purpose in Medieval-Renaissance Europe, helping to keep open the alternatives to the orthodox Church channels for individual spiritual and psychological transformation. And in *Cien años* the Tarot, like alchemy, seems to receive considerable development. Presenting and commenting on this development is an exercise included here, because it both strengthens and facilitates conclusions concerning the use of alchemy and its relation to narrative theory in García Márquez' work.

In *Cien años*, the Tarot is presented as Pilar Ternera's province, as her key to knowledge normally outside the ken of mortals, in a way akin to how alchemy and Melquíades are associated in the novel. Two passages seem to suggest that she, like Melquíades, has power over events in the work. The first of these describes her reading of her son Aureliano José's cards. She sees him marked by the sign of death, and she pleads with him not to go out that night. He ignores her and is subsequently killed, shot in the back, and the narrator offers this comment:

> Aureliano José estaba destinado a conocer con ella [Carmelita Montiel] la felicidad que le negó Amaranta, a tener siete hijos y a morirse de viejo en sus brazos, pero la bala de fusil que le entró por la espalda y le despedazó el pecho, estaba dirigida por una mala interpretación de las barajas (136).

This power to influence events in the narrative is echoed toward the end of the novel, when Aureliano Buendía-Babilonia cries on Pilar's lap from unrequited love for Amaranta Úrsula and she tells him simply: "No te preocupes.... En cualquier lugar en que esté ahora, ella te está esperando" (334). Immediately, these words of unassuming authority are borne out by events. According to the narrator, her power, or knowledge, is the result of "un siglo de naipes y de experiencia" (334).

Examining the Tarot as an esoteric system, several fundamental parallels to alchemy emerge. First, like alchemy, Tarot cards were understood in more than one way. They were regarded as a game, as a tool for divination, and as a vehicle for secret rites of passage, designed to effect a psychological transformation in the initiate. The Tarot deck today is composed of seventy-eight cards, divided into twenty-two "major trumps" (also called the major arcana), and fifty-six "minor trumps" (the minor arcana). The minor arcana are not very different from an American poker deck, having four suits, each with one extra court card, the page. Although used in conjunction with the major arcana for purposes of divination, these fifty six cards of the minor arcana seem to have played no role in the use of the Tarot as a catalyst for the transmission of esoteric knowledge. For this purpose, the major trumps, exclusively, were employed:

> if the twenty-two cards of the greater arcana, the major trumps, are viewed in sequence—commencing with the unnumbered card *The Fool* and finishing with XXI, *The World*—they reveal the theme of Classical Gnosticism remarkably well.[15]

Once more we confront the Hermetic tradition, and, as with alchemy, once more it stands in a compensatory relationship to Medieval-Renaissance Christianity. It is believed that when the Church began supressing ideas it considered dangerous, the twenty-two Tarot cards mentioned above became a kind of visual aid for the initiation of illiterate adepts into esoteric confraternities. Again, like alchemy, the Tarot cards display a universal symbolism. According to authorities, they became popular when many streams of ideas were converging upon Europe: "The designs were executed in Europe, but seem to incorporate not only Christian, Gnostic and Islamic imagery, but Celtic and Norse elements as well."[16]

There are several other connections between alchemy and the Tarot which are particularly relevant to *Cien años*. One author writes:

> The word Tarot comes from the Sanskrit [Melquíades' mother tongue] and means "fixed star", which in its turn signifies immutable tradition, theosophical synthesis, symbolism of primitive dogmatism, etc. Graven on golden plates, the designs were used by Hermes Trismegistus and their mysteries were only revealed to the highest grade of the priesthood of Isis.[17]

Another author makes this comment:

> The game of cards called the Tarot, which the gypsies possess, is the Bible of Bibles. It is the book of Thoth Hermes Trismegistus, the book of Adam, the book of the primitive Revelation of the ancient civilizations.[18]

Their links to Sanskrit, gypsies, "the primitive Revelation of the ancient civilizations" and Hermes Trismegistus integrate the esoteric Tarot cards well into the world of the novel.

The pictures portrayed on these twenty-two cards of the major arcana reflect archetypal characters or situations. Some examples are the cards depicting a male magician, a female counterpart, the King or all-Father, the corresponding Queen /all-Mother, warrior, virgin, lovers, Death, Judgment and Resurrection. The description of the twenty-two card major arcana as a "Bible of Bibles" reflects the idea that the Tarot cards graphically represent initiatory motifs common to many religions and other mystical systems involved with the rites of passage.

I do not intend an exhaustive scrutiny of Tarot related material in *Cien años*, but its presence in the narrative should be duly noted, in order to establish that, like alchemy, the Tarot is more than just a name for an esoteric pursuit as García Márquez employs it. Two kinds of Tarot inclusions in the novel will be considered: one at the level of content, involving the correspondence of characters in the narrative to figures in the twenty-two card greater arcana; another at the level of structure, which suggests a parallel between one aspect of the work taken as a whole, and the rites of passage associated with the Tarot initiation.

The major arcana consists of twenty-one numbered cards and one, *The Fool*, which is unnumbered, or designated as zero. Alfred Douglas makes the following comments about the esoteric Tarot as a tool for assisting psychological passage:

> The Tarot speaks in the language of the unconscious, and when approached in the right manner it may open doors into the hidden reaches of the soul.
>
> If the major arcana of the Tarot pack illustrates twenty-two important stages in the path of life, then each card can be interpreted at several levels. It can point to important principles and forces operating in the world; it can unveil significant processes in the expansion of mystical consciousness; [when upright] it can indicate the emergence of as yet unevolved aspects of personality, and when reversed, it can warn of physical or psychic pitfalls which may be encountered... [19]

The Fool represents the initiand, and is considered a floating card in the Tarot. It corresponds to the seeker of knowledge who passes successively through the phases symbolized by the other twenty-one cards. Its "placement" in this sequence of major trumps has evoked some polemic in the past, but this confusion has arisen out of ignorance that the major arcana was used in esoteric initiations, something discovered quite recently, according to Douglas and Waite. Because this fact was unknown, or forgotten, until the present, persons writing about the Tarot attempted to establish the "true place" or places of *The Fool*, or tried to explain the traditional placements which they had discovered. Three of *The Fool's* positionings are readily understood: he is found 1) at the beginning of the major trumps; 2) at the end; 3) in both places.

For purposes of initiation, the last sequence, *Fool*—cards I through XXI—*Fool* might seem the most logical, the first *Fool* representing a true fool, one without the secret knowledge, while, when placed at the end of the sequence, this figure would signify the sage, whose indifference to the material world might make him appear to the "unenlightened" as a fool. However, while perhaps the most apparently likely, the sequence is not the most common traditionally. *The Fool* is most often located between the last two numbered cards, *Judgement* (XX) and *The World* (XXI). These four positionings yield a fifth one: *The Fool*—cards I through XX—*The Fool*—card XXI. The logic of this synthetic ordering, which makes the most sense from the point of view of initiatory scenarios, will become clearer below, when the comparison of the structure of *Cien años* to the Tarot initiation is discussed.

Several of the twenty-two cards in the major trumps are personified to a greater or lesser degree in the novel. The most obvious case, perhaps, involves the card numbered One in this pack, *The Magician*. This card is generally accepted to represent Hermes Trismegistus (the guide of alchemists), and, as the first character described in the novel is the alchemical magus Melquíades, the correspondence is patent. In certain Tarot decks, the magician is portrayed with a hat having stylized wings, a description which recalls Melquíades' "sombrero grande y negro, como las alas extendidas de un cuervo" (13). More significantly, the roles of the gypsy in *Cien años* and the magician in the Tarot initiation are equivalent: each orchestrates the quest of the initiate and assists him to its successful completion.

The Fool, also, can be seen to receive considerable development in the narrative. In José Arcadio Buendía, who initiates the quest for gold in the opening paragraph of the narrative, we encounter an apt representation of the "true fool", the unenlightened seeker who stands at the front of the Tarot major arcana. Like *The Fool* starting on his journey, José Arcadio first meets "the Magician":

> José Arcadio Buendía, cuya desaforada imaginación iba siempre más lejos que el ingenio de la naturaleza, y aun más allá del milagro y la magia, pensó que era posible servirse de aquella invención inútil [Melquíades' magnets] para desentrañar el oro de la tierra (9).

In the first chapter of this study the founder was compared to the literal-minded alchemist, in other words a fool, and in this light the following observation can be introduced: "the conventional explanations say that...its [*The Fool's*] subsidiary name was at one time the alchemist..."[20] Similarly, at the end of the novel we find a "transformed" character, an initiate, Aureliano Babilonia, who completes the other branch of the quest begun by José Arcadio Buendía. Another relevant commentary, from a different source, tells us this: "*The Fool* can indicate the imminent start of a new cycle of destiny, and can refer to a type of person—the creative dreamer".[21] The patriarch of the family might be described as a "creative dreamer", and both he, as the novel opens, and Aureliano Babilonia, as it closes, can be seen as characters involved with "the imminent start of a new cycle".

The Fool, or seeker, in progressing through the initiatory Tarot sequence, becomes associated with many characters and situations, and, not surprisingly, Aureliano Babilonia and José Arcadio Buendía are not the only two characters who can be linked with this card. In the novel, all of the characters involved in the quest for "true gold" can be connected with *The Fool* in one way or another. The descriptions of José Arcadio Segundo, "todo el mundo lo tenía por loco" (296), and of his sister Remedios the Beauty, believed to be a "restrasada mental" (172), identify these characters as fools in the eyes of others, though both are actually extraordinarily lucid. The Colonel, the other Buendía associated with the quest for intangible gold, can be linked with *The Fool*, too. He is the first character mentioned in the novel, and, therefore, like his father, he can be seen as standing at the beginning of the narrative. He is also the first person born in Macondo, thereby "initiating a new cycle", and his "rara intuición alquímica" provides another link between him and *The Fool*, or alchemist. Finally, Colonel Aureliano Buendía is identical in appearance to Aureliano Babilonia, the "transformed fool" who stands at the end of the novel. (Curiously, both of these characters are *literally* standing at the beginning and ending of the narrative: the Colonel in front of the firing squad, and Aureliano Babilonia as he deciphers the manuscripts). This physical likeness between the first and last characters mentioned in the novel exactly corresponds to the case of *The Fool* card, which changes in role and significance as it moves from beginning to end of the Tarot sequence, but not in appearance:

When he appears at the end of the sequence *The Fool*
has completed his journey, and he passes through the
World, the appearance of which has been transformed by
his own inner transformation.[22]

This parallel between *The Fool* and the two characters,
Colonel Aureliano Buendía and Aureliano Babilonia, can be
extended if the visual imagery of this card is examined (see
Appendix, following the notes of this chapter). *The Fool* card
depicts a youth who is apparently about to meet his death.
He has one foot on a cliff, and, in some decks, the other in
the air. He is walking forward, off the precipice, seemingly
oblivious to his situation. (Compare the beginning and the
ending of the novel, where characters who look exactly alike
are facing apparently fatal situations.) When found at the
beginning of the Tarot sequence, *The Fool* represents someone
whose mind wanders after transient beauty (the butterfly),
someone who is in an extremely dangerous predicament, and
oblivious to it. (The Colonel's youthful idealism, which leads
him to war, and its subsequent evolution into ruthlessness,
could be one exemplary situation.) At the end of the Tarot
sequence, the passage of the fool from earth to air represents
the liberation of ethereal Spirit from gross Matter, the successful completion of the rites of passage. The butterfly the
fool follows symbolizes transformation, the transmutation of
the earth-bound caterpillar into its winged and aerial metamorphosed state.

As Aureliano Babilonia is also, ultimately, a reader as well
as a character, this parallel to the Tarot can be extended, by
bringing the other, "external" reader of *Cien años* into this
discussion. He too passes through a sequence of twenty
phases, the twenty chapters of the narrative, and, like the
characters and the novel itself, is bounded by "the World". In
addition, the identification of Aureliano Babilonia and the
"other, real life" reader, suggests a parallel "revelation" for
the external participant, a point treated in the next chapter,
when novelistic theory is considered.

Another correspondence, perhaps the most intriguing of
the possible links between the Tarot and *Cien años*, can be
seen if card number ten, *The Wheel of Fortune*, is scrutinized.
This card signals the end of one cycle and the beginning of a

new one, for in Tarot the numbers 1 and 10 are equivalent: 10, as 1 + 0, reduces to unity. If, now, the opening lines of chapter ten of the novel are compared to those which open chapter one, how the text explicitly reflects the idea that a new cycle is commencing becomes patent:

> Años después, en su lecho de agonía, Aureliano Segundo había de recordar la lluviosa tarde de junio en que entró en el dormitorio a conocer a su primer hijo (159).

> Muchos años después, frente al pelotón de fusilamiento, el coronel Aureliano Buendía había de recordar aquella tarde remota en que su padre lo llevó a conocer el hielo (9).

From this juxtaposition, similarities too strong to be the result of mere coincidence emerge. And, as with the number of cards in the Tarot sequence, only nine of the twenty chapters, and not ten, or half of them, have passed at this point. This similarity, coupled with those above, encourages a comparison between the structure of the novel and the sequence of cards used for the Tarot initiation. Both begin with *The Fool* meeting the Magician, start a new cycle at the tenth card and tenth chapter respectively, and both end (card and chapter XX) with an enlightened fool and Judgment. Both sequences, finally, are also bounded by the World. This comparison between the structure of the novel and the Tarot sequence is undertaken after a few other parallels involving specific Tarot cards and characters and events in the narrative have been presented.

Card number XVII, *The Star*, suggests another example of how the Tarot might be employed in the narrative, and this concerns Remedios, the Beauty. The name Remedios is as common among the Buendía women as Aureliano and José Arcadio are among the men. Of the associations to this name that develop in the course of the work, one of the most obvious and significant is its connection with the Virgin. On three occasions there are references to *La Virgen de los Remedios* (pp. 83, 124, 141), and of course the most dramatic link between the name Remedios and the Virgin Mary occurs when Remedios the Beauty is assumed into heaven. This character is in fact a virgin, the personification of innocence. The Tarot card *The Star* depicts a nude young women, traditionally considered to be a virgin, pouring water out of two goblets she holds in her hands. One of her feet (in some decks it is her knee) is on the land, or in the fire, while the other is in the water (see Appendix). In either case she is the mediatrix between two elements, generally regarded as symbolizing the profane and sacred worlds. For an even more direct connection of this card's depiction and Remedios the Beauty, it is useful to recall one specific manifestation of this archetypal motif, the Greco-roman myth of Astrelia, the virgin goddess who dwelt among men during the Golden Age. When man's nature became more base, she left the earth, flying away to join the gods in the sky. She was placed among the stars, and became the constellation Virgo.[23]

Other resemblances between characters in the novel and the major arcana emerge. Pilar Ternera, in many ways Melquíades' counterpart, fits neatly into the image of *The High Priestess*, or female magus, the second card in this sequence. *Death*, the thirteenth card, also makes an appearance in the novel, when she tells Amaranta to prepare her *mortaja* (p. 283). José Arcadio Buendía is once referred to as "el rey" by Cataure (p. 125), suggesting a correlation with *The Emperor*, card IV, and Úrsula, by association, can be seen as *The Empress*, which comes third in the deck. [The characteristics ascribed to these cards, which I will not enter into here, strongly reinforce these parallels. (See Waite, and especially Douglas).] Cards like *The Pope*, V, *The Hermit* (who, according to Douglas, "shuts out the outer world, and an inner animation takes over"), IX, and *The Lovers*, VI, recall respectively: the last José Arcadio; José Arcadio Segundo (also Aureliano Babilonia, and possibly even the Colonel); and the pairs Aureliano Buendía-Babilonia—Amaranta Úrsula, and Aureliano Segundo—Petra Cotes. The seventh card, *The Chariot* or *The Warrior*, can be seen to represent the Colonel very aptly. *The Warrior* is considered the offspring of *The Emperor* and *The Empress*, figures which correlate well with the Colonel's parents, and is described as follows: "he who has taught himself to concentrate all his faculties on a single goal... He may believe himself to be an idealist, but his only answer to those who question his aims is oppression".[24]

Perhaps the most bizarre image encountered in the major arcana is depicted in card number XII, *The Hanged Man*, a human figure suspended from a tree by a rope tied about his ankle. Another card, XV, is *The Devil*, imaged as a half-man, half-beast hybrid, hirsute and winged. In the novel, curiously, we meet an admixture of these two Tarot representations. The Wandering Jew, a hirsute, half-human, half-animal creature with scars of truncated wings, is captured by the inhabitants of Macondo. Its final fate is portrayed in these words: "Lo colgaron por los tobillos en un almendro de la plaza" (292). (*The Hanged Man* of the Tarot deck is also traditionally associated with the suspension of a deity, or mythological figure, in the "World Tree", a motif related earlier to José Arcadio Buendía [*supra.* pp.67-68], the character who plants the "almendros eternos", one of which is used to hang the Wandering Jew, in Macondo (p. 40).)

While the above comments could easily be expanded, and additional arguments could be framed to include similar reflections of the remaining twenty-two major arcana in *Cien años*, the purpose here is not to show how the content of the novel can be "fitted" into any one esoteric framework (it cannot), but rather to demonstrate that the author has included references to such practices, which are integrated creatively into his story, at once a history of a family and a myth in its own right. Instead, a somewhat different approach to possible Tarot inclusions will be taken at this point, one concerned more with the significance of the Tarot initiation sequence, *The Fool*—cards I-XX—*The Fool*—*The World*, to an overall interpretation of the narrative.

How *The Fool* card, which is found at the beginning and again in the penultimate position in the Tarot initiation sequence, can be integrated into *Cien años* has been described already. The relevance of card XX, Judgement, to chapter twenty should be patent after the discussion of the material related to initiation and rites of passage contained in the final paragraphs of the novel. [This card's central motif is resurrection; its central image a child arisen from the tomb (see Appendix)]. "The angel of resurrection blows his mighty horn and the psyche is released from the walls that imprison it", remarks one commentator about the imagery of the Judgement card.[25] This passage can be seen as a paraphrase of the simultaneous processes of parchment deciphering and the blowing away of the Buendía house and Macondo which occur in the final paragraph of the novel. The child in the center of the card has been called "the Divine Child ... a symbol of the Philosopher's Stone, the treasure hard to attain; ... the youthful 'God within'".[26] This "Divine Child" is reflected in the narrative as *El Niño de Oro*, a designation which has been applied to Aureliano Babilonia above.

In the initiation sequence, *The Fool* reappears after *Judgement* and before *The World*. And, once again, the traditional interpretation of *The Fool* in this position, that he represents the "enlightened fool" or sage, reinforces what was said earlier concerning the transfiguration of Aureliano Babilonia. Looking now at *The World*, the final card in the sequence of Tarot major trumps, we see a human figure inside of a wreath which is surrounded by the tetramorphs of Christian iconography (see Appendix). The figure is holding two wands, and is traditionally regarded as an androgyne, the union of male and female principles. One commentator relates *The World* both to alchemy and psychology, two threads that have reappeared time and again in the present study, and which will emerge once more when narrative theory is considered:

> The figure seen here represents the goal of the alchemists, the *anima mundi* freed from the bonds of matter. The conclusion of the Great Work is symbolized by the cosmic egg within which all chaos is reduced to order ... The search is ended, the goal has been reached. The self has at last reached true unity and is indivisible. The contrasexual elements have been reconciled; the psyche no longer holds any illusions concerning its own separateness and is aware that it is coterminous with the entire universe ... The dancer is seen at the still point where past and future, evolution and involution, action and inaction all intersect and interact ...
>
> Viewed in terms of the whole Tarot sequence, *The World* can be seen ... as containing the seeds of fresh endeavor on higher planes.[27]

Several points in this commentary, which links the goals of Tarot and alchemical initiations, can be directly related to *Cien años*. First, there are two explicit references to the *anima mundi* in the novel, and both are significant. This alchemical reference is mentioned initially by Melquíades, in the inaugural words spoken by a character in the narrative: "Las cosas tienen vida propia—pregonaba el gitano con áspero acento—todo es cuestión de despertarles el ánima" (9). The other time the *anima mundi* is referred to, it is done so in a less dramatic way:

> en sus prolongados encierros, mientras manipulaba la materia, rogaba en el fondo de su corazón que el prodigio esperado no fuera el hallazgo de la piedra filosofal, ni la liberación del soplo que hace vivir los metales, ni la facultad de convertir en oro las bisagras y cerraduras de la casa, sino lo que ahora había ocurrido: el regreso de Úrsula (38).

This mention, though less striking than the previous one, can be seen, nonetheless, as significant. "La liberación del soplo que hace vivir los metales" refers to the divine breath or wind that recalls the final destruction and transformation of the Buendía house and of Macondo by the "huracán bíblico", and also the zephyr which carries off Remedios. (At one point, the house is described as "una casa a la que sólo le hacía falta un último soplo para derrumbarse" (345).)

Aside from specific narrative references to this alchemical phenomenon, the tenor of the entire passage concerning the *anima mundi* integrates well into the conclusions drawn before in the discussion of initiatory material in the closing paragraphs of the novel. Specifically, the "reconciliation of contrasexual elements" has been addressed in the examination of Aureliano Buendía-Babilonia's and Amaranta Úrsula's mutual identification. Also germane to the conclusion of *Cien años* is the fact that, as the narrative closes, Aureliano is explicitly "coterminous with the entire universe", as external events correspond exactly to his manuscript deciphering as the work ends.

The World card aptly portrays a successful rite of psychological passage. Besides the alchemical imagery, this card also includes the tetramorphs of Christianity, symbolizing inspired writers who brought God's revelation to man. As pictured on this Tarot card, Christianity is seen as one emanation of the central, unchangeable, androgynous (or non-dual) being, which has been called atman by the Hindus, Being by the pre-Socratics, Yahweh by the Jews, God by the Christians, the philosophers' stone by alchemists and the Self by Jungians.

Furthermore, the novel echoes the phrase " ... *The World* can be seen ... as containing the seeds of fresh endeavor on higher planes". Not only is this an apt description of successful rites of passage, but the entire past of Macondo and the Buendía family has been literally erased. The last chapter deals explicitly with the death and destruction of the past: Amaranta Úrsula reflects traits of all Buendía women as Aureliano Buendía-Babilonia reflects those of the men, and their child, who dies, embodies the entire family past; the destruction of the house, completed by the wind, is begun by the rain, continued by the ants and also by Amaranta Úrsula's and Aureliano's lovemaking; the death of Pilar Ternera and the *sabio catalán*, who bears a marked resemblance to Melquíades, are also contained in this final chapter. Aureliano Babilonia's separation from all of this death and destruction at the beginning of the last paragraph ("olvidó sus muertos y el dolor de sus muertos" (349)), signals the potential for fresh endeavors on higher planes, as does his mystic light experience and his ultimately becoming one with the universe—in short, his rites of passage to the "ciudad luminosa". And the relevance of all Aureliano Babilonia's personal experience to the external reader of the narrative is implicit in the bisemic ending of the novel (this is developed in the next chapter), and made explicit in the identification of Aureliano as reader, in the final paragraph, when he is described as "profetizándose a sí mismo en el acto de descifrar la última página de los pergaminos, como si se estuviera viendo en un espejo hablado" (350).

Finally, the passage on *The World* card, and especially the image of the "dancer at the still point," can also be related to literature, as it bears a remarkable resemblance to the definition of art André Breton gives in "The Second Surrealist Manifesto":

> The bugaboo of death, the simplistic theatrical portrayal of the beyond, the shipwreck of the most beautiful reason in sleep, the overwhelming curtain of the future, the tower of Babel, the mirrors of inconstancy, ... these all too gripping images of the human catastrophe are, perhaps, no more than images. Everything tends to make us believe that there exists a certain point of the mind at which life

and death, the real and the imagined, past and future, the communicable and incommunicable, high and low, cease to be perceived as contradictions. Now, search as one may one will never find any other motivating force in the activities of the Surrealists than the hope of finding and fixing this point.[28]

Some final comments on androgyny seem in order in this discussion of alchemy and the Tarot in *Cien años*. Eliade cites symbolic and/or ritualistic androgyny as an element in many initiation ceremonies, as an expression of the *Symplegades* motif of the apparently paradoxical or impossible quest. Androgyny symbolizes the union of opposites, and in Aureliano Babilonia, several contraries developed in the novel are brought together. Earlier, androgyny was discussed when the incest between Aureliano and Amaranta Úrsula was considered as an alchemical motif. Here Aureliano's "androgyny" will be considered against the background of a comparison of the characters Melquíades and Pilar Ternera.

Earlier we saw how Pilar Ternera treats him maternally and acts as his sexual counselor and assistant, and in Melquíades we can see the spiritual father of the lonely orphan Aureliano. From an alchemical point of view, Pilar's association with night and Melquíades' with light and the day, are consistent with their roles of sexual and spiritual assistants to Aureliano. (In the novel, these associations are established in several ways. A few examples are: José Arcadio and his brother the Colonel visit Pilar by night, the former "every night" for awhile; her brothel, *El Niño de Oro*, is involved with nocturnal activity; her death, described in the opening sentence of the final chapter, occurs "una noche de fiesta." Turning to Melquíades, the phrase "alumbrando con su profunda voz de órgano los territorios más oscuros de la imaginación" is one example; "Un mediodía ardiente", related to Melquíades at least four times (13, 161, 301, 348), is another; the perpetual flame in his room and the images of light mentioned when Aureliano Babilonia begins his deciphering are two more.) The union of night and day, or *Sol* and *Luna*, called sometimes the "alchymical marriage", is one of the most common descriptions of the attainment of the philosophers' stone. At a more obvious level, Melquíades and Pilar

Ternera can represent the masculine and feminine principles, which are also unified when the *opus* is successfully completed.

Another "complementary contrast" emerges, apropos of these two characters, if we compare *Cien años* to a day and consider its "dawn" and "nightfall". Melquíades, the first character to speak, the first described in the novel, is linked to Macondo's beginning. His first words, "Las cosas tienen vida propia, todo es cuestión de despertarles el ánima," can be seen as the conjuring phrase of a magus, awakening the world of Macondo and bringing it to life. On the other hand, Pilar's death is tied up with the end of Macondo. We see this association explicitly established in the second paragraph of the last chapter, immediately succeeding the description of Pilar Ternera's death and burial, with which this final chapter begins:

> Era el final. En la tumba de Pilar Ternera, entre salmos y abalorios de putas, se pudrían los escombros del pasado, los pocos que quedaban después de que el sabio catalán remató la librería y regresó a la aldea mediterránea donde había nacido...(336).

Again, when the figure death appears to Amaranta in the novel, she is described as "una mujer vestida de azul con el cabello largo, de aspecto un poco anticuado, y con un cierto parecido a Pilar Ternera" (238).

The alchemical concept of the *coniunctio oppositorum*, while often depicted as the joining of two opposing principles, truly symbolizes the attainment of a state of consciousness wherein all oppositions are seen to be merely apparent, and, consequently, a unity results. This "point of view", which has been discussed before, constitutes the most significant link between Melquíades, Pilar Ternera and Aureliano Babilonia, a common perspective outside of "el tiempo convencional de los hombres". From this perspective, as we have seen, Melquíades' chronicle is written and deciphered, and it is from this perspective that Pilar lives out the last part of her long life:

> Años antes, cuando cumplió los ciento cuarenta y cinco, había renunciado a la perniciosa costumbre de llevar las cuentas de su edad, y continuaba viviendo en *el tiempo*

*estático y marginal de los recuerdos, en un futuro perfectamente
revelado y establecido*, más allá de los futuros perturbados por
las acechanzas y las suposiciones insidiosas de las barajas
[my emphasis] (333).

In a sense, then, Aureliano Babilonia can be seen as an
"androgynous" figure, the "synthesis", or product, of the
influences Melquíades and Pilar Ternera, representative of
alchemy, and the Tarot, have brought to bear upon the
Buendía family.

CONCLUSION

As in the gold quest and its development, alchemy figures
prominently in the bisemic ending of *Cien años de soledad*. Here,
however, its role is rather generic than specific. That is,
alchemy represents a certain kind of religious or philosophic
al belief system, one designed to assist a psychological passage in an individual from a profane or unenlightened understanding of self and world to a truer, more complete comprehension of reality. Like the major trumps of the Tarot deck,
the initiatory scenarios of tribes and ancient mystery cults,
alchemy seeks to put man in touch with hitherto unseen, or
unexperienced, realms.

Alchemy and practices whose ultimate aims are similar,
and references to them, are used in the closing paragraphs of
Cien años de soledad to construct an exercise in perspectivism,
an ending which can be interpreted in two very different
ways. Moreover, disciplines like alchemy offer insights into
how such a bisemic ending should be understood, for in the
Symplegades motif the union of apparent opposites is brought
about, stressing the integral role that resolution of paradoxes
plays in successful "passages". So, "alchemically", these systems suggest that the two opposing interpretations should
not be seen as black and white chess players who confront
each other on the board, one set to be eliminated eventually,
but rather as the game of chess in its totality, a game whose
purpose is to entertain, and to develop the mind. Their use in
Cien años de soledad intimates that alchemy, and these other
practices and belief systems, can be seen as metaphors for
literature, which, as the novel presents it, can be a vehicle for
the transformation of point of view, an exercise in perspec-

tivism, at least when it is properly understood. It is to the development of this idea that the present study now turns, taking up the specifics of narrative theory, as these are presented in the novel.

NOTES

[1] C. G. Jung, *Aion: Researches into the Phenomenology of the Self*, 2nd ed., trans. R. F. C. Hull (Princeton: Bollingen Foundation, 1970), Vol. IX of *The Collected Works of Carl Gustav Jung*, p. 210 and *Mysterium Coniunctionis: An Inquiry into the Separation and Synthesis of Psychic Opposites in Alchemy*, trans. R. F. C. Hull (New York: Bollingen, 1963), Vol. XIV of *The Collected Works*, p. 423. In alchemical literature, this figure is associated with the Ethiopian woman Moses marries (*Numbers*, 12:10). (Moses, Thomas Aquinas and other such personages are often found in this literature, sometimes as the "true authors" of the tracts.) It is interesting that Aureliano Buendía-Babilonia is, in fact, linked to the Old Testament hero at one point in the novel, when the nun brings him to Macondo in a basket and presents him to Fernanda and the following humorous exchange transpires:

—Diremos que lo encontramos flotando en la canastilla—sonrió [Fernanda].

—No se lo creerá nadie—dijo la monja.

—Si se lo creyeron a las Sagradas Escrituras—replicó Fernanda—, no veo por qué no han de creérmelo a mí (254).

[2] C. G. Jung, *Psychology and Alchemy*, trans. R. F. C. Hull, 2nd ed. (Princeton: Bollingen, 1968), Vol. XII of *The Collected Works*, p. 81. In the context of the alchemists' ultimate goal being thrown on a dunghill, it is interesting that Melquíades' parchments, in one sense the goal of the "true quest", are stored in "el cuarto de las bacinillas".

[3] Aureliano's search for links to his past displays several points of contact with the Jungian Individuation process of personal discovery and integration. While this process does not directly concern us here, the direction of Aureliano's regression, in relation to Individuation, can be noted. His search for his past identity moves through four phases: 1) his quest to regain group consciousness (his four friends and Mercedes, now all gone); 2) his attempts to recapture the paternal contacts with the *sabio catalán* (now dead); 3) next, his search for the mother (Pilar Ternera, who is also dead), a stage of development prior to the father-child relationship (which, in turn, is antecedent to the group consciousness); 4) the regression to alcohol induced unconsciousness—a state prior to all conscious relation-

ships.

The significance of Aureliano's attempts at regression in terms of Individuation is cast into relief fully with the opening sentence of the final paragraph, when he proceeds with the passage from his old Buendía consciousness to his new Babilonia consciousness, and the enlightenment and self discovery which accompany this change:

> Aureliano no había sido más lúcido en ningún acto de su vida que cuando olvidó sus muertos y el dolor de sus muertos, y volvió a clavar las puertas y las ventanas con las crucetas de Fernanda para no dejarse perturbar por ninguna tentación del mundo, porque entonces sabía que en los pergaminos de Melquíades estaba escrito su destino (349).

4 Mircea Eliade, *The Quest: History and Meaning in Religion* (Chicago: Univ. of Chicago Press, 1969), p. 112.

5 Mircea Eliade, *The Forge and the Crucible* (London: Rider and Co., 1962), p. 165.

6 Eliade, *Rites and Symbols of Initiation: The Mysteries of Birth and Rebirth*, trans. W. R. Trask (New York: Harper and Row, 1958), p. 124.

7 Eliade, *The Quest*, pp. 112-16.

8 Ibid., p. 113.

9 Ibid., p. 112.

10 Ibid., p. 114.

11 J. E. Harrison, *Prolegomena to the Study of Greek Religion* (Cambridge: Univ. Press, 1903), pp. 150-60.

12 Jung, *Psychology and Alchemy*, p. 21.

13 Jung, *Alchemical Studies*, trans. R. F. C. Hull, Vol. XIII of *The Collected Works*, pp. 197-99.

See also *Psychology and Alchemy*, p. 232.

14 The context of this Biblical quotation is interesting in light of this discussion on initiatory rebirth. It comes from *John*, Chapter 3, from Jesus' talk with Nicodemus:

> "Truly, truly, I say to you, unless one is born anew, he cannot see the kingdom of God." Nicodemus said to him, "How can a man be born when he is old? Can he enter a second time into his mother's womb and be born?" Jesus answered, "Truly, truly, I say to you, unless one is born of water and the Spirit, he cannot enter the kingdom of God. That which is born of the flesh is flesh, and that which is born of the Spirit is spirit. Do not marvel that I said to you, 'You must be born anew'. The wind blows where it wills, and you hear the sound of it, but you do not know whence it comes or whither it goes; so it is with every one who is born of the Spirit (verses 3-8).

15 Alfred Douglas, *The Tarot: The Origins, Meaning and Uses of the Cards* (New York: Taplinger, 1972), p. 32.

[16] Ibid., p. 33

[17] R. Falconnier. *Les XXII Lames Hermetiques du Tarot Divinatoire*, trans. by A. E. Waite in *The Pictorial Key to the Tarot: Being Fragments of a Secret Tradition Under the Veil of Divination* (New York: University Books, 1959), p. 32.

[18] Dr. Gerard Encausse, *Le Tarot des Bohémiens*, trans. by, and found in, A. Douglas, *The Tarot*, p. 122. Whether this information is true or false is, of course, another question entirely, and one of no concern to us here. The point to be made is that, historically, this information was believed to be true by persons interested in the Tarot.

[19] Douglas, *The Tarot*, p. 43.

[20] A. E. Waite, *The Pictorial Key to the Tarot: Being Fragments of a Secret Tradition Under the Veil of Divination* (New York: University Books, 1959), p. 155.

[21] Douglas, *The Tarot*, p. 49.

[22] Ibid. p. 116.

[23] For the myth of Astrelia I am indebted to Ms. Audrey Aaron's "The Total Innovation in García Márquez' *Cien años de soledad*", a talk given at Wheaton College on February 28, 1976.

The assumptions of Astrelia and the Blessed Virgin Mary, like the Carnival in *Cien años*, provide one concrete example of syncretism, the "mixing" or fusing of mythologies, in the novel. Syncretism tends to generalize the contents of the myths involved, emphasizing the *mythologem*, or archetypal motif underlying the specific Christian or pagan version of the myth. I feel an appreciation of this technique is essential to an understanding of García Márquez' novel, although the treatment of this subject in any depth must lie outside the scope of the present study.

[24] Douglas, *The Tarot*, p. 47.

[25] Ibid., p. 111.

[26] Ibid., p. 112.

[27] Ibid., pp. 113-14.

[28] André Breton, *Manifestoes of Surrealism*, trans. R. Seaver and H. R. Lane (Ann Arbor: Univ. of Michigan, 1972), pp. 122-23.

APPENDIX

LE BATELEUR
THE MAGICIAN

THE MAGICIAN

THE FOOL

THE FOOL.

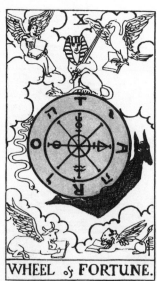

WHEEL of FORTUNE.

JUDGEMENT.

LE JUGEMENT
JUDGEMENT

THE WORLD.

THE HANGED MAN.

THE DEVIL.

THE HERMIT

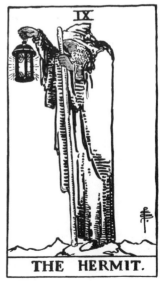

THE HERMIT.

¿Cuál sería la novela ideal? Una novela absolutamente libre, que no sólo inquiete por su contenido político y social, sino por su poder de penetración en la realidad; y mejor aun si es capaz de voltear la realidad al revés para mostrar cómo es del otro lado.

GABRIEL GARCÍA MÁRQUEZ

A tiny particle of the Philosopher's Stone, if cast upon the surface of water, will...immediately begin a process of recapitulating in miniature the history of the universe...A miniature universe is formed which the philosophers affirm actually rises out of the water and floats in the air, where it passes through all the stages of cosmic unfoldment and finally disintegrates into dust again.

MANLY P. HALL

La dirección analógica inherente al hombre sobrevive en el inconsciente y halla apertura en el poeta, el mago contemporáneo.

JULIO CORTÁZAR

Art is never real and always true.

ANTONIN ARTAUD

In that potential unitary world...all the "pious" will be united outside time, for the *unus mundus* does not exist within the space-time continuum.

Aurora Consurgens, Anonymous Alchemical Treatise

Ora,
Lege, lege, lege, relege, labora.
Et invenies.

Alchemical motto

 3

Narrative Theory
in *Cien años de soledad*

THE PRECEDING CHAPTERS have established the presence of alchemy and other initiation related material in *Cien años de soledad*, and the question of why such inclusions are employed may now be addressed. The general focus of all the discussions in this chapter is alchemy and literature, and, more specifically, an exposition and analysis of the narrative theory —ideas about author, literary creation and reader—which the novel seems to present. In considering these ideas, particular characteristics of alchemy, as well as those that it has in common with other belief systems designed to effect a spiritual passage, or a psychological transformation in an individual's consciousness, will be used, as before, as convenient scaffolding for developing the discussions. The connection of alchemy to Melquíades and Aureliano Babilonia, as well as their respective roles as analogue author and analogue reader, are also examined. Some of the topics expostulated below include point of view, time and memory in the novel, as they relate to literature, and also to each other. Some links between literature and psychology which are relevant in the context of the quest for "true gold" in the narrative, are also scrutinized.

POINT OF VIEW
AND THE UNION OF OPPOSITES

In the previous chapters we have seen how the philosophers' stone of alchemy ultimately signifies a point of view, what might be called an enlightened *Weltanschauung*. Aureliano Babilonia's experience of the "mystic light", and the corresponding transformation of Macondo into a "celestial city", can be seen as reflections in the novel of the attainment of such a unique, synoptic perspective. Other, related reflections, have also been mentioned above: Remedios' assumption; Melquíades' "mirada asiática"; and the perspective Pilar Ternera develops in her old age. In alchemy, one of the most popular representations of this ineffable outlook on the world is the *coniunctionis oppositorum*, the "great mystery" of the union of opposites. Earlier, this relation between point of view and the conjoining of opposites was traced, in the discussion of the Symplegades motif of initiation rites, where it symbolizes the successful resolution of an apparent paradox, one usually signifying the presumable impossibility of the quest. Another example of united opposites emerged in an examination of Aureliano Babilonia, who finally attains such an alchemical perspective: he can be seen to represent the synthesis of the male-female, and the sexual-spiritual polarities inherent in man. In the novel, this alchemical concept of the *coniunctionis oppositorum* also pertains at the technical and structural levels.

The idea that *Cien años* reconciles various sets of traditional opposites is a popular one among critics. Structuralists

have described it as "conjuntive literature", because it joins
or equates elements which are by definition disparate. "Novela total," "una ficción total," "clásica y moderna" and "tragic
and comic", represent a sampling of phrases commonly found
in the critical literature. Vargas Llosa, in the following excerpt from a study entitled "Realidad total, novela total: *Cien
años de soledad*," makes an observation which can be regarded
as typical:

> Esta totalidad se manifiesta ante todo en la naturaleza
> plural de la novela que es, simultáneamente, cosas que se
> creían antinómicas: tradicional y moderna, localista y uni-
> versal, imaginaria y realista. Otra expresión de esta "tota-
> lidad" es su accesibilidad ilimitada ... [1]

A few of these pairs of apparent opposites can be commented
upon briefly. A considerable body of critical studies has
already analyzed the techniques employed by the author in
synthesizing or superseding labels frequently used to define
literary "opposites". For this reason, the examples presented
here will be illustrative rather than exhaustive. Of central
interest here is not the means whereby synthesis is gener-
ated in *Cien años*, but rather the phenomenon of synthesis
itself, and how the idea of the union of opposites, prominent
in alchemical literature, emerges as one element in the narrative theory implicit in the work.

The first of three syntheses to be considered is the fusion
of real and fantastic elements in the novel. The net effect of
García Márquez' treatment of these elements is the creation
of a homogeneous "reality", what might be called a synthetic
ontological plane, whereupon natural and supernatural e-
vents coexist. One set of examples which casts this phenomenon into clear relief is provided by the presentation of
Melquíades' artifacts in the narrative. The gypsy's magnets,
his magnifying glass and Daguerrotype, and above all his
false teeth, are received by the inhabitants of Macondo
("quienes recordaban sus encías destruidas por el escorbuto"),
as sheer sorcery:

> El pavor se convirtió en pánico cuando Melquíades se sacó
> los dientes, intactos, engastados en las encías, y se los
> mostró al público por un instante—un instante fugaz en

que volvió a ser el mismo hombre decrépito de los años anteriores—y se los puso otra vez y sonrió de nuevo con un dominio pleno de su juventud restaurada. Hasta el propio José Arcadio Buendía consideró que los conocimientos de Melquíades habían llegado a extremos intolerables, pero experimentó un saludable alborozo cuando el gitano le explicó a solas el mecanismo de su dentadura postiza (14-15).

Presenting such everyday products of science and technology as if they were really magical, serves to erode any distinction between them and truly supernatural phenomena, such as the assumption of Remedios the Beauty, the levitation of the local priest, and the presence of magic carpets in Macondo. These latter events, for their part, are presented matter-of-factly, and this type of portrayal contributes to establishing a convincing homogenization of these scientifically disparate worlds.

In *Cien años*, then, the real and fantastic are "con-fused", coexisting in a single reality whose nature is dependent solely upon the narrative itself, and not upon the laws of the universe as twentieth century man has come to understand it. And this synthetic ontological plane ultimately includes the non-fictional world as well, by identifying Aureliano Babilonia with the external reader when this character:

empezó a descifrar el instante que estaba viviendo, descifrándolo a medida que lo vivía, profetizándose a sí mismo en el acto de descifrar la última página de los pergaminos, como si se estuviera viendo en un espejo hablado (350).

At this point in the story, both Aureliano and the external reader are reading the exact same text.

In passing, the basic similarity between the world as it appears to be in Macondo, and the world as it was understood by the alchemist, can be noted. In alchemy, the imagination is regarded as a critically important instrument in the transformation of the apparently real world into the *unus mundus*, the one, true world. Alchemy represents the interaction of the physically real with the imaginatively subjective world, and the attainment of the point from which this apparent antinomy is resolved forms the goal of the alchemical quest. Insofar as *Cien años* successfully unites real and fantastic elements, it reflects a unifying perspective. To what degree this occurs must remain moot, but the attempt to effect such a fusion is clearly being made, and this fact alone suggests that the author is seeking to present an all-encompassing, synthetic viewpoint.

Another example of the union of opposites in the novel involves the interaction and combination of humorous and tragic elements. A great deal of literary criticism has concerned itself with the terms "comic" and "tragic"; in what follows they are used in two separate senses: first, as that which induces, respectively, laughter, or sadness and melancholy, and secondly, as formal literary descriptions of types of dramatic *dénoument*, i.e., comic and tragic "endings". Each will be considered in turn, beginning with the former.

Here the playfulness reflected in the tone and style of the work is of central interest. In the narrative, humor and absurdity often stand in sharp contrast to the suffering and solitude of the characters, and to specific events, which are described in a way belying their otherwise "serious" or "tragic" nature. One such occurrence involves the murder of the first José Arcadio (the older son of José Arcadio Buendía and Úrsula), a crime described as "tal vez el único misterio que nunca se esclareció en Macondo:"

> Tan pronto como José Arcadio cerró la puerta del dormitorio, el estampido de un pistoletazo retumbó en la casa. Un hilo de sangre siguió en un curso directo por los andenes disparejos, descendió escalinatas y subió pretiles, pasó de largo por la Calle de los Turcos, dobló una esquina a la derecha y otra a la izquierda, volteó en ángulo recto frente a la casa de los Buendía, pasó por debajo de la puerta cerrada, atravesó la sala de visitas pegado a las paredes para no manchar los tapices, siguió por la otra sala, eludió en una curva amplia la mesa del comedor, avanzó por debajo de la silla de Amaranta que daba una lección de aritmética a Aureliano José, y se metió por el granero y apareció en la cocina donde Úrsula se disponía a partir treinta y seis huevos para el pan.
> —¡Ave María Purísima —gritó Úrsula (118).

The presence of the fantastic element of the blood flow

finding its way to Úrsula is only one of many ways in which
the tragic side of an apparent murder is attenuated. Lengthy
concatenation of phrases which introduce diverse, unrelated
material [such as "...una lección de aritmética"], or introduce an absurd dimension into the narration [such as "atravesó la sala de visitas pegado a las paredes para no manchar
los tapices"], are other techniques contributing to the vitality
of this description of a violent death, a vitality which casts
the murder itself into the background. The foreground is
occupied by the humor of the description, not by what is
being described. The compelling language and the highly
entertaining images serve to dampen, and nearly extinguish,
the essentially tragic content of a violent death. It is worth
emphasizing here that the humor in this passage is not of the
type commonly referred to as black or sick. On the contrary,
the muting of the tragedy inherent in such a death is achieved
through its genuinely humorous, non-morbid, situational
context. This light treatment of essentially serious matter is
reinforced in the next paragraph, which begins with another
marathon sentence, a mirror image of the one excerpted
above, wherin Úrsula retraces the line of blood back to her
dead son. Whether she sheds tears or not is never mentioned. Rather than dwell on slow-moving portrayals of emo-
tional states, the narrative continues to move swiftly, describing the prodigious proportions of José Arcadio's coffin and
the smell of gunpowder which is to permeate the cemetery
"hasta muchos años después" (119).

While other examples could be enumerated to demonstrate how humor appears to dampen specific tragic events in
the narrative, such particular cases, like those involving the
fusion of the real and the imaginary elements, are only
isolated manifestations of a more general phenomenon, the
conjoining in the novel of elements traditionally regarded as
antagonistic. In the specific case of comic and tragic con-
stituents in *Cien años*, the pervasiveness of their interaction
has been recognized by several critics, one of whom sum-
marizes it as follows:

> Porque la última paradoja que revela el análisis es ésta: el
> humor y la felicidad del estilo, la vitalidad y rapidez de la
> obra, su magia y su fábula, están edificados sobre la mirada
> más triste, más solitaria, más lúcida.[2]

A reflection of this interpenetration of comic and tragic elements in the work can be seen in the ending, which was analyzed in the preceding chapter. In this context, the terms tragic and comic will be used to refer to the manner in which the action of the work is ultimately resolved. In comedy, the *dénoument* either presents or promises the reintegration and/or renewal of society, whereas tragedy emphasizes its disintegration (often portrayed as the death or isolation of the protagonist). Such clear-cut definitions can be questioned, but here they will be used only as convenient approximations with which to approach the conclusion of *Cien años*.

From a strictly literal reading of the final pages, the novel represents an extreme case of a tragic ending: everything is destroyed, everyone dies, the destruction is explicitly irreparable, and, to make matters even worse, the overall mythological matrix within which the work moves, its encyclopaedic nature and the apocalyptic imagery with which it closes, raises this irremediable destruction to the plane of cosmic proportions. If the arguments in the earlier chapters have been convincing, however, the conclusion of *Cien años* can also be seen in a radically different way, as the transformation of Aureliano Buendía-Babilonia, the character-reader, and the transfiguration of his world. The ending, seen this way, heralds a new heaven and a new earth, which replace the dead Aureliano Buendía and the pre-initiation Macondo.

Such total interpenetration of disparate elements, the simultaneously positive and negative endings which *Cien años* presents, is the culmination of the *coniunctio oppositorum*, the all-inclusiveness that informs the novel. From the point of view of literature, the ending of the narrative is an exercise in perspectivism. Both interpretations, the literal and the symbolic, are consistent on their own terms. The former is exclusive and requires no "deciphering" or reading between the lines; the latter is inclusive, as death and destruction form part of the scenarios used in initiatory rites of passage, and requires "decoding". (Moreover, according to Eliade, it is only within an initiatory context that death takes on an exclusively positive value: "Death prepares the new, purely spiritual birth, access to a mode of being not subject to the destroying action of Time".[3]) Obviously, arguments in defense of one or the other of these interpretations can be framed, but I think such exercises would miss an important point, one embodying another element in the narrative theory *Cien años* seems to present: literature is designed, ideally, not only as a mirror held up to society or as a series of pleasant mirages ("la ciudad de los espejos (o los espejismos)" (351)), but also as a vehicle for the transformation of individual consciousness. Literature, and, more generally, art, can change our outlook on the world in a meaningful way. And while the entertainment quotient of literature ends with each reading, any permanent changes induced in the reader live on for an indefinite time. Hans Meyerhoff, a philosopher and literary critic, offers a definition of literature which, as I hope to demonstrate, reflects very well the ideas *Cien años* explicitly expresses on this subject:

> [Literature] may bring to light, or may set us free to see, certain aspects of human experience and existence from an entirely different perspective.[4]

The bisemic nature of the novel's ending (and of literature), parallel the mythological explanation of the origin of Tarot cards. Thoth-Hermes, the Egyptian god of writing and magic, decided to transmit the esoteric secrets of enlightenment as a vice, and invented playing cards. He did this to assure the ubiquity and immortality of the secrets, as well as to protect them from all who were not spiritually ready to receive them. To some the cards were merely a very pleasant pastime, but to others they were a vehicle of transformation, the keys to true wisdom and enlightenment. For this latter, symbolic use, of course, deciphering by one who was properly prepared was required.

THREE LITERARY ANALOGUES

The technique of uniting opposites, the motif of deciphering and the idea of changing the perspective of the reader, then, are three facets of alchemy and alchemical literature that *Cien años* reflects. A helpful prelude to a further description and discussion of the narrative theory presented in García Márquez' work is a brief examination of the three literary analogues contained in the novel: Melquíades, an analogue author, the manuscripts, an analogue work, and Aureliano Babilonia, an analogue reader who is successful in understanding the author's work completely.

THE ANALOGUE AUTHOR

If we look at Melquíades, it can be seen that his "authorial point of view" is explicitly presented, one could say "encoded", in the scientific discoveries he brings to Macondo. He establishes himself as an adept manipulator of space and time, suggesting that he can serve as an ideal, or theoretical, literary creator. When Melquíades introduces the telescope to the townspeople, he announces: "la ciencia ha eliminado las distancias" (10). This mastery over space is paralleled by a similar one over time when he demonstrates the Daguerrotype, which elicits chagrin from José Arcadio Buendía, "cuando se vio a sí mismo y a toda su familia plasmados en *una edad eterna*" [my emphasis] (49). Melquíades also brings the magnifying glass to Macondo, and, like the telescope, this is an instrument for altering one's perception of reality: both induce "unconventional" points of view in the observer. Operating in time, Melquíades uses a corresponding process of alteration to arrange the events of the Buendía family history in a "non-conventional", synchronic, fashion:

> Melquíades no había ordenado los hechos en el tiempo convencional de los hombres, sino que concentró un siglo de episodios cotidianos, de modo que todos coexistieran en un instante (350).

Melquíades' special time ordering is examined in more detail later, when the relationship between time, alchemy and literature is discussed.

Also considered in a subsequent discussion on mechanical versus creative memory, are the ramifications of Melquíades' first "invention", "lo que él mismo llamaba la octava maravilla de los sabios alquimistas de Macedonia," his magnets. These are described as "fierros mágicos" and they permit him to "awaken" not only the visible metal objects, but "aun los objetos perdidos desde hacía mucho tiempo aparecían por donde más se les había buscado" (9). This first event of the novel can be seen as a humorous description of an author's roles as entertainer and magician, as one who can not only delight, but can also bring to light what has been lost or forgotten.

In the novel, Melquíades' unique point of view is not only "encoded" in his scientific apportations to Macondo, it is also explicitly described. His "mirada asiática que parecía conocer el otro lado de las cosas" (13) has been referred to several times already. In literature, the author's point of view is, of course, extremely important, and it is interesting that Melquíades' "mirada" should be described as it is. Responding in an interview once, García Márquez answered the question "¿Cuál sería la novela ideal?" with these words:

> Una novela absolutamente libre, que no sólo inquiete por su contenido político y social sino por su poder de penetración en la realidad; *y mejor aun si es capaz de voltear la realidad al revés para mostrar cómo es del otro lado* [my emphasis].[5]

Melquíades' literature, written by one who knows "the other side of things", would seem to fit this description.

One final comment on Melquíades' role as analogue author seems warranted at this time, and it involves his similarities to the Greek god Hermes. Earlier, this association came up in connection with both alchemy and the Tarot. The greek Hermes descended from the Egyptian Thoth-Hermes. (Thoth-Hermes was the god of magic and writing. It would be difficult to find a more fitting description of Melquíades.) Among the offices of Hermes was familiar, or guide, of alchemists, a role Melquíades explicitly plays in *Cien años*. Another explicit Hermetical office portrayed by the gypsy in the novel is Psychopomp, conductor of souls to Hades, the link between man and the Underworld, his past. Melquíades' physical death links Macondo to the world of the dead for the first time. The gypsy is the first person who dies in the town, and as a result of his journey to the underworld, Prudencio Aguilar is finally able to locate his old friend and murderer, José Arcadio Buendía. Hermes is also traditionally regarded as the messenger of the gods, and, in particular, of Almighty Zeus; he links man with the higher world, too. Finally, Hermes is a renowned story teller, and it is this attribute, his nonpareil art of narrative improvisation, which makes him the preferred traveling companion of Zeus when the father-god takes long journeys. Associating the analogue author Melquíades with Hermes leads to a view of a literary creator as one who tells a good story; brings divine messages to earth; places men in contact with their past, and with the underworld; and guides the quest for true enlightenment.[6]

THE ANALOGUE LITERARY CREATION

The parchment manuscripts are the work created by the analogue author Melquíades. Their development in the novel supports several additional elements of the narrative theory *Cien años* seems to contain. Written by a magus, whose special point of view allows him to "see the other side of reality", they are encoded, and require deciphering. Like the Tarot cards of Thoth-Hermes, the manuscripts can be seen in two ways: as an entertaining pastime (which is what they are, originally, for José Arcadio Segundo), and as the potential vehicle for psychological passage and self-discovery (what they are ultimately for Aureliano Babilonia).

These manuscripts recall the earliest kind of literature, oral and sung. At one point in the novel, Melquíades reads to Arcadio from them, in the original Sanskrit, and we are told: "al ser leídas [the pages] en voz alta parecían encíclicas cantadas" (68). As the work closes, Aureliano Babilonia is reading them aloud, and earlier their appearance is associated with a musical score: "Las letras parecían ropa puesta a secar en un alambre, y se asemejaban más a la escritura musical que a la literaria" (161). This last image, while humorous, nonetheless describes the parchment manuscripts well, for they have the same relation to literature as a musical score does to the piece of music: they need an interpreter, someone who can translate the curious signs and symbols into a meaningful statement. A musical score is not the music any more than the literal sense of the manuscripts (the sense before the "claves definitivas" are decoded) is meaningful writing.

That Melquíades' work is written in Sanskrit is interesting. Sanskrit literature is divided into two groups, *sruti* ("hearing, i.e. revealed"), and *smitri* ("memory or tradition"). The *sruti*, or revealed literature, is older, and considered sacred, coming from the mouths of the gods, while the *smitri* constitutes the profane, or man-made, body of writing. In *Cien años*, Melquíades' written creation would pertain to the first type, *sruti*, as it is, literally, both heard, in the case of Arcadio, and revealed, to Aureliano Babilonia: "en aquel instante prodigioso se le revelaron las claves definitivas de Melquíades, y vio el epígrafe de los pergaminos perfectamente ordenado en el tiempo y el espacio de los hombres" (349). A further link between the manuscripts and sacred literature involves the location of the Sanskrit primer Aureliano uses to prepare himself for the final revelation:

> Por primera vez en su larga vida Santa Sofía de la Piedad dejó traslucir un sentimiento, y era un sentimiento de estupor, cuando Aureliano le pidió que le llevara el libro que había de encontrar entre la *Jerusalén Libertada* y los poemas de Milton...(302).

Another relevant fact about Melquíades' chronicle is that the final protection, the last key Aureliano needs to decipher them, concerns their unconventional temporal ordering:

> La protección final, que Aureliano empezaba a vislumbrar cuando se dejó confundir por el amor de Amaranta Úrsula, radicaba en que Melquíades no había ordenado los hechos en el tiempo convencional de los hombres, sino que concentró un siglo de episodios cotidianos, de modo que todos coexistieran en un instante (349-50).

The manuscripts are, in fact, organized into the time of myths, a timeless time, an eternal instant, a sacred time outside of man's conventional and profane temporal setting. When the final keys reveal themselves to Aureliano, he is able to see these writings "perfectamente ordenado en el tiempo y el espacio de los hombres" (349), because his psychological passage is complete and he can operate simultaneously in both sacred and profane worlds.

Melquíades' literature, then, like all literature, exists in a special time and space. To properly decipher a literary creation a reader must discover the correct point of view, the perspective from which it was written. In the case of Melquíades' creation, the most important clue to establishing this point of view ("la protección final") seems to be its atemporality, the synchronous concentration of all the events in the story into a single instant. This instant might be called poetic time, mythical time, literary time, an "eternal instant", or something else. Whatever the designation, however, such time is graphically represented in the novel, as *mediodía*, and its links to Melquíades' point of view are well developed and merit explication.

MEDIODÍA

Mediodía, like light, is repeatedly associated with Melquíades in the narrative. It forms part of the Buendía's hereditary memory of the gypsy sage, a memory mentioned four times in the course of the novel (pp. 13, 161, 225, 301):

El sofocante mediodía en que reveló sus secretos, José Arcadio Buendía tuvo la certidumbre de que aquel era el principio de una grande amistad. Los niños se asombraron con sus relatos fantásticos. Aureliano, que no tenía entonces más de cinco años, había de recordarlo por el resto de su vida como lo vio aquella tarde, sentado contra la claridad metálica y reverberante de la ventana, alumbrando con su profunda voz de órgano los territorios más oscuros de la imaginación, mientras chorreaba por sus sienes la grasa derretida por el calor. José Arcadio, su hermano mayor, había de transmitir aquella imagen maravillosa, como un recuerdo hereditario, a toda su descendencia (13).

In the second paragraph of the novel, Melquíades' tribe combusts dry grass with the aid of a giant magnifying glass: "Un mediodía ardiente hicieron una asombrosa demostración con la lupa gigantesca" (10). In his room it is always high noon. His disappearance from the narrative is described like this: "Melquíades iba haciéndose cada vez menos asiduo y más lejano, esfumándose en la claridad radiante del mediodía" (302). And when Aureliano Babilonia begins deciphering Melquíades' manuscripts, we read the following lines:

no tuvo serenidad para sacarlos a la luz, sino que allí mismo, de pie, sin la menor dificultad, como si hubieran estado escritos en castellano bajo el resplandor deslumbrante del mediodía, empezó a descifrarlos en voz alta (349).

Earlier Melquíades' point of view was linked with his room, and now it has been linked to *mediodía*, the omnipresent time in his room, as well. This latter connection receives significant treatment in the novel. The development of *medio-día* and its links to point of view, offer several parallels to the handling of the *nigredo* and *separatio* discussed in the first chapter of this study. Like this alchemical motif, the one involving *mediodía* presents both literal and symbolic facets, and contains an element of quest.

How the literal quest for gold, initiated by José Arcadio Buendía, begins in the opening paragraph of the work, has been examined already. The "literal quest for *mediodía*," initiated by the same character, has its genesis in paragraph two. Following his failure to harness Melquíades' magnifying glass for use as a weapon of war, José Arcadio Buendía, using some materials the gypsy has left him (among which are the first writings in his own hand left to a Buendía):

> permaneció noches enteras en el patio vigilando el curso de los astros, y estuvo a punto de contraer una insolación por tratar de establecer un método exacto para encontrar el mediodía (11).[7]

Something in the literature left by Melquíades, it seems, has led José Arcadio Buendía on his quest to establish *mediodía* precisely. No more is said about this search for "exact midday", but later the founder is once more linked to *mediodía*, in a reference which explicitly involves clocks and time, and seems directly relevant to our discussion of Melquíades' manuscripts:

> Emancipado al menos por el momento de las torturas de la fantasía, José Arcadio Buendía impuso en poco tiempo un estado de orden y trabajo, dentro del cual sólo se permitió una licencia: la liberación de los pájaros que desde la época de la fundación alegraban el tiempo con sus flautas, y la instalación en su lugar de relojes musicales en todas las casas. Eran unos preciosos relojes de madera labrada que los árabes cambiaban por guacamayas, y que José Arcadio Buendía sincronizó con tanta precisión, que cada media hora el pueblo se alegraba con los acordes progresivos de una misma pieza, hasta alcanzar la culminación de un mediodía exacto y unánime con el valse completo (40).

A parallel is suggested here between the literal and symbolic middays of the novel, between the complete waltz which the synchronized clocks play exactly at noon, and the synchronized episodes of Melquíades' manuscripts, which are ordered so that "todos coexistieran en un instante" (350).

Parallels also emerge between the development of the literal and symbolic middays of the novel, and the quest for gold theme, and these deserve to be emphasized. Both are initiated, at the literal level, by the first Buendía, José Arcadio, the founder, and both are finally resolved, at the symbolic level, by the last survivor of the line, Aureliano Babilonia. Just as José Arcadio Buendía manages to achieve some "literal" success in the quest for gold, with the first *nigredo* and *separatio* of the narrative, he also realizes a literal midday, with the synchronization of Macondo's timepieces and the complete waltz at noon. His misunderstanding of the *Gran Magisterio* of alchemy (he begins as the archetypical literal alchemist), is paralleled in the work by his eventual discovery that time has ceased to progress, a realization which costs him his sanity and transports him to a state of blissful oblivion (pp. 73-74). At the symbolic level, we see Aureliano Babilonia ultimately installed in a perspective from which he comprehends the synchronous ordering of the events in his family chronicle, something corresponding to the symbolic *nigredo* and *separatio* in which he participates.

THE TITLE OF THE NOVEL

Finally, one hundred years, the time span mentioned in the title of the novel, is explicitly linked to Melquíades' parchments, the analogue literary creation, in at least two places in the narrative. The first such mention occurs in chapter ten, when Aureliano Segundo and the gypsy's presence are conversing in Melquíades' room:

> Melquíades le hablaba del mundo, trataba de infundirle su vieja sabiduría, pero se negó a traducir los manuscritos. "Nadie debe conocer su sentido mientras no hayan cumplido cien años," explicó (161).

There is at least one other reference associating Melquíades' literature with exactly one century:

> Melquíades le reveló que sus oportunidades de volver al

cuarto estaban contadas. Pero se iba tranquilo a las pra-
deras de la muerte definitiva, porque Aureliano tenía tiempo de aprender el sánscrito en los años que faltaban para
que los pergaminos cumplieran un siglo y pudieran ser
descifrados (301-02).[8]

It is possible to interpret the title of the novel in several
different ways, but a case can be made for relating the one
hundred years primarily to Melquíades' manuscripts. The
total action related in the narrative, as well as the existence
of Macondo, would seem to span more than a century in its
literal sense of one hundred years. (Pilar Ternera's age can be
used to verify this. She is in her early twenties when brought
along to Macondo [p. 31], and towards the end of the story
we read: "Era Pilar Ternera. Años antes, cuando cumplió los
ciento cuarenta y cinco, había renunciado a la perniciosa
costumbre de llevar las cuentas de su edad" (333). Macondo
would be at least 120 years old at this point, and perhaps
considerably more, as the phrase "años antes" indicates.)

The explicit connection between the title phrase and the
manuscripts encourages an investigation of narrative theory
in *Cien años de soledad*, for it suggests that this subject, literary
creation, may be a cardinal focus of the novel. The association of the title phrase and the time Melquíades' manuscripts
remain undeciphered would seem to postulate that literature,
properly written and understood, can remedy solitude. More
will be said about this idea below.

THE ANALOGUE READER

Having looked at the analogue author and the analogue
work, the analogue reader can be considered now. Actually,
the novel presents two manuscript readers, José Arcadio
Segundo and Aureliano Buendía-Babilonia. (In fact, a number
of Buendías read writings Melquíades has left. José Arcado
Buendía, while he never sees the manuscripts, does read
other treatises written or left by the gypsy, and eventually
reaps some benefits: his conquering of space (p. 11), his
discovery of how to make the almond trees immortal (p. 40),
and his blissful oblivion are examples. Aureliano, José Arcadio Buendía's son, also probably reads the alchemical writings
Melquíades gives his father, and Aureliano Segundo visits

the gypsy's room every day for a few years, reading what he can (pp. 160-61). He tries, fruitlessly, to decipher the manuscripts, and abandons the enterprise quickly.)

For José Arcadio Segundo, reading the manuscripts is literally a form of escape, as he locks himself in Melquíades' room, refusing to leave, until he dies there. Although he never deciphers the manuscripts, his repeated "readings" seem to protect him from the false ideas held by those outside: the belief that there was no massacre in Macondo, and the history of the Banana Company which the propaganda had disseminated. From the time he spends with the manuscripts he gains confidence in what he knows to be true.

The peace and repose José Arcadio Segundo finds while sequestered seems to stem at least as much from the room as from his reading:

> En el cuarto de Melquíades...protegido por la luz sobre-natural...por la sensación de ser invisible, encontró el reposo que no tuvo un solo instante de su vida ante-rior.... A salvo de todo temor, José Arcadio Segundo se dedicó entonces a repasar muchas veces los pergaminos de Melquíades, y tanto más a gusto cuanto menos los enten-día (265).

The phrase "se dedicó entonces a repasar muchas veces los pergaminos de Melquíades, y tanto más a gusto cuanto menos los entendía", suggests that José Arcadio Segundo reads primarily for enjoyment, even though the benefits of his repeated perusals are undeniable. He is described as "el habitante más lúcido de la casa" (296), and "iluminado por un resplandor seráfico" (266).

José Arcadio Segundo is a reader who is not properly prepared to understand Melquíades' work completely. This fact is developed in the novel both literally and symbolically. He does not know Sanskrit, and this proves an insurmountable, literal obstacle to decipherment. But his lack of preparation is also presented in another way, one which integrates into the quest for "true gold" that evolves, by degrees, through the actions of the Colonel, José Arcadio Segundo and Aureliano Buendía-Babilonia. The development of this non-literal lack of preparation involves the concept of war, and José Arcadio Segundo's relationship with Colonel Aureliano Buendía.

In the first chapter of this study, how Aureliano Buendía, who later becomes the Colonel, can be seen as the initiator of the non-literal quest for gold was established. His "rara intuición alquímica", his revaluation of this precious metal, and his repeated reworking of the twenty-five gold fishes were cited then as links between this character and the spiritual quest for gold. Of all the family members, however, the Colonel is the only one who perceives Melquíades' room through different eyes. To him, time has not stood still there, but has continued its passage, leaving the marks of its ravages in the room the other members see as fresh and clean always. When José Arcadio Segundo is hiding in this room after the plaza massacre, it is registered by a young military official who also sees Melquíades' room "con los mismos ojos con que lo vio el coronel Aureliano Buendía" (265): "Es verdad que nadie ha estado en ese cuarto por lo menos en un siglo—dijo el oficial a los soldados—. Ahí debe haber hasta culebras" (265).

The link between this difference in perception and a fascination with war is firmly established in the sentences which immediately follow this one by the official:

Al cerrarse la puerta, José Arcadio Segundo tuvo la certidumbre de que su guerra había terminado. Años antes, el coronel Aureliano Buendía le había hablado de la fascinación de la guerra y había tratado de demostrarla con ejemplos incontables sacados de su propia experiencia. El le había creído. Pero la noche en que los militares lo miraron sin verlo, mientras pensaba en la tensión de los últimos meses, en la miseria de la cárcel, en el pánico de la estación y en el tren cargado de muertos, José Arcadio Segundo llegó a la conclusión de que el coronel Aureliano Buendía no fue más que un farsante o un imbécil. No entendía que hubiera necesitado tantas palabras para explicar lo que se sentía en la guerra, si con una sola bastaba: miedo. En el cuarto de Melquíades, en cambio, protegido por la luz sobrenatural, por el ruido de la lluvia, por la sensación de ser invisible, encontró el reposo que no tuvo un solo instante de su vida anterior...(265).

The Colonel's fascination with war, which José Arcadio Segundo had shared before, is now rejected by him. Significantly, the Colonel's attitude and Melquíades' room are explicitly opposed: "lo que se sentía en la guerra ... :miedo. En el cuarto de Melquíades, *en cambio* ..." [my emphasis]. While the Colonel, who originally shared a room with Melquíades (the old workshop), returns from his twenty years of war with an incorrigibly different perspective, José Arcadio Segundo rejects war, and the Colonel's perspective, in favor of Melquíades' room and perspective. And Aureliano Buendía-Babilonia, the third character who is involved in the quest initiated (and abandoned) by the Colonel, and continued and passed on by José Arcadio Segundo, is described as physically identical to the Colonel as he was *before the wars*:

> Estaba [Pilar Ternera] viendo otra vez al coronel Aureliano Buendía, como lo vio a la luz de una lámpara mucho antes de las guerras, mucho antes de la desolación de la gloria y el exilio del desencanto ... (333).

The Colonel shares a workshop with Melquíades before he goes to war, but never sees the manuscripts. His first namesake, Aureliano Segundo, visits Melquíades' room for several years, but abandons it definitively, and never makes any progress with the manuscripts. His twin brother, José Arcadio Segundo, begins the preparation necessary for deciphering the manuscripts, installing himself in Melquíades' room for the rest of his life, classifying the Sanskrit alphabet and helping to prepare Aureliano Buendía-Babilonia, who eventually succeeds in deciphering them. In Melquíades' room, or "el cuarto de las bacinillas" as it is temporarily renamed, José Arcadio Segundo goes through a process of purification (traced earlier, *supra.* p. 20), and one part of this process involves the emendation of the Colonel's perspective. Aureliano Buendía-Babilonia is the beneficiary of José Arcadio Segundo's purification and preparation, and the character who eventually brings the work José Arcadio Segundo has begun to fruition, when he deciphers the manuscripts, something he does after he is "transformed" into Aureliano Babilonia.

Parallels can be seen here in the actions of the three characters who carry forward the psychological quest, the

Colonel, José Arcadio Segundo and Aureliano (Buendía)—Babilonia. José Arcadio Segundo initially shares the Colonel's perspective, but after a symbolic death in the plaza massacre he rejects his former life of involvement and retires to Melquíades room, just as the Colonel retired to his workshop (which originally housed Melquíades' laboratory), after his symbolic death, his attempted suicide. Aureliano Babilonia ultimately retires from the outside world, too, after his symbolic death and resurrection, the *nigredo, separatio* and *albedo* sequence at the end of the novel, when he forgets his dead, boards up the house, and goes to Melquíades' room to decipher the manuscripts. José Arcadio Segundo, in his retirement in Melquíades' room, becomes a different person, as changed, in his own way, as is the Colonel when he retires to his workshop after his return from the wars. Aureliano Buendía-Babilonia continues José Arcadio Segundo's work on the manuscripts, in a way similar to the one in which José Arcadio Segundo, as a young union chief, continued the Colonel's struggles; and Aureliano Buendía-Babilonia also undergoes a change as great as the Colonel's or José Arcadio Segundo's, a change explicitly reflected in his transformation from Aureliano Buendía-Babilonia to Aureliano Babilonia.

In Aureliano *Buendía*-Babilonia we are presented with a reader who is essentially identical to José Arcadio Segundo. Like his great uncle, he never succeeds in deciphering the manuscripts (it is Aureliano *Babilonia* who does this). Aureliano Babilonia, however, is a different type of analogue reader, for he goes beyond mere enjoyment to complete understanding. Deciphering the manuscripts is, for him, truly a revelation: a mystical experience of self-discovery and total integration with the cosmos. He literally leaves one role, that of character, behind, and assumes another, that of character-reader, for Aureliano *Babilonia* does only one thing in *Cien años*, he deciphers / reads the parchment manuscripts.

Aureliano's transformation occurs after Melquíades' final keys reveal themselves to him and he is installed successfully in the gypsy author's point of view. Because he has been properly prepared, Aureliano Babilonia can understand Melquíades' literary creation. The manuscripts can only be deciphered when they have reached one hundred years of age, but it is clear that even then a specially prepared reader is required, and that Aureliano is such a reader:

> Pero se iba [Melquíades] tranquilo a las praderas de la muerte difinitiva porque Aureliano tenía tiempo de aprender el sánscrito en los años que faltaban para que los pergaminos cumplieran un siglo y pudieran ser descifrados (301-02).

While José Arcadio Segundo reads for escape and enjoyment, primarily appreciating the entertainment value of literature (although he realizes the manuscripts are very important), Aureliano is ultimately drawn to the literature because "sabía que en los pergaminos de Melquíades estaba escrito su destino" (349). For Aureliano Babilonia, literature, when properly understood, is self-discovery and revelation; it is, magically, not the mere reflection of things (la ciudad de los espejos), but the things themselves, seen from a different perspective, "el otro lado de las cosas"; the realization that "Las cosas tienen vida propia... todo es cuestión de despertarles el ánima", and an experience of this soul-awakening, his own and that of the world at once.

If the description of the letters of the manuscripts as "se asemejaban más a la escritura musical que a la literaria" is recalled, then José Arcadio Segundo is soothed and fascinated by the appearance of the notes of the score, sensing something of the potential therein, while Aureliano Babilonia is capable of translating these same notes into music. The novel suggests that a comparable difference exists between reading for escape and enjoyment, without really understanding the sense of what is read (as José Arcadio Segundo does), and reading with complete comprehension of the truths represented by the words on the page.

Conclusion

Literature, in *Cien años*, emerges as the relationship between a participant-observer (which is exactly what Aureliano Babilonia, the character-reader, is) and a literary creation, in which the author, like Melquíades, provides hints designed to help a properly prepared reader "decipher", or understand, the work. It is Melquíades who tells Aureliano where to find the Sanskrit primer, and the gypsy's "fading away" is linked to the orphan's domination of this single most important tool of his eventual deciphering:

> Aureliano avanzaba en los estudios del sánscrito, mientras Melquíades iba haciéndose cada vez menos asiduo y más lejano, esfumándose en la claridad radiante del mediodía (302).

Ultimately, it is the relationship of the participant-observer and the work of art that is important, and in *Cien años* this is symbolized by the "light" by which Aurelaino Babilonia deciphers the manuscripts. This light, as we have seen in the previous chapter, radiates simultaneously from the character-reader and the *pergaminos*. The author has definitively disappeared, but his point of view, which is "la protección final" (as well as the catalyst to an understanding or "deciphering" of his work), endures, having been "transmitted" to the participant-observer Aureliano Babilonia. Put another way, the novelistic theory developed in *Cien años* establishes point of view as the common meeting ground of the reader and author, and as the vehicle for the soteriological potential of literature. Through his reading Aureliano experiences a self-revelation and is transfromed, and from this we can develop a definition of "exemplary literature" as literature which has the potential to help the reader alter the way he perceives reality, which, in the words of Meyerhoff:

> may bring to light, or may set us free to see, certain aspects of human experience and existence from an entirely different perspective ... [Literature] does, in fact, make an intellectual contribution to ... the *orientation* of man in the world of experience [emphasis Meyerhoff's].[9]

MEMORY

The preceeding discussions on the three literary analogues and the union of opposites have provided several tenets of what can be called the narrative theory contained in *Cien años de soledad*. Another subject, memory, and its treatment in the novel, provides perhaps the most important insights into the literary ideas that are to be found in the work. The importance of memory is emphasized in the final sentence of the novel, where it is linked to Aureliano's reading:

estaba previsto que la ciudad de los espejos (o los espejismos) sería arrasada por el viento y desterrada de la
memoria de los hombres en el instante en que Aureliano
Babilonia acabara de descifrar los pergaminos (351).

Memory receives ample development in *Cien años*, and, as
with the quest for gold and the treatment of *mediodía*, it
displays a literal and a symbolic facet. Again, like these other
two motifs, memory is associated with Melquíades, José
Arcadio Buendía and Aureliano Babilonia. It is during the
plague of forgetfulness that two kinds of recollection, one
linked to Melquíades, the other to José Arcadio Buendía, are
concretely juxtaposed:

José Arcadio Buendía decidió entonces construir la máquina de la memoria que una vez había deseado para acor-
darse de los maravillosos inventos de los gitanos. El arte-
facto se fundaba en la posibilidad de repasar todas las
mañanas, y desde el principio hasta el fin, la totalidad de
los conocimientos adquiridos en la vida. Lo imaginaba
como un diccionario giratorio que un individuo situado en
el eje pudiera operar mediante una manivela, de modo que
en pocas horas pasaran frente a sus ojos las nociones más
necesarias para vivir. Había logrado escribir cerca de catorce mil fichas, cuando apareció por el camino de la ciénaga
un anciano estrafalario con la campanita triste de los
durmientes, cargando una maleta ventruda amarrada con
cuerdas y un carrito cubierto de trapos negros. Fue direc-
tamente a la casa de José Arcadio Buendía.
   ...Abrió la maleta atiborrada de objetos indescifrables,
y de entre ellos sacó un maletín con muchos frascos. Le dio
a beber a José Arcadio Buendía una sustancia de color
apacible, y la luz se hizo en su memoria. Los ojos se le
humedecieron de llanto, antes de verse a sí mismo en una
sala absurda donde los objetos estaban marcados, y antes
de avergonzarse de las solemnes tonterías escritas en las
paredes, y aun antes de reconocer al recién llegado en un
deslumbrante resplandor de alegría. Era Melquíades (48-
49).

The mechanistic nature of José Arcadio Buendía's pro-
posed "máquina de la memoria", and the "magical", trans-

formative elixir produced by Melquíades from his satchel, correspond remarkably well to two types of remembering described by Meyerhoff, "mechanical memory" and "creative memory". Using the example of Proust, Meyerhoff distinguishes between these two terms as follows:

> What appears forgotten and lost is only pushed aside, buried, or repressed, i.e. not accessible to our conscious selves; the creative as against the mechanical act of recollection for Proust consists precisely in descending "like a diver" to the deep "strata" of the "unconscious self" and bringing to light those traces, impressions and associations which seem to have been lost.[10]

With its thousands of notecards, the founder's machine presents, according to the narrative, only a shadowy reality, "una realidad escurridiza, momentáneamente capturada por las palabras, pero que había de fugarse sin remedio cuando olvidaran los valores de la letra escrita" (47). On the other hand, the "sustancia" produced by Melquíades from among his "objetos indescifrables", attacks the cause and not merely the consequences of the "forgetfulness plague". Memory is cast as the bedrock of reality, the link to the direct understanding of things-in-themselves, the support of the written word. With the quotation from Meyerhoff in mind, it is noteworthy that Melquíades' act of recuperating what has been lost occurs after he has died, or "descended to the depths", and has been resurrected. And when the gypsy saves the townspeople from the plague of forgetfulness, he literally resurrects them, too, as the novel explicitly equates the loss of memory with death:

> Se sintió [Melquíades] olvidado, no con el olvido remediable del corazón, sino con otro olvido más cruel e irrevocable que él conocía muy bien, porque era el olvido de la muerte (48-49).

In the context of Meyerhoff's distinction between creative and mechanical memory, it is also useful to focus again on the description of Melquíades' first "miracle" in Macondo:

> Fue de casa en casa arrastrando dos lingotes metálicos, y todo el mundo se espantó al ver que los calderos, las pailas, las tenazas y los anafes se caían de su sitio, y las maderas

crujían por la desesperación de los clavos y los tornillos tratando de desenclavarse, y aun los objetos perdidos desde hacía mucho tiempo aparecían por donde más se les había buscado, y se arrastraban en desbandada turbulenta detrás de los fierros mágicos de Melquíades. "Las cosas tienen vida propia—pregonaba el gitano con áspero acento—, todo es cuestión de despertarles el ánima" (9).

This initial act of Melquíades' can symbolize the activity of a creative author who brings to light what seems to have been lost to the conscious mind. It is significant that the gypsy brings objects out from "donde más se les había buscado", because it shows how he, the analogue author of the novel, has a power to retrieve what others, although they try repeatedly, cannot. The objects Melquíades brings out into the light of day once more are like contents in the unconscious mind that are resurrected into consciousness.

It should be noted that in both of the instances examined here, the forgetfulness plague and the recupertion of "aun los objetos perdidos desde hacía mucho tiempo," Melquíades does not create anything new, but rather is instrumental in recovering what has been lost. He acts as a catalyst of rediscovery, an assistant who helps people uncover what they have forgotten or encounter what they cannot find by themselves. Here the similarities between the offices of the analogue author Melquíades and the god Hermes, familiar of alchemists and the one who assists them in their quest to liberate Spirit from Matter, surface again.

Another association connecting Melquíades and memory, one which also involves Hermes and figures like him, is the "recuerdo hereditario", the image of the gypsy sage passed on from generation to generation of Buendías. This memory, part of each Buendía, is activated in his special room, and it is through contact with this "presence" that Melquíades' knowledge and assistance in the quest to decipher his writings is passed on to the characters directly concerned. As a primordial image transmitted by heredity, Melquíades is quite literally established as an archetype in the psychological sense of this term. He is easily identified as "the wise old man", one of several archetypes hypothesized by Jung. This figure, according to Jung, is popular in fairy tales, folklore and mythology, and examples he cites include Merlin, Hermes-Mercury, and Prometheus. Such characters possess great powers and act as intermediaries between man and other, supernatural realms. This figure generally appears at times when an individual's consciousness is undergoing a transformation, usually a development to a state of expanded knowledge. The wise old man acts as guide and/or helper during the quest, usually disappearing when the hero is totally prepared. In *Cien años* Melquíades eventually disappears, but not, as we have seen, before the success of the quest is assured:

> Melquíades le reveló [to Aureliano] que sus oportunidades de volver al cuarto estaban contadas. Pero se iba tranquilo a las praderas de la muerte definitiva, porque Aureliano tenía tiempo de aprender el sánscrito en los años que faltaban para que los pergaminos cumplieran un siglo y pudieran ser descifrados. Fue él quien le indicó que en el callejón que terminaba en el río, y donde en los tiempos de la compañía bananera se adivinaba el porvenir y se interpretaban los sueños, un sabio catalán tenía una tienda de libros donde había un *Sanskrit Primer* que sería devorado por las polillas seis años después si él no se apresuraba a comprarlo...
>
> Aureliano avanzaba en los estudios del sánscrito, mientras Melquíades iba haciéndose cada vez menos asiduo y más lejano, esfumándose en la claridad radiante del mediodía. La última vez que Aureliano lo sintió era apenas una presencia invisible que murmuraba: "He muerto de fiebre en los médanos de Singapur." El cuarto se hizo entonces vulnerable al polvo, al calor, al comején, a las hormigas coloradas, a las polillas que habían de convertir en aserrín la sabiduría de los libros y los pergaminos (301-02).

Returning to the passage concerning the plague of forgetfulness, which depicts the creative and mechanical types of memory, we see that José Arcadio Buendía is portrayed as a foil to Melquíades. As with his desire to discover "literal" gold with Melquíades' magnets, or his attempt to "establecer un método exacto para encontrar el mediodía", the founder is once more the vehicle for suggesting a non-literal understanding of Melquíades' instruments and actions. And again, as before, Aureliano Babilonia is the character involved with the true meaning of memory, just as he was the "symbolic realizer" in the other two quests (for gold and for *mediodía*) where José Arcadio Buendía is cast as "literal initiator".

There are links between the founder's "enlightenment", his reaction to Melquíades' magic elixir, and the enlightenment of Aureliano Babilonia when he, at the end of the novel, comes into contact with what might be called the primordial memory of the race. Two connections can be seen, and they both involve light. José Arcadio Buendía, as a result of ingesting Melquíades' potion, finds that "la luz se hizo en su memoria", and Aureliano Babilonia's mystic light experience occurs just as he sets to deciphering the manuscripts, which are the source of his self-discovery and his recovery of the entire past of the family, much of which has been lost. The phrase used to describe José Arcadio Buendía's delight after he regains his memory and recognizes Melquíades, "un deslumbrante resplandor de alegría", unmistakably resembles "el resplandor deslumbrante del mediodía", the phrase describing the intensity of Aureliano Babilonia's mystic light experience. And this experience accompanies (in fact, causes), the exile of profane memory described in the final sentence of the novel, and the recovery of mythic or sacred memory which is concomitant with the transformation of individual and world discussed in chapter two. Seen this way, the deciphering at the end of the work represents the recuperation of something previously lost, and this remembering or rediscovery marks the end of the one hundred years of solitude to which the Buendías, as the final phrase of the narrative puts it, were "condemned". One might say that when Aureliano recovers this sacred memory, the plague of solitude comes to an end.

In *Cien años*, the first and last sentences of the final paragraph of the novel relate to memory, and this seems significant. Aureliano's personal discovery is linked to "memory" in the two phrases "olvidó sus muertos y el dolor de sus muertos" (349), and "desterrada de la memoria de los hombres en el instante en que Aureliano Babilonia acabara de descifrar los pergaminos" (350), and the transpersonal recollection suggested by Aureliano's loss of profane memory and recovery of sacred memory can be linked to a transpersonal memory: the *recuerdo hereditario* of Melquíades. Above it was mentioned that Melquíades is developed not only as an archetype in the literary sense of this term, but also in its psychological sense, as a kind of "species memory", as well. The subsequent development of Melquíades as "light-bearer", and specifically as the one who is responsible for rekindling the light of memory ("y la luz se hizo en su memoria"), suggests that this "transpersonal memory" may be reactivated as the novel ends; and it perhaps terminates the solitude of what might be called "a transpersonal plague of forgetfulness", whose ultimate literal manifestation is described as the loss of "aun la conciencia del propio ser, hasta hundirse en una especie de idiotez sin pasado" (44).

These comments can support some further elaboration. In the novel, the Buendía's transpersonal memory, while associated with Melquíades in general, is especially concerned with his point of view, the organizing principle behind his literary creation, the manuscripts. We have, then, at the thematic level of *Cien años*, an interdependence of the following: memory, the process of artistic creation, and the self. In the next section, when the treatment of time in the narrative is discussed we shall return to this relationship.

There are a couple of indications which encourage the interpretation that the revelation Aureliano encounters in the manuscripts may signify more than merely his personal destiny, and the discovery of who he is and what his origins were. Besides the name Babilonia, which recalls the traditional "cradle of civilization", or the origins of mankind itself, the description of where Aureliano finds the manuscripts strongly suggests a time before recorded history and man's presence on earth:

> sabía que en los pergaminos de Melquíades estaba escrito su destino. Los encontró intactos, entre las plantas prehistóricas y los charcos humeantes y los insectos luminosos que habían desterrado del cuarto todo vestigio del paso de los hombres por la tierra (349).

Also, the context of rites of spiritual passage reinforce the idea of a transpersonal, transhistorical discovery. As was mentioned earlier, alchemy and Tarot (and other such belief systems) were aids to recovering what had been lost in Medieval-Renaissance Europe, a primordial revelation which would reintegrate the initiate into the cosmic fabric.

Melquíades, through his manuscripts, is a catalyst for Aureliano Babilonia's self-discovery, and for his proper understanding of history. To Aureliano, the manuscripts are, literally, a revelation: through them he finds truth. The descriptions of his deciphering, however, suggest that it is not so much the content of the manuscripts, or at least not exclusively their content, which makes the experience so intense. What Melquíades has written reveals itself to Aureliano in a flash: "en aquel instante prodigioso se le revelaron las claves definitivas de Melquíades" (349). It is this flash, representing Aureliano's transformed point of view, which is truly important. His discovery is only partially linked to the words of the manuscripts. The lucidity he experiences is comparable to that of José Arcadio Segundo, a "reader" who never understood the words at all, but who nonetheless "estaba iluminado por un resplandor seráfico" (266). What this seems to tell us, in terms of narrative theory, is that the essence of literature is not to be found exclusively in the words, but also in the preparation of the reader and his reaction to what is beyond the words. José Arcadio Buendía bases his "máquina de la memoria" on language, and the reality he captures is tenuous and ultimately forgotten, when the meaning of words is forgotten. Melquíades' manuscripts, for José Arcadio Segundo and Aureliano Babilonia, are based on experiences (the plaza massacre and the ants dragging the dead baby away), and the words serve to trigger a revelation of the truths that such experiences contain. (For José Arcadio Segundo, in fact, it is the truth and not the words, which he never does understand, that he gains from the manuscripts. They reinforce his memory, when the propaganda has caused everyone else to lose theirs.) Creative memory, then, puts the properly prepared reader into contact with truths that have been forgotten, as with the plaza massacre and the role of the banana company, or hidden, as with Aureliano Babilonia's origins. The manuscripts assist these two characters and let them see in ways they have never seen before: José Arcadio Segundo dies with his eyes open, after repeating the truth about the plaza massacre; Aureliano Babilonia deciphers the manuscripts without the aid of light ("no tuvo serenidad para sacarlos a la luz" [349]), and without difficulty.

So, in terms of the treatment of memory, too, the narrative theory in *Cien años* suggests that literature, as Meyerhoff puts it, "may bring to light, or may set us free to see, certain aspects of human experience and existence from an entirely different perspective". Melquíades does "bring light" to three of the Buendías, and in each case, though in different ways, this light is related to memory. He saves José Arcadio Buendía from forgetting "los valores de la letra escrita", by illuminating his recollection ("la luz se hizo en su memoria"). José Arcadio Segundo, in his repeated perusals of the indecipherable manuscripts, is eventually suffused by "un resplandor seráfico," explicitly linked to his memory of Macondo's recent history, a memory no longer extant in the other inhabitants. He has been set free to see the events from a different point of view, the special perspective of Melquíades' room, which he never again relinquishes. Finally, Aureliano Babilonia's experience as the novel ends is a graphic portrayal of events "being brought to light" and of a reader seeing things from an entirely different perspective. And this revelation, directly tied to Melquíades' writings, exiles "sus muertos y el dolor de sus muertos", and the solitude of the entire Buendía line, from his memory.

TIME

The handling of time is another important element in the narrative theory *Cien años* presents. Revealed in the last paragraph of the novel is the fact that "la protección final" of Melquíades' literary creation is related to his temporal ordering of the chronicle's events:

> La protección final, que Aureliano empezaba a vislumbrar cuando se dejó confundir por el amor de Amaranta Úrsula, radicaba en que Melquíades no había ordenado los hechos en el tiempo convencional de los hombres, sino que concentró un siglo de episodios cotidianos, de modo que todos coexistieran en un instante (350).

With this discovery, Aureliano Babilonia comes to share Melquíades' point of view completely, and is led directly to his deciphering. This most critical realization arrives in a flash, in the "instante prodigioso" when Aureliano sees the baby being dragged off by "todas las hormigas del mundo":

> Aureliano no pudo moverse. No porque lo hubiera
> paralizado el estupor, sino porque en aquel instante prodi-
> gioso se le revelaron las claves definitivas de Melquíades, y
> vio el epígrafe de los pergaminos perfectamente ordenado
> en el tiempo y el espacio de los hombres (349).

Aureliano's mystic light experience, the revelation which
leads to his self-discovery and his proper understanding of
history, ultimately depends upon a transformation of time-
consciousness. This unconventional, sychronic ordering of
the manuscripts is reflected in the following passage from
the final paragraph, one wherein the complementary processes of internal self-discovery and external metamorphosis
culminate:

> Sólo entonces descubrió [Aureliano] que Amaranta Úrsula
> no era su hermana sino su tía, y que Francis Drake había
> asaltado a Riohacha solamente para que ellos pudieran
> buscarse por los laberintos más intrincados de la sangre,
> hasta engendrar el animal mitológico que había de poner
> término a la estirpe (350).

To cite a meeting between two characters as the reason for
an event which preceded it by several centuries constitutes a
distortion of the conventional order of cause and effect. Such
a statement challenges chronologically based causality, and
parallels Melquíades' non-conventional synchronic arrange-
ment of the "historical" events contained in the Buendía
chronicle. Both phenomena establish the priority of an a-
historical, or a-chronological, temporality in which all times
coexist.

The similarity between the inverted causality described in
this excerpt and the properties of the "mythical time" within
which religious initiations have taken place historically is
noteworthy. The final step along the road to the realization
concerning Francis Drake's pirate attack, and its unconventional relation to Aureliano Babilonia's destiny, is precisely
this character's dis-covering of "la protección final" of the
manuscripts, their synchronous ordering. Therefore, just as
in initiation ceremonies, where "sacred history" and "sacred
time" underlie and explain the world of profane historical

events, so too in Melquíades' parchments we see diachrony, the apparent organizing principle of past occurrences, finally revealed as a false standard. It is ultimately explained by the true, underlying principle of simultaneous, synchronic coexistence.

Earlier it was seen how, in the eternal and timeless "mythic time" of initiations, the initiate is believed to be (and believes himself to be) coexistent with the mythical heroes, and even identical to the central heroic figure. The initiate is not separated from the "original time" by the passage of historical time: he participates in what might be called a "timeless time", one which bridges the apparent chronological distance between him and the mythical "past". In the novel, in parallel fashion, Aureliano Babilonia gains his enlightened, mystical perspective, precisely when his past, or "profane" perception of time, is fundamentally transformed.

Here, in connection with the treatment of time in literature that *Cien años* can be seen to suggest, a few comments on the use of myths in the novel, as this relates to time, are germane. As regards time, it has been said that myths are adopted and adapted by modern writers for two purposes:

> to suggest, within a secular setting, a timeless perspective of looking upon the human situation; and to convey a sense of continuity and identification with mankind in general.[11]

In the phrase "a timeless perspective of looking upon the human situation", Melquíades' manuscripts are well reflected, and, as has been mentioned previously, their connections with myth and the mythical mode are many. Also patent is the fusion of personal and typical identities, a primary literary technique for achieving a "sense of continuity and identification with mankind". The archetypal dimension of the characters in the novel is coupled with personal idiosyncrasies. Names as well as personal resemblances repeatedly occur among the family members, and Babilonia, the surname of the ultimate character, reinforces generalizing the continuity and identification which accompanies the Buendías throughout their history, to the history of man. It is useful to recall, here, that Aureliano Babilonia (as opposed to Aureliano Buendía-Babilonia), has only one role in the novel, that of reader-decipherer, and in this role he is identified with the "other", external reader (us). His surname serves to identify him with each reader and all men. If seen as a psychological revelation, a reestablishing of contact with contents of his mind which have been buried or forgotten, then Aureliano's recovery of his personal past, and his family's past, symbolizes what literature can do for each one of us, at least ideally. Aureliano's dis-covery, which is set within a mythic matrix, can assume mythic proportions and be seen as a recovery of mankind's past, a retracing of human steps back to the "cradle of civilization", and beyond it to the primordial revelation, a perfect reintegration of man and universe, and the end of solitude. Aureliano Babilonia would represent the second Adam of the alchemists, the Christ of *Revelation*, the individual after complete self-discovery, or the reader of literature contacting truth, installed in mythic, or psychological, or "creative" time. Such a retracing of steps back to and beyond man's earliest history is reflected in the events and descriptions of the final paragraph of the novel. The manuscripts, the catalyst in the revelation, are found "entre las plantas *prehistóricas* y los charcos humeantes y los insectos luminosos *que habían desterrado del cuarto todo vestigio del paso de los hombres por la tierra*" [my emphasis] (349). The destruction of the house and the city reflect the dissolution of man-made structures, of the work of civilization, and a return to a time before these existed, to a time when they were, perhaps, like the "huevos prehistóricos" mentioned in the second sentence of the novel (p. 9).

The treatment of time in *Cien años* reflects mythical time in another way also. Literature, like myth, exists outside of the conventional time and space of man, in a special time, represented in the novel by *mediodía*. As stated earlier, the readers installed in such a time, José Arcadio Segundo and Aureliano Babilonia, experience revelations of truths which are forgotten, a recapturing of what has been lost, and a transformation of point of view, which allows them to see things more lucidly.

Perhaps the most interesting comment to be made about the treatment of time as this is presented in the narrative theory *Cien años* can be seen to contain, is its similarity to time as this is perceived in psychology. While it is not surprising that the synchronic ordering of the manuscripts, as "la protección final", can be linked with the other elements of the literary theory the novel seems to advance, it is striking that the link between memory and time is psychological in nature. By this I mean that both "creative memory" and the achronological ordering of events in the manuscripts are in close accord with corresponding concepts from the field of psychology. Earlier, in the discussion of creative versus mechanical memory, a comment by Hans Meyerhoff was presented, and now his observation can be extended to include a relevant comment on time and literature:

> What appears forgotten and lost is only pushed aside, buried, or repressed, i.e. not accessible to our conscious selves; the creative as against the mechanical act of recollection for Proust consists precisely in descending "like a diver" to the deep "strata" of the "unconscious self" and bringing to light those traces, impressions and associations which seem to have been lost. It is interesting to note that the literary discovery of timeless elements buried in the unconscious strata of the self is remarkably similar to Freud's description of the temporal characteristics of unconscious processes in the mind. "The events of the unconscious system are timeless, that is, they are not ordered in time, are not changed by the passage of time, have no relation whatever to time.[12]

The "creative time" in which Melquíades arranges his manuscripts explicitly suggests just such an "eternal" or "timeless" time. This is also the treatment received by time in mythology, what Eliade has called "sacred time", and before leaving the subject of how time is treated in the analogue literary creation in *Cien años*, a few of Eliade's comments concerning "modern" and "primitive" conceptions of time, and their relations to alchemy, deserve to be considered.

According to Eliade, the most significant difference between so-called primitive and modern perceptions or world views, lies precisely in their distinct conceptions of time: the former is circular and/or synchronous, the latter linear and/or diachronic.[13] He sees alchemy's relation to time as standing exactly at the interface of these two disparate perceptions, transitional between linear and non-linear time. Eliade observes, too, that as the freeing of nature from the laws of time (the "perfection" of baser metals into gold—according to alchemy, all metals, given enough time, become pure gold, a process the artifex assisted and hastened) goes hand in hand with the deliverance of the alchemist himself, then:

> on the plane of cultural history it is therefore permissible to say that the alchemists, in their desire to supersede Time, anticipated what is in fact the essence of the ideology of the modern world.[14]

From alchemy, he claims, modern man inherited, besides the rudiments of chemistry, his faith in the transmutation of nature and his ambition to control time. He concludes:

> The tragic grandeur of modern man is bound up with the fact that he was the first to take on the role of Time in relation to Nature...the modern world feels at one with Time in the way that nineteenth-century science and industry urged it to be.[15]

But Eliade insists that today's complete identification with time, along with a consequent and tragic "philosophic awareness of the vanity of all human existence", also differentiates modern man from the alchemist. The latter, "although he put himself in the place of Time, took good care not to assume its role", never considering himself to be an essentially temporal being, but rather pursuing immortality, and ultimately "mastering Time when...he underwent initiatory 'death and resurrection.'" And in the closing comments of this alchemical study Eliade states that a viable reconciliation with temporality remains a possibility for modern man, but only if he discovers a "more correct conception of Time", that is, a different point of view.[16] Aureliano Buendía-Babilonia's "death and resurrection", its connection to a transformation of time consciousness and also to alchemy, integrate well with the ideas Eliade expresses here.

Meyerhoff echoes Eliade's reflections on the modern conception of time, arguing that the increasing dominance of time's role in the contemporary world has been reflected in literature in two ways: as a preoccupation with time, and as an identification of time and the self. He asserts that "literary works have always acknowledged the interdependence of the two unities of time and the self".[17] Citing the phrases "stream of consciousness" and "river of time" as examples, he comments that this interrelatedness is reflected in common images. In *Cien años* this interdependence is explicitly established in the deciphering of the manuscripts, for it is only when Aureliano Babilonia penetrates "la protección final" and alters his conception of time that he can decipher the manuscripts and discover who he is, what his origins were, and what his destiny is to be. Meyerhoff links this relation between time and the self to a recurrent theme in modern fiction in the following excerpt, one which seems particularly applicable to the ending of *Cien años*:

> Finally, the frequent, intense search for a recapture of the past, one's own, the family's, the nation's or mankind's...may [now be] seen as an attempt to recover oneself by discovering this sense of continuity with and belongingness to something that seems forever lost.[18]

In Aureliano Babilonia we have a character who literally discovers his true self, recaptures his past in his family's "captured past" (the manuscripts), and whose "sense of continuity with and belongingness to something that seems forever lost", is well established, and seems to extend back to the most remote past of mankind, as his name, Babilonia, suggests.

Cien años de soledad, then, seems to make the following observations about time in literature. First, a statement that a literary creation stands outside the conventional time of man, in an a-chronological temporal state. (One could paraphrase Freud, here, and say: The events of literature are timeless, that is, they are not ordered in time, are not changed by the passage of time, have no relation whatever to time.) The novel suggests, further, that this non-linear, a-temporal ordering of events is more correct than the conventional, linear one, and this agrees with the view of time held in psychology, and is congruent with time as it is presented in myths. In terms of narrative theory, a proper participation in this "literary time" can activate creative memory, putting the reader in touch with truths heretofore hidden or forgotten, and with buried or lost aspects of the self.

The link which emerges between literature and psychology, traced above, is an important one, as it casts the narrative theory the novel presents more sharply into relief. Such a connection has been noted before, by psychologists. Freud said:

> The poets and philosophers before me discovered the unconscious; what I discovered was the scientific method by which the unconscious can be studied.

> The poets are valuable allies, and their testimony is to be rated highly; for they tend to know a great many things between heaven and earth not yet dreamt of in our academic knowledge. In the study of the mind, in particular, they are far ahead of us ordinary people, because they draw upon sources which have not yet been tapped by science.[19]

And Jung grounds the Individuation process, his prescription for overcoming personal feelings of alienation, on the mythic, and literary, motif of the hero on the quest for "the treasure hard to attain". Psychologists talk about mediating between the conscious and unconscious parts of the mind, of helping the individual to recapture a unity and wholeness which seem to have been lost. Organized religion, the traditionally accepted mediator between man and his unconscious in the Western World until the advent of psychology, has failed, for whatever reasons, to provide many with the means to a successful quest for personal wholeness. Jungian depth psychology, as well as other psychological techniques and numerous psychic cults and pseudo-religious practices, have attempted to bridge this gap of "alienation", and to recapture the "at-one-ment" which the "atonements" of major religions have effected in the past.

Eliade, as a religious historian, feels that literature, too, has taken over, at least for some people, the role of mediator previously consigned exclusively to religion:

> Literature plays an important part in contemporary civilization. Reading itself, as a distraction and escape from the historical present, constitutes one of the characteristic traits of modern man. Hence it is only natural that modern man should seek to satisfy his suppressed or inade-

quately satisfied religious needs by reading certain books that, though apparently "secular", in fact contain mythological figures camouflaged as contemporary characters and offer initiatory scenarios in the guise of everyday happenings.[20]

Meyerhoff concurs:

since the decline of religious faith, the aesthetic way of life has become one of the most significant secular responses both to the challenge of death and to the general pessimism pervading the intellectual climate of our age ... Aestheticism has gained by default, as it were, because of the decline or bankruptcy of previously accepted "ways of life".[21]

CONCLUSION

Emerging from this examination of the literary analogues and related subjects in *Cien años de soledad*, is a narrative theory which links literature with man's eternal quest for truth and wholeness. An author is seen as a contemporary magician, like Melquíades or Thoth-Hermes, the god of magic and writing; as one who is in contact with lost or buried knowledge, and who has the ability to transmit this knowledge to others. Not bounded by either time or space, nor by any other conventional notions, the ideal author is able to write "la novela ideal ... una novela ... capaz de voltear la realidad al revés para mostrar como es del otro lado". The literary creation exists outside of the "tiempo convencional de los hombres", in a "creative instant", reflecting an achronological ordering akin to those visible in psychology, religion and mythology. In the past, myths have been religious and literary in nature, and literature may have a potentially "religious", or soteriological facet, at least according to humanists from the fields of philosophy (Meyerhoff), religious history (Eliade) and psychology (Freud and Jung). The narrative theory presented in Garcia Márquez' novel is in agreement with this idea that literature can put man into contact with transpersonal truths and can meaningfully alter his perspective.

From the treatment of the manuscripts, the analogue

literary creation in *Cien años*, it becomes obvious that a proper understanding of literature depends a great deal upon the preparation of the reader. This preparation is both universal and personal. The manuscripts cannot be deciphered until the Buendía family has moved through an entire cycle of solitude, culminating in the birth of "el animal mitológico que había de poner término a la estirpe" (350). Nor can they be successfully penetrated until Aureliano Buendía-Babilonia is prepared for the final revelation, the mystical experience wherein his creative memory is activated and the entire family past and his personal destiny become perfectly clear. Aureliano Babilonia's mystic light experience represents, literally, self-discovery, and symbolizes a reintegration of internal and external processes, of man and cosmos, an at-one-ment that had been lost.

Aureliano's literary preparation is described explicitly in the opening lines of chapter eighteen:

> Aureliano no abandonó en mucho tiempo el cuarto de Melquíades. Se aprendió de memoria las leyendas fantásticas del libro desencuadernado, la síntesis de los estudios de Hermann, el tullido; los apuntes sobre la ciencia demonológica, las claves de la piedra filosofal, las centurias de Nostradamus y sus investigaciones sobre la peste, de modo que llegó a la adolescencia sin saber nada de su tiempo, pero con los conocimientos básicos del hombre medieval (301).

His studies in these esoteric pursuits expressly establish Aureliano's capacity to complete the quest that alchemy and these other disciplines and investigations had in common, to reach a goal which has been described in many ways: as passage from a mundane to a sacred world, as immortality, as the primordial revelation, as true self-discovery, as experience of the *numinosum*, as im-mediate perception of reality, or, more generally, in the words of Eliade, as "an ontological mutation of the existential condition". Whatever the designation chosen for this goal, the picture of the reader which emerges from *Cien años* is one of a transformed participant, who ultimately passes into the world with a changed point of view, one who has been set free to see the prevailing cultural canon from a different perspective, and who has recovered truths, or aspects of himself, that had been lost.

Contact between author and reader is also an important element of the narrative theory in the novel, as the transformative potential of literature finally depends upon the reader's sharing the author's point of view. It is only from this new perspective that one sees "el otro lado de las cosas", the side heretofore hidden, and the complement to the partial reality accepted by the general public. In *Cien años* this process, the assumption of a new, unpopular perspective by a reader occurs at least twice. José Arcadio Buendía, to the great horror of Úrsula, announces that the earth is round, "like an orange," after reading material left behind by Melquíades. The townspeople believe he is crazy. José Arcadio Segundo holds views concerning the Banana Company and the plaza massacre which contradict the popularly held ideas espoused by official historians. His certainty is explicitly, if mysteriously, grounded in his repeated readings of the manuscripts. I would suggest that there is a third example, involving Aureliano Babilonia and literature in general. At the end of the novel, when Aureliano Buendía-Babilonia becomes Aureliano Buendía (the character whose death marks the end of the Buendía line), and Aureliano Babilonia (the character-reader, or participant-observer), the external reader becomes identified with him, as an "observer-participant". This identification represents a facet of the magic of literature, a statement that *literature is true*, an observation contrary to the popularly held belief that fiction is just that, fiction, and no more. A comment by Antonin Artaud makes this point cogently: "Art is never real and always true". An external reader can never really participate in fictional events, but he can, and should, participate in the truth contained in such events. Artaud's statement helps to reconcile the bisemic ending of *Cien años*, the literal, terminal destruction, and the apparently successful "rites of passage" suggested by the same events and descriptions. Macondo and the Buendías are destroyed "para siempre", because they are unreal, a mere fiction. On the other hand, the transformed Macondo, and the correspondingly immortal Aureliano Babilonia, would represent the *truth* contained in the manuscripts, the analogue literary creation. The century of daily occurrences written in the manuscripts, and the characters who performed them, are like a "ciudad de los espejos (o los espejismos)" and are irrevocably "exiled from the memory of men". The truth behind this fictional one hundred years of activity, however, is eternal, and exists in "creative time". To use an image from the novel, the events of the manuscripts might be compared to the description of their letters as "escritura musical" (161), while the truth behind them would be the music itself. As the narrative closes, Aureliano Babilonia knows he will never leave Melquíades' room, and at the literal level of interpretation he dies, just as the unreal fictional characters, who never truly exist in the first place, apparently cease to be. At the symbolic level, however, where Melquíades' room represents the transformed point of view, the statement that Aureliano Babilonia never again leaves this room means this character-reader's perspective has been definitively changed. Like Melquíades (and to a lesser degree, José Arcadio Buendía and José Arcadio Segundo), Aureliano now sees "el otro lado de las cosas", the truth behind the mere fiction. The bisemic nature of the ending of *Cien años*, then, reflects the central idea contained in the narrative theory which the novel presents, that literature itself is bisemic, it is "never real and always true".

Finally, a very obvious element of narrative theory, as this can be seen in *Cien años de soledad*, should not be overlooked. Like Hermes, the author must be not only a magus, a messenger between the common man and other realms, but also a good story teller. Thoth-Hermes employed a vice, playing cards, to transmit the secrets of personal integration contained in the Tarot, because he knew the entertainment value would ensure their immortality and accessiblity. In *Cien años* these two aspects of literature, literature as entertainment and as potential vehicle for meaningfully altering a reader's orientation in the world, are united: it is at once *dulce et utile*. However, while the pleasing nature of literature is patent in the novel, its "usefulness" requires patience and preparation, that is, it must be deciphered.

To conclude this discussion on the narrative theory García Márquez' novel presents, a quotation from Meyerhoff, one cited before, is offered as a summary statement of the view of literature which emerges from *Cien años de soledad*:

literature—a reminder of aspects of time and the self which may be neglected, buried or lost because of our enslavement to the physical and social categories of time and the self—may bring to light, or may set us free to see, certain aspects of human experience and existence from an entirely different perspective... It does, in fact, make an intellectual contribution to what I shall call the *orientation* of man in the world of experience [emphasis Meyerhoff's].[22]

NOTES

[1] M. Vargas Llosa, *Historia de un deicidio* (Barcelona: Barral, 1971), pp. 479-80.

[2] E. Rodríguez-Monegal, "Novedad y anacronismo de *Cien años de soledad*," *NNH*, 1 (Jan. 1971), p. 38.

[3] Mircea Eliade, *Rites and Symbols of Initiation: The Mysteries of Birth and Rebirth*, trans. W. R. Trask (New York: Harper and Row, 1958), p. 36.

[4] Hans Meyerhoff, *Time in Literature* (Berkeley: Univ. of Calif., 1968), p. 119.

[5] M. Fernández-Braso, *Gabriel García Márquez* (Madrid: Edit. Asur, 1969), p. 65.

[6] Two other divine offices exercised by Hermes can also be related to *Cien años* and the present study, though the connections are somewhat casual. They are offered here for the interested reader. W. K. C. Guthrie, in *The Greeks and Their Gods* (Boston: Beacon Press, 1951), writes that Hermes signifies "he of the stone heap", and that the god is regarded as "the stone spirit". This may explain why the alchemists, who sought the philosophers' stone, were devoted to him. Guthrie notes, in another place: "his worship flourished particularly, and from a very early date, in Arkadia" (p. 91), a fortuitous link to the oft repeated name José Arcadio Buendía.

    Finally, Hermes eventually comes to be the patron of thieves also, probably because of his cleverness, and even this "divine attribute" of thievery has been associated with the novel. It has been ascribed to García Márquez, and within the context of literary creation, by Vargas Llosa. He maintains, in *Historia de un deicidio*, that an author of a literary fiction is not only a deicide, but also a thief, one who robs from "reality" the building blocks of personal literary creation (p. 102).

[7] The result of this and other experiments is a profound transformation of José Arcadio Buendía's "orientation in the world", and his

overall world view, a change humorously described as this second
paragraph of the novel concludes:

> Cuando se hizo experto en el uso y manejo de sus instrumentos,
> tuvo una noción del espacio que le permitió navegar por mares
> incógnitos, visitar territorios deshabitados y trabar relación con
> seres espléndidos, sin necesidad de abandonar su gabinete. Fue
> esa la época en que adquirió el hábito de hablar a solas, paseándo-
> se por la casa sin hacer caso de nadie... De pronto, sin ningún
> anuncio, su actividad febril se interrumpió y fue sustituida por
> una especie de fascinación. Estuvo varios días como hechizado,
> repitiéndose a sí mismo en voz baja un sartal de asombrosas
> conjeturas, sin dar crédito a su propio entendimiento. Por fin, un
> martes de diciembre, a la hora del almuerzo, soltó de un golpe
> toda la carga de su tormento. Los niños habían de recordar por el
> resto de su vida la augusta solemnidad con que su padre se sentó
> a la cabecera de la mesa, temblando de fiebre, devastado por la
> prolongada vigilia y por el encono de su imaginación, y les reveló
> su descubrimiento:
> —La tierra es redonda como una naranja—(11-12).

This humorous treatment betrays the triviality of José Arcadio
Buendía's "changed perspective" at this point in the narrative, yet it
is interesting that García Márquez chooses the natural phenomenon
historically linked to the discovery of the New World for this
example of "transformed perspective". Aside from the importance
this discovery had upon the history of Latin America, "discovering
the 'New World'" is a motif which also integrates well with 1)
alchemy, 2) the interpretation of Aureliano Babilonia's ultimate
deciphering of Melquíades' parchments and the transformation of
Macondo, when these are seen in the light of psychological rites of
passage, and 3) with the playfulness with which the author treats
these themes on two levels, the literal and non-literal. Curiously, it
is in the paragraph following this pronouncement that the earth is
round, when Melquíades returns and dispels the generally held
belief that José Arcadio Buendía has gone crazy ("llegó Melquíades a
poner las cosas en su punto"), and erects the alchemical laboratory
that is to exercise "una influencia terminante en el futuro de la
aldea".

8 This relation of the title to the manuscripts has not attracted
critical attention, to my knowledge. In fact, there is a mistranslation
in the English version of the novel. The sentence "Nadie debe
conocer su sentido mientras no hayan cumplido cien años" (161), is
rendered: "No one must know their meaning until he has [sic]
reached one hundred years of age" [p. 177 of Gregory Rabassa's
translation, *One Hundred Years of Solitude* (New York: Harper and Row,
1970), Avon paperback printing.]

9 Meyerhoff, *Time in Literature*, p. 119.

10 Ibid., p. 57.

11 Ibid., p. 80.

12 Ibid., pp. 57-58.

13 Mircea Eliade, *The Myth of the Eternal Return*, trans. W. R. Trask (New York: Bollingen, 1954), pp. 90-92. See also, by the same author, *The Forge and the Crucible* (London: Rider and Co., 1962), pp. 171-73.

14 Eliade, *The Forge and the Crucible*, pp. 171 and 173.

15 Ibid., pp. 175-76.

16 Ibid., pp. 174-75.

17 Eliade cites the secularization of work as the cause for the contemporary identity of the individual with time, and the accompanying popular belief that man is essentially a temporal being. To this compression of time into the historical dimension and the ultimate failure of history to encounter a unifying and meaningful structure, Meyerhoff adds the discrete fragmenting of time by scientific measurement.

   Among the results of this phenomenon, the most important is "the sharp decline or virtual collapse of the dimension of 'eternity' as seen within the religious, philosophical, political or social realms" (Meyerhoff, p. 89). Time, more and more, is regarded as constant change, becoming increasingly fragmented, as does the self which is identified with it. See Eliade, *The Forge and the Crucible*, pp. 171-75, and Meyerhoff, especially pp. 89-90 and 134.

18 Meyerhoff, *Time in Literature*, p. 37, and p. 113.

19 Ibid., p. 88. Meyerhoff introduces these quotations with these words: "Freud himself, it must be remembered, always acknowledged a sense of priority for literature".

20 Eliade, *Rites and Symbols of Initiation*, pp. 134-35.

21 Meyerhoff, *Time in Literature*, p. 58.

22 Ibid., p. 119.

Conclusion

WHY ALCHEMY IS EMPLOYED in *Cien años de soledad*, and how examining its use can contribute to a better understanding of the novel are questions which have served as guiding threads throughout this study. These questions have been addressed in various ways. One of the most significant facts about alchemy concerns its general connection with a large number of mystical belief systems. Alchemy is representative of many disciplines whose common goal is the transformation of the individual through personal contact with the *numinosum*, defined by Jung as "a dynamic agency or effect not caused by an arbitrary act of the will". Such numinous experience is always psychological, and often religious, in nature, and results in a significant change in an individual's perception of himself and his world. This common goal of "primordial revelation", associated with initiations and rites of passage, is linked with narrative theory in *Cien años*, where literature is seen as a vehicle for transmitting truths to a prepared discoverer. But what alchemy has in common with other esoteric disciplines, while perhaps its most important contribution to an enhanced understanding of the novel, is by no means its only point of integration into the narrative. Both historically and philosophically alchemy reveals characteristics that establish numerous points of contact with the novel, and suggest many possible reasons for its inclusion.

As regards its history, several attributes of alchemy which might be attractive to García Márquez for a novel like *Cien años* emerge. Alchemists have a guide or familiar, Hermes or Thoth-Hermes, and this god's qualities describe Melquíades' actions in the narrative well. Thoth-Hermes is the Egyptian god of magic and writing, and the one who invented the alphabet, the writer's medium, according to the myths. Hermes is a renowned story teller, one who could enchant with words. He is also called psychopomp, the god who guides souls to the lower realms, which, psychologically, represent the unconscious part of the mind, and psychological contents which are buried there. Another attribute of the alchemical art is that it was practiced universally in one form or another, with treatises from India, China, Egypt and Greece joining those of Europe. In this sense alchemy serves as a metaphor for literature, if this is seen as a universal art form designed to transmit truth, and to bring apparently lost or hidden truths to light.

Alchemy also produced a considerable amount of literature, and several parallels between this literature and *Cien años* can be drawn. First, much alchemical literature was entertaining, and a good amount was written by persons whose sole interest in this art was literary. Secondly, all alchemical literature, like Melquíades' manuscripts, required deciphering. Moreover, literature written by alchemists is "never real and always true". It is fantastic literature, but it always has a real meaning which, according to Jung, is psychologically true. For instance, the dissolution and death of the "prima materia" in the flask refers to the liberation of the alchemist from the bonds of the superego. This essential phase of the alchemical *opus* commonly calls for the death of the artifex, but this is to be understood literally only at the psychological level. Melquíades' physical death by drowning, from which he returns, Remedios' assumption and many other events and descriptions in *Cien años* reflect a similar technique and, as I have suggested, can support a similar interpretation. Literature, as it is portrayed in the narrative requires an internal correspondence of external events, that is, it requires that the reader discover the truth behind the unreal fiction, just as the artifex deciphered the instructions for changing lead into gold, and understood them as transformations of his point of view. Furthermore, the alchemist, like the modern reader, uses his hands and his head, and the flask, which symbolized the artifex' head, was "read" by the alchemist as a book is today. What occurs in the flask or book corresponds, at least ideally, to internal mental metamorphoses. Alchemy, when successful, involved not the words of the operations themselves, but the artifex' personal reactions to them; the same holds true for literature according to the narrative theory in *Cien años*.

Another "accidental" characteristic which integrates alchemy well into *Cien años* is the quest for gold, the central alchemical metaphor which informs the artifex' search for truth. In this central quest, the bisemic nature of alchemy is cast into relief. The thirst for symbolic, "true" gold, was not to be confused with a lust for the physical metal. The philosophers' stone, the substance that permitted one "to turn vulgar lead into purest gold", represents an ineffable state of mind, a perspective from which the secrets of the universe, its hidden truths and reality, are perceived. Again, the treatment of the quest for gold in alchemy is reflected in the narrative theory presented in the novel. As in alchemy, the narrative presents a dual quest, with the literal branch ending in the discovery of Úrsula's gold and the resulting death of the last José Arcadio, and the symbolic branch terminating in the successful deciphering of Melquíades' manuscripts, and the symbolic death and resurrection of Aureliano Babilonia. The simultaneous literal death and symbolic transformation of the character-reader (identified in the last paragraph with the external reader), and the destruction of Macondo (which represents all that has happened in the novel), parallels the alchemical treatment of the quest for gold exactly. Like literature, alchemical gold was "never real but always true", and, once again, alchemy is seen as a useful metaphor for the narrative theory in García Márquez' novel. The philosophers' stone corresponds to the proper point of view, the perspective which lets one see "the other side of things", and "wake up their souls". And this perspective, according to alchemical belief, is not discovered as much as it is revealed, another idea echoed in the concept of literature set forth in the novel.

One more historical fact about alchemy, its compensatory relationship to the Medieval-Renaissance Church in Europe, can also provide a convenient focusing of ideas about literature that are found in the novel. According to Jung, alchemy offered Europe one of few channels to direct numinous experience at a time when Church dogma had a near monopoly on mediating such experiences between individuals and God, or the numinous realm. In the literary theory contained in *Cien años*, literature, too, is set up as a force which can free the individual from the prevailing cultural canon (José Arcadio Buendía's discovery that the earth is round), and from societal prejudices or disbeliefs (José Arcadio Segundo's ideas on the Banana Company and the plaza massacre). One writer states:

> During the middle ages, alchemy was not only a philosophy and a science, but a religion. Those who rebelled against the religious limitations of their day concealed their philosophic teachings under the allegory of gold-making. In this way they preserved their personal liberty and were ridiculed rather than persecuted.[1]

Alchemy, then, can serve as an exercise in perspective, for its purpose was to draw individuals out of a blind acceptance of popular modes of thought, out of the prevailing world view. Ideally, literature can help one achieve an orientation in the world that results in "im-mediate" experience, a perception "más allá de cualquier formalismo", a point of view which is, like Remedios the Beauty, no longer earth-bound, but rather pure light. This idea, also, is reflected in the narrative theory of the novel.

Eliade cites the role of alchemy as a preserver of ancient, pre-Christian ideas, commenting that, through alchemy, the substance of the ancient mysteries was preserved down into modern times. Especially in terms of time-consciousness, alchemy stands at the crossroads of past and present. Similarities to the time of ancient myth and the time of modern psychology, and to that of literature, make alchemy's inclusion in a modern novel much less surprising than it might at first appear.

From a more philosophical standpoint, the *coniunctio oppositorum* or union of opposites, so crucial to alchemy, is also reflected in the novel, not only in the final paragraphs, but also in techniques used throughout the narrative. Although many examples of this principle can be identified at a number of different levels of the work, ultimately, perhaps, this *modus operandi* of the union of opposites culminates in the statement that, according to *Cien años*, fiction conjoins the unreal with the true.

Alchemy, then, for several reasons, can be seen as a metaphor for literature as this is portrayed in García Márquez' novel. Just as Jung cited alchemy as a forerunner of depth psychology, saying that the processes and goal were the same for both, alchemy can be considered as a relative of

serious literature. Like alchemy, serious literature is potentially a transformative vehicle which puts man into contact
with truths lost or hidden, or frees him to see things in a
different way. If men like Jung, Eliade and Meyerhoff are
correct, the importance of literature as such a potential
mediator has become greater as the secularization of the
world has increased, for the need of man to understand
remains even when religion can no longer satisfy it for many.
A recognition of this transformative purpose of literature,
and art in general, has precedents among twentieth century
artists, too. (For Breton's comments, see *supra*. pp. 91-92).

Another use to which alchemy lends itself is humor and
irony, and it is possible that García Márquez also takes
advantage of this facet of the esoteric discipline in *Cien años*. It
is known that alchemy's dual, literal/psychological, nature
was the source of jokes even several centuries ago, when
literal-minded alchemists wasted time and money just as José
Arcadio Buendía does when he fuses Úrsula's gold with a
host of "vulgar substances". And alchemy, from the scientific
point of view, is an example of superstition and man's irra-
tional gullibility. From another perspective, however, alchemy is a valid and systematic process for achieving psychological integration. Seen this way, the fact that it was misunderstood by minds ignorant of psychology, who dismissed
it out of hand, is an indictment of the parochialism and
blindness of their world view. If understood literally, alchemy is a source of humor, but when understood properly,
it is involved with nothing less than man's eternal quest for
truth and wisdom. The literature of alchemy was purpose-
fully ironic, not only to protect its "secrets" from the "un-
worthy", but also to protect its practitioners from persecu-
tion. The manner in which alchemically related material is
included in *Cien años* permits some interesting conjecture on
irony in the novel. The underlying pessimism some critics
have attributed to the work, based in large part upon a literal
reading of the final paragraphs, may be ironic in nature. Such
a perception of the narrative is certainly consistent with the
prevailing ideas of a troubled world, but it is possible that the
novel is attempting to undermine the exclusivity of such a
world view rather than reinforce it. I think it is significant
that a "literal" reading of the ending reflects the pessimistic,

angst-ridden *Weltanschauung* of modern, "alienated man", so prevalent in the twentieth century, while the "non-literal" or symbolic reading heralds a resurrected individual and world, a transformed world view, and an exuberant praise of literature and its transformative potential. If *Cien años*, like Melquíades' manuscripts and alchemical tracts, is literature requiring deciphering, the presence and use of alchemy suggests that the relativity of point of view is, perhaps, the underlying theme of the novel. The bisemic ending, like alchemical literature, can be seen as an attempt to reveal the relativity of the prevailing cultural canon, to demonstrate how our preconceptions influence our perceptions, often to the complete exclusion of "the other side of things". The ending of the novel can be seen as a statement that literature can free us from the domination of a "single vision", by revealing to us "aun los objetos perdidos desde hacía mucho tiempo", which appear precisely "por donde más se les había buscado" (9). Irony would be important in such a process of transforming point of view, because it forces the reader to participate, to try to decipher; and, as in alchemy, if the artifex is properly prepared, the deciphering will be possible, for the secrets will reveal themselves.[2] Suggested by this type of irony, which mixes the comic and the tragic, might be a comparison of *Cien años* and the literature of the Baroque Age, particularly as regards the phenomenon known as "Baroque melancholy", which flourished throughout Europe, and especially in Spain and England.[3]

Besides a comparison to Baroque literature, the use of alchemy in *Cien años de soledad* opens up several other interesting avenues of approach to the novel, and in this way, too, contributes to an overall understanding of the work. Alchemy's relationship to religion, psychology and mythology indicate areas of investigation which have not been addressed, or which have been treated only partially to date. A few of these are: a systematic examination of the archetypes and mythologems in the narrative; the presence of Freudian and Jungian psychology; and a comparison of the concept of harmony as this is presented in *Cien años*, to classical and modern ideas on this subject. While such topics have fallen outside the present study for the most part, they are related to the quest theme and the theme of perspectivism, and to the narrative theory set forth in the novel, the areas of investigation whose corners alchemy has helped illuminate. Gabriel García Márquez' *Cien años de soledad* is a fecund field for exploration, and perhaps the most useful advice alchemy can offer is expressed in the following alchemical motto:

> Ora,
> Lege, lege, lege, relege, labora.
> Et invenies.

NOTES

[1] M. P. Hall, *An Encyclopedic Outline of Masonic, Hermetic, Quabbalistic and Rosicrucian Symbolical Philosophy* (Los Angeles: The Philosophic Research Society, Inc., 1977), p. CLIV.

[2] The following statement, by García Márquez, comes from an interview with M. Fernández-Braso: "tarde o temprano, la realidad termina por darle la razón a la imaginación". For this and related comments see M. Fernández-Braso, *Gabriel García Márquez* (Madrid: Edit. Asur, 1969), pp. 65-67.

[3] Lope and Cervantes explicitly describe themselves as "melancólicos" upon several occasions. For general background on the subject of melancholy and Baroque melancholy, see R. Klibansky, E. Panofsky and F. Saxl, *Saturn and Melancholy* (Cambridge: Thos. Nelson and Sons Ltd., 1964).

BIBLIOGRAPHY

Aaron, Audrey. "The Total Innovation of García Márquez' *Cien años de soledad*," a lecture presented February 28, 1976, at Wheaton College.

Aínsa, Fernando. "Integración y pseudonimia en la novela latinoamericana contemporánea." *Nueva Narrativa Hispanoamericana*, 5 (Jan. and Sept. 1975), pp. 239-49.

Amorós, Andrés. "*Cien años de soledad.*" In *Introducción a la novela hispanoamericana actual*. Salamanca: Ediciones Anaya, 1971, pp. 155-61.

Anderson Imbert, Enrique. "'Literatura fantástica,' 'realismo mágico' y 'lo real maravilloso.'" In *Otros mundos otros fuegos: fantasía y realismo mágico en Iberoamérica; memoria del XVI Congreso Internacional de Literatura Iberoamericana*, ed. Donald A. Yates. East Lansing: Latin American Studies Center at Michigan State University, 1975, pp. 39-44.

Armando, Octavio. "Sobre las comparaciones de Rulfo." *Nueva Narrativa Hispanoamericana*, II, 2 (Sept. 1972), pp. 173-77.

Arnau, Carmen. *El mundo mítico de Gabriel García Márquez*. Barcelona: Ediciones Insula, 1971.

Bacstrom's Alchemical Anthology, ed. J. W. Hamilton-Jones. London: John M. Watkins, 1960.

Balla, Andrés. "Clasicismo e innovación en *Cien años de soledad, La casa verde* y *Rayuela*." *Insula*, No. 303 (Feb. 1972), p. 12.

Benedetti, Mario. "García Márquez o la vigilia dentro del sueño." In *Letras del continente mestizo*. Montevideo: Arca, 1967, pp. 180-89.

—————, ed. *Nueve asedios a García Márquez*. Santiago de Chile: Edit. Universitaria, 1969.

Benet, Juan. "De Canudos a Macondo." *Revista de Occidente*, Ser. 2, 24-25 (1969), pp. 49-57.

The Book of Revelation. In *The Bible Designed to be Read as Literature*, ed. Ernest S. Bates. London: Folio Society, 1958, II, pp. 523-49.

The Oxford Annotated Bible With the Apocrypha: Revised Standard Version, ed. H. G. May and B. M. Metzger. New York: Oxford University Press, 1965.

The Reader's Bible: Being the Authorized Version of the "Holy Bible" Containing the Old and New Testaments and the Apocrypha Translated Out of the Original Tongues. London: Oxford and Cambridge University Presses, 1951.

Booth, Wayne C. *A Rhetoric of Irony*. Chicago: University of Chicago, 1974.

──────. *The Rhetoric of Fiction*. Chicago: University of Chicago, 1961.

Breton, André. *Manifestoes of Surrealism*, trans. R. Seaver and H. R. Lane. Ann Arbor: University of Michigan, 1972.

Burckhardt, T. *Alchemy: Science of the Cosmos, Science of the Soul*, trans. William Stoddart. Baltimore: Penguin, 1967.

Campbell, Joseph. *The Hero With A Thousand Faces*. New York: The Bollingen Foundation, 1949.

Campos, Jorge. "García Márquez: fábula y realidad." *Insula*, No. 258 (Mayo 1968), p. 11.

Castagnino, Raul H. "Sintaxis de personajes y seudopersonajes en una pequeña gran novela de Gabriel García Márquez." *Nueva Narrativa Hispanoamericana*, 4 (Jan. and Sept. 1974), pp. 105-09.

Ciplijauskaité, Birutė. "Foreshadowing as Technique and Theme in *One Hundred Years of Solitude*." In *Books Abroad*, 47, No. 3 (Spring 1973), pp. 478-84.

The Complete Prophecies of Nostradamus, trans. and ed. Henry C. Roberts. New York: Crown Publishers, 1947.

Conte, Rafael. "Gabriel García Márquez o el mito." In *Lenguaje y violencia: introducción a la nueva novela hispanoamericana*. Madrid: Al-Borak, S. A., 1972, pp. 157-83.

Dauster, Frank. "The Short Stories of García Márquez." In *Books Abroad*, 47, No. 3 (Spring 1973), pp. 466-70.

Debus, Allen C. "Renaissance Chemistry and the Work of Robert Fludd." In *Alchemy and Chemistry in the Seventeenth Century*. Los Angeles: Andrews Clark Memorial Library, 1966, pp. 3-29.

Díez, Luis Alfonso. "Torquemada en Macondo." *Nueva Narrativa Hispanoamericana*, 4 (Jan. and Sept. 1974), pp. 360-63.

Domingo, José. "Entrevistas: Gabriel García Márquez." *Insula*, No. 259 (Junio 1968), pp. 6 and 11.

Dorfman, Ariel. "La muerte como acto imaginativo en *Cien años de soledad*." In *Imaginación y violencia en América*. Santiago de Chile: Edit. Universitaria, S. A., 1970, pp. 138-80.

Douglas, Alfred. *The Tarot: The Origins, Meaning and Uses of the Cards*. New York: Taplinger, 1972.

Earle, Peter G. "Muerte y transfiguración del realismo mágico." In *Otros mundos otros fuegos: fantasía y realismo mágico en Iberoamérica: memoria del XVI Congreso Internacional de Literatura Iberoamericana*, ed. Donald A. Yates. East Lansing: Latin American Studies at Michigan State University, 1975, pp. 39-44.

Edinger, Edward F. *Ego and Archetype: Individuation and the Religious Function of the Psyche.* Baltimore: Penquin, 1972.

Ehrmann, Jacques, ed. *Game, Play, Literature.* Boston: Beacon Press, 1968.

Eliade, Mircea. *The Forge and the Crucible.* London: Rider and Co., 1962.

——. *The Myth of the Eternal Return*, trans. W. R. Trask. New York: Bollingen, 1954.

——. *The Quest: History and Meaning in Religion.* Chicago: University of Chicago, 1969.

——. *Rites and Symbols of Initiation: The Mysteries of Birth and Rebirth*, trans. Willard R. Trask. New York: Harper and Row, 1958.

——. *The Two and the One*, trans. J. M. Cohen. New York: Harper and Row, 1965.

Eyzaguirre, Luis B. "Sobre tiranía y 'métodos' de 'supremos' y 'patriarcas.'" In *INTI: Revista de Literatura Hispánica*, 3 (abril 1976), pp. 64-74.

Fernández Bonilla, Magali and Raimundo. "Los fundamentos cosmológicos del lenguaje en el cuento 'Un día después del sábado,' de Gabriel García Márquez." *Nueva Narrativa Hispanoamericana*, 4 (Jan. and Sept. 1974), pp. 17-68.

Fernández-Braso, Miguel. *Gabriel García Márquez.* Madrid: Editorial Azur, 1969.

Foster, David William. "García Márquez and Solitude." *Américas*, 21, No. 11-12 (Nov.-Dec. 1969), pp. 36-41.

Franco, Jean. "A New Visitation of Hell: Comala, Macondo and Santa María" and "Gabriel García Márquez." In *A Literary History of Spain: Spanish American Literature Since Independence.* London: Ernest Benn Ltd., 1973, pp. 246, 256-58.

Franz, Marie-Louise von. *Aurora Consurgens: A Document Attributed to Thomas Aquinas on the Problem of Opposites in Alchemy*, trans. R. F. C. Hull and A. S. B. Glover. New York: Bollingen Foundation, 1966.

Frye, Northrop. *Anatomy of Criticism: Four Essays.* Princeton: University Press, 1971.

——. *Fables of Identity: Studies in Poetic Mythology.* New York: Harcourt, Brace and World, 1963.

García Márquez, Gabriel. *Cien años de soledad.* Buenos Aires: Editorial Sudamericana, 1967.

——. *One Hundred Years of Solitude*, trans. Gregory Rabassa. New York: Harper and Row, 1970.

————. *El coronel no tiene quien le escriba*. Buenos Aires: Sudamericana (Colección Indice), 1973.

————. *La hojarasca*, 3rd ed. Buenos Aires: Sudamericana, 1969.

————. *La increíble y triste historia de la cándida eréndira y de su abuela desalmada: siete cuentos*. México: Editorial Hermes, 1972.

————. *La mala hora*. México: Era, S. A., 1966.

————. El otoño del partiarca, 2nd ed. Buenos Aires: Editorial Sudamericana, 1975.

————. *Relato de un náufrago que estuvo diez días a la deriva en una balsa sin comer ni beber, que fue proclamado héroe de la patria, besado por las reinas de la belleza y hecho rico por la publicidad, y luego aborrecido por el gobierno y olvidado para siempre*. Barcelona: Tusquets, 1970.

Gertel, Zunilda. "La novela de espacio totalizador." In *La novela hispanoamericana contemporánea*. Buenos Aires: Nuevos Esquemas, 1970, pp. 150-58.

————. "Tres estructuras fundamentales en la narrativa hispanoamericana actual." In *Nueva Narrativa Hispanoamericana*, 5 (Jan. and Sept. 1975), pp. 215-27.

Giacoman, Helmy F., ed. *Homenaje a García Márquez: variaciones interpretivas en torno a su obra*. Madrid: Las Américas, 1972.

Graubard, Mark. *Astrology and Alchemy: Two Fossil Sciences*. New York: Philosophical Library, 1953, pp. 81-101, 237-360.

Guthrie, W. K. C. *The Greeks and Their Gods*. Boston: Beacon Press, 1951.

Hall, Manly P. *Masonic, Hermetic, Qabbalistic and Rosicrucian Symbolic Philosophy*. Los Angeles: The Philosophical Research Society, Inc., 1977.

Hamilton, Edith. *Mythology: Timeless Tales of Gods and Heroes*. New York: The New American Library Inc., 1940.

Harrison, J. E. *Prolegomena to the Study of Greek Religion*. Cambridge: University Press, 1903.

Harss, Luis. "Gabriel García Márquez, or the Lost Chord." In *Into the Mainstream: Conversations with Latin-American Writers*. New York: Harper and Row, 1967, pp. 310-41.

Heidel, Alexander. *The Gilgamesh Epic and Old Testament Parallels*, 2nd ed. Chicago: University of Chicago Press, 1949.

Hopkins, Arthur John. *Alchemy: Child of Greek Philosophy*. New York: Columbia University Press, 1934.

Hornedo Si, R. María de. "*Cien años de soledad*." *Razón y Fe*, 857 (June 1969), pp. 647-51.

Ivask, Ivar. "Allegro Barbaro, or Gabriel García Márquez in Oklahoma." *Books Abroad*, 47, No. 3 (Spring 1973), pp. 439-40.

————. "Freedom of Imagination Regained." *Books Abroad*, 47, No. 1 (Winter 1973), pp. 7-10.

Jaramillo Levi, Enrique. "Tiempo y espacio a través del tema del doble en 'La isla al mediodía' de Julio Cortázar." *Nueva Narrativa Hispanoamericana*, 4 (Jan. and Sept. 1974), pp. 299-305.

Jung, Carl Gustav. *The Collected Works of Carl Gustav Jung*. Vol. IX, 2: *AION: Researches into the Phenomenology of the Self*, 2nd ed. Translated by R. F. C. Hull. Princeton: Bollingen Foundation, 1970.

—————. *The Collected Works of Carl Gustav Jung*. Vol. XIII: *The Alchemical Studies*. Translated by R. F. C. Hull. Princeton: Bollingen, 1967.

—————. *The Collected Works of Carl Gustav Jung*. Vol. IX, 1: *The Archetypes and the Collective Unconscious*, 2nd ed. Translated by R. F. C. Hull. Princeton: Bollingen, 1968.

—————. *The Collected Works of Carl Gustav Jung*. Vol. X: *Civilization in Transition*. Translated by R. F. C. Hull. Princeton: Bollingen, 1957.

—————. *Four Archetypes: Mother/Rebirth/Spirit/Trickster*. Translated by R. F. C. Hull. Princeton: Bollingen, 1970.

—————, ed. *Man and His Symbols*. Garden City: Doubleday and Co., 1964.

—————. *The Collected Works of Carl Gustav Jung*. Vol. XIV: *Mysterium Coniunctionis: An Inquiry Into the Separation and Synthesis of Psychic Opposites in Alchemy*. Translated by R. F. C. Hull. Princeton: Bollingen, 1963.

—————. *The Portable Jung*. Translated by R. F. C. Hull. Edited by Joseph Campbell. New York: Viking Press, 1971.

—————. *Psychological Reflections: A New Anthology of His Writings 1905-1961*. Edited by Jolande Jacobi. Princeton: Bollingen, 1973.

—————. *The Collected Works of Carl Gustav Jung*. Vol. XII: *Psychology and Alchemy*, 2nd ed. Translated by R. F. C. Hull. Princeton: Bollingen, 1968.

—————. *The Collected Works of Carl Gustav Jung*. Vol. XI: *Psychology and Religion: West and East*, 2nd ed. Translated by R. F. C. Hull. Princeton: Bollingen, 1969.

—————. *The Spirit in Man, Art and Literature*. Translated by R. F. C. Hull. Princeton: Bollingen, 1971.

Kerényi, C. and Jung, C. G. *Essays on a Science of Mythology: The Myth of the Divine Child and the Mysteries of Eleusis*. Translated by R. F. C. Hull. Princeton: Bollingen, 1969.

Lagmanovich, David. "De la lingüística a la crítica literaria: consecuencias para la nueva narrativa." *Nueva Narrativa Hispanoamericana*, 5 (Jan. and Sept. 1975), pp. 229-37.

Leadbeater, C. W. *The Chakras*. Wheaton, Illinois: The Theosophical Publishing House, 1977.

Leek, Sybil. *The Sybil Leek Book of Fortune Telling*. New York: Macmillan, 1969.

Lerner, Isaias. "A propósito de *Cien años de soledad*." *Cuadernos Americanos*, 162 (Feb. 1969), pp. 186-200.

Levine, Suzanne Jill. "*Cien años de soledad* y la biografía imaginaria." *Revista Iberoamericana*, 36 (1970), pp. 453-63.

——————. "La maldición del incesto en *Cien años de soledad*." *Revista Iberoamericana*, 37 (July-Dec. 1971), pp. 711-24.

——————. "*One Hundred Years of Solitude* and *Pedro Páramo*: A Parallel." *Books Abroad*, 47, No. 3 (Spring 1975), pp. 490-95.

Lévi-Strauss, Claude. *The Savage Mind*. Translated by George Weindenfeld and Nicholson Ltd. Chicago: University Press, 1966.

——————. *Structural Anthropology*. Translated by C. Jacobson and B. Grundfest Schoepf. New York: Basic Books Inc., 1963.

Lucas, F. L. *Gilgamesh, King of Erech*. Great Britain: The Golden Cockerel Press, 1948.

Luchting, Wolfgang A. "Lampooning Literature: *La mala hora*." *Books Abroad*, 47, No. 3 (Spring 1973), pp. 471-78.

Ludmer, Josefina. *Cien años de soledad: una interpretación*, 2nd ed. Buenos Aires: Edit. Tiempo Contemporáneo, 1974.

d'Lugo, Marvin. "Caminos de re-encuentro." *Nueva Narrativa Hispano-americana*, 4 (Jan. and Sept. 1974), pp. 380-84.

Martínez, Z. Nelly. "Realismo mágico y lo fantástico en la ficción hispanoamericana contemporánea." In *Otros mundos otros fuegos: fantasía y realismo mágico en Iberoamérica; memoria del XVI Congreso Internacional de Literatura Iberoamericana*. Edited by Donald A. Yates. East Lansing: Latin American Studies Center at Michigan State University, 1975, pp. 45-52.

Maturo, Graciela. *Claves simbólicas de García Márquez*. Buenos Aires: Fernando García Cambero, 1972.

Mendilow, A. A. *Time and the Novel*. New York: Humanities Press, 1972.

Metzner, Ralph. Maps of Consciousness: *I Ching, Tantra, Tarot, Alchemy, Astrology, Actualism*. New York: Collier Macmillan, 1971.

Meyerhoff, Hans. *Time in Literature*. Berkeley: University of Calif., 1968.

Morello Frosch, Marta. "The Common Wonders of García Márquez' Recent Fiction." *Books Abroad*, 47, No. 3 (Spring 1973), pp. 496-501.

Muller-Bergh, Klaus. "*Relato de un náufrago*: Gabriel García Márquez' Tale of Shipwreck and Survival at Sea." *Books Abroad*, 47, No. 3 (Spring 1973), pp. 460-66.

Multhauf, Robert P. "Some Non-existent Chemists of the Seventeenth Century: Remarks on the Use of the Dialogue in Scientific Writing." In *Alchemy and Chemistry in the Seventeenth Century*. Los Angeles: Wm. Andrews Clark Memorial Library, 1966, pp. 33-50.

Neumann, Erich. *Amor and Psyche: The Psychic Development of the Feminine: A Commentary on a Tale by Apuleius.* Translated by Ralph Manheim. Princeton: Bollingen, 1971.

————. *Art and the Creative Unconscious: Four Essays.* Translated by Ralph Manheim. Princeton: Bollingen, 1971.

————. *The Great Mother: An Analysis of the Archetype.* Translated by Ralph Manheim. Princeton: Bollingen, 1972.

————. *The Origins and History of Consciousness.* Translated by R. F. C. Hull. Princeton: Bollingen, 1970.

Ortega, Julio. "Gabriel García Márquez: *Cien años de soledad.*" In *La contemplación y la fiesta: ensayos sobre la nueva novela latinoamericana.* Lima: Editorial Universitaria, 1968, pp. 45-58.

Osorio, Nelson. *"Nueve asedios a García Márquez." Nueva Narrativa Hispanoamericana,* 1 (Jan. 1971), pp. 140-42.

Pascual Buxó, José. "García Márquez o la crisis de la realidad." *Insula,* No. 303 (Feb. 1972), pp. 3 and 12.

Paz, Octavio. *Claude Lévi-Strauss: An Introduction.* Translated by J. S. Bernstein and Maxine Bernstein. Ithaca: Cornell University Press, 1970.

Poulet, Georges. *Studies in Human Time.* Translated by Elliott Coleman. New York: Harper and Brothers, 1959. [First published by the Johns Hopkins Press, 1956.]

Rabassa, Clementine. "El aire como materia literaria: la épica, la nueva narrativa, y Demetrio Aguilera-Malta." *Nueva Narrativa Hispanoamericana,* 4 (Jan. and Sept. 1974), pp. 261-68.

Rabassa, Gregory. "Beyond Magic Realism: Thoughts on the Art of Gabriel García Márquez." *Books Abroad,* 47, No. 3 (Spring 1973), pp. 443-50.

Read, John. *Prelude to Chemistry: An Outline of Alchemy, Its Literature and Relationships.* New York: Macmillan Co., 1937.

Rodríguez Monegal, Emir. "Los maestros de la nueva novela" and "Nueva y vieja nueva novela." Chapters 3 and 4 in *El Boom de la novela latinoamericana.* Caracas: Edit. Tiempo Nuevo, 1972, pp. 56-85.

————. "Novedad y anacronismo de *Cien años de soledad.*" *Nueva Narrativa Hispanoamericana,* 1 (Jan. 1971), pp. 17-39.

————. "*One Hundred Years of Solitude*: The Last Three Pages." *Books Abroad,* 47, No. 3 (Spring 1973), pp. 485-89.

————. "Tradición y renovación." In *América Latina en su literatura.* Edited by César Fernández Moreno. México: Siglo XXI Editores, S. A. and UNESCO, 1972, pp. 139-66.

Sauné, Luis. *L'influence des Chercheurs de la "Médecine Universelle" sur l'Oeuvre de François Rabelais.* Paris: Librairie E. Le François, 1935.

Scholes, Robert, ed. *Approaches to the Novel: Materials for a Poetics.* Revised edition. Scranton: Chandler Publishing Co., 1966.

Segre, Cesare. *Semiotics and Literary Criticism.* Translated by John Meddemmen. Paris: Mouton, 1973.

Shakespeare, Wm. *Macbeth.* Edited by Kenneth Muir. New York: Random House, 1962.

—————. *The Tempest.* Edited by Frank Kermode. London: Methuen and Company Ltd., 1964.

Soto, Lilvia. "El hombre: víctima de sus intuiciones arquetípicas." *Nueva Narrativa Hispanoamericana,* 4 (Jan. and Sept. 1974), pp. 367-70.

Spitzer, Leo, *Classical and Christian Ideas of World Harmony: Prolegomena to an Interpretation of the Word "Stimmung."* Edited by Anna Granville Hatcher. Baltimore: Johns Hopkins Press, 1963.

Urondo, Francisco. "La buena hora de García Márquez." *Cuadernos Hispanoamericanos,* 232 (April 1969), 163-68.

Valle-Inclán, Ramón del. *La lámpara maravillosa: ejercicios espirituales.* Madrid: Artes de la Ilustración, 1922.

Vargas Llosa, Mario. *Historia de un deicidio.* Barcelona: Barral, 1971.

Vilhjalmsson, Thor. "Presentation of Gabriel García Márquez." *Books Abroad,* 47, No. 1 (Winter 1973), pp. 10-11.

Waite, Arthur E. *The Pictorial Key to the Tarot: Being Fragments of a Secret Tradition Under the Veil of Divination.* New York: University Books, 1959.

Wellek, René and Warren, Austin. *Theory of Literature,* 3rd edition. New York: Harcourt Brace and World, 1956.

APPENDIX

What follows are the English translations of the non-obvious Spanish quotations in the text of my study. The majority of these translations come from *One Hundred Years of Solitude* by Gabriel García Márquez, trans. Gregory Rabassa (New York: Harper and Row, 1970). Each entry consists of four parts: (1) the number of the page in my text where the Spanish quotation, to which the English entry corresponds, appears, or an indentation signifying that the page is the same as for the previous quotation; (2) the first word, or words, of the Spanish quotation; (3) the English translation of the quotation; (4) a number in parenthesis, which identifies the page in Rabassa's translation where the English quotation can be found. If no number appears parenthetically, then the translation is mine, not Rabassa's. You will need to have Professor Rabassa's translation on hand for some of the longer quotations (these are duly identified), but in all other cases the English translations are given in their entirety.

Chapter 1

1. "Las cosas...
   "Things have a life of their own," the gypsy proclaimed with a harsh accent. "It's simply a matter of waking up their souls (11)."

   "los hierros mágicos"—the magical irons

   "la octava...
   The eighth wonder of the learned alchemists of Macedonia (11).

"un regalo...
a gift that was to have a profound influence on the
future of the village (14).

2. "Un gitano corpulento...
A heavy gypsy with an untamed beard and sparrow
hands, who introduced himself as Melquíades, put on a
bold public demonstration of what he himself called the
eighth wonder of the learned alchemists of Macedonia
(11).

"Usaba...
He wore a large black hat that looked like a raven with
widespread wings, and a velvet vest across which the
patina of the centuries had skated (15).

3. "había revelado...
had revealed a strange intuition for alchemy (32).

"un chicharrón...
a large piece of burnt hog cracklings that was firmly
stuck to the bottom of the pot (16-17).

"jarabe...—thick and pestilential syrup (16)

11. "José...
José Arcadio Buendía, whose unbridled imagination always went beyond the genius of nature and even beyond miracles and magic, thought that it would be
possible to make use of that useless invention [Melquía-
des' magnets] to extract gold from the bowels of the
earth (11).

"la liberación...
the freeing of the breath that makes metals live (42).

"Muy pronto...
Very soon we'll have gold enough and more to pave the
floors of the house (12).

"Además...
Along with those items, Melquíades left samples of the
seven metals that corresponded to the seven planets,
the formulas of Moses and Zosimus for doubling the
quantity of gold, and a set of notes and sketches concerning the processes of the Great Teaching that would

permit those who could interpret them to undertake the manufacture of the philosopher's stone. Seduced by the simplicity of the formulas to double the quantity of gold, José Arcadio Buendía paid court to Úrsula for several weeks so that she would let him dig up her colonial coins and increase them by as many times as it was possible to subdivide mercury... Then José Arcadio Buendía threw three doubloons into a pan and fused them with copper filings, orpiment, brimstone, and lead. He put it all to boil in a pot of castor oil until he got a thick and pestilential syrup which was more like common caramel than valuable gold (16).

12. "quien supiera...
of those who could interpret the notes and sketches concerning the processes of the Great Teaching (16).

"un día en que...
one day when he awoke in a merry mood, Aureliano Segundo appeared with a chest full of money, a can of paint and a brush, and singing at the top of his lungs the old songs of Francisco the Man, he papered the house inside and out and from top to bottom with one-peso banknotes (183).

"En el último año...
During the second year she had sent pressing messages to Aureliano Segundo and he had answered that he did not know when he would go back to her house, but that in any case he would bring along a box of gold coins to pave the bedroom floor with (306).

"que ella...
that she had buried underneath her bed in hopes of a proper occasion to make use of it (12).

"la fortuna enterrada...
the fortune buried in some place only Úrsula knew (302).

13. "sus súplicas...
Her prayers were answered in reverse. One of the workmen removing the bills bumped into an enormous plaster statue of Saint Joseph that someone had left in

the house during the last years of the war and the hollow figure broke to pieces on the floor. It had been stuffed with gold coins. ... Úrsula had put candles on it and had prostrated herself before it, not suspecting that instead of a saint she was adoring almost four hundred pounds of gold. The tardy evidence of her involuntary paganism made her even more upset (184).

"Presa...
Overcome by an exploratory delirium comparable only to that of his great-grandfather when he was searching for the route of inventions, Aureliano Segundo lost the last layers of fat that he had left and the old resemblance to his twin brother was becoming accentuated again, not only because of his slim figure, but also because of the distant air and the withdrawn attitude (304).

14. "Una noche...
One night in the room where Úrsula had slept they [José Arcadio and a friend] saw a yellow glow coming through the crumbling cement, as if an underground sun had changed the floor of the room into a pane of glass (342).

"José Arcadio...
José Arcadio, who left the seminary as soon as he reached Rome, continued nourishing the legend of theology and canon law so as not to jeopardize the fabulous inheritance of which his mother's delirious letters spoke and which would rescue him from the misery and sordidness he shared with two friends in a Trastevere garret. When he received Fernanda's last letter, dictated by the foreboding of imminent death, he put the leftovers of his false splendor into a suitcase and crossed the ocean in the hold of a ship where immigrants were crammed together like cattle in a slaughterhouse, eating cold macaroni and wormy cheese (339f).

"Una armadura...
a suit of fifteenth-century armor which had all of its pieces soldered together with rust... When José Arcadio Buendía and the four men of his expedition managed to

take the armor apart, they found inside a calcified skeleton with a copper locket containing a woman's hair around its neck (12).

15. ...José Arcadio...
José Arcadio was finishing his daily bath when through the openings in the tiles the four children he had expelled from the house burst in. Without giving him time to defend himself, they jumped into the pool fully clothed, grabbed him by the hair, and held his head under the water until the bubbling of his death throes ceased on the surface and his silent and pale dolphin body slipped down to the bottom of the fragrant water. Then they took out the three sacks of gold from the hiding place which was known only to them and their victim. It was such a rapid, methodical, and brutal action that it was like a military operation. Aureliano... looked for José Arcadio all over the house and found him floating on the perfumed mirror of the pool, enormous and bloated and still thinking about Amaranta (345f).

"que pareció un asalto de militares"
that seemed like a military operation (346).

"rizo de mujer"
woman's tress (or "woman's curl")

"todavía pensando en Amaranta"—still thinking of A-maranta (346).

16. "ojos abiertos"—eyes open

"Pero no tardó...
But it did not take her long to realize that he [José Arcadio Segundo] was as insensible to her begging as the colonel would have been, and that they were armoured by the same impermeability of affection. Although she never knew, nor did anyone know, what they spoke about in their prolonged sessions shut up in the workshop, she understood that they were probably the only members of the family who seemed drawn together by some affinity (246).

17. "Cuando Úrsula...
When Úrsula had the door of Melquíades' room opened

he began to linger about it, peeping through the half-opened door, and no one knew at what moment he bacame close to José Arcadio Segundo in a link of mutual affection (321).

"escapó a catorce...
survived fourteen attempts on his life, seventy-three ambushes (104).

"escapó de milagro...
miraculously escaped four revolver shots taken at him by an unknown party as he was leaving a secret meeting (276).

18. "Soy Aureliano Buendía... "Es verdad...
"I'm Aureliano Buendía."..."That's right"... "And now it's time for you to start learning how to be a silversmith (314)."

"...la espléndida...
the splendid and taciturn old woman who guarded the entrance in a wicker rocking chair felt that time was turning back to its earliest origins when among the five who were arriving she saw a bony, jaundiced man with Tartar cheekbones, marked forever and from the beginning of the world with the pox of solitude.
     "Lord, Lord," she sighed, "Aureliano."
     She was seeing Colonel Aureliano Buendía once more as she had seen him in the light of a lamp long before the wars, long before the desolation of glory and the exile of disillusionment...(363).

"la concentración...
the implacable concentration awarded him with peace of spirit.

"Estaba seguro de que...
He was certain that they corresponded to an alphabet of forty-seven to fifty-three characters (322).

19. "Melquíades...se iba...
Melquíades...would go in peace to the meadows of the ultimate death because Aureliano would have time to learn Sanskrit during the years remaining until the parchments became one hundred years old, when they could be deciphered (329).

"el habitante...
the most lucid inhabitant of the house (319-20).

"el cuarto de las bacinillas" — the chamberpot room

20. "Desde que abrió..."
As soon as he opened the door he felt the pestilential attack of the chamberpots, which were placed on the floor and all of which had been used several times. José Arcadio Segundo...was still reading and rereading the unintelligible parchments. He was illuminated by a seraphic glow....

"There were more then three thousand of them," was all that José Arcadio Segundo said. "I'm sure now that they were everybody who had been at the station (290)."

21. "Si no...
If he did not persevere in his attempts to build an ice factory, it was because at that time he was absolutely enthusiastic over the education of his sons, especially that of Aureliano, who from the very first had revealed a strange intuition for alchemy. The laboratory had been dusted off. Reviewing Melquíades' notes, serene now,...in prolonged and patient sessions they tried to separate Úrsula's gold from the debris that was stuck to the bottom of the pot (32).

"alborotaron...
aroused the household with the news that they had succeeded in penetrating the metalic debris and had separated Úrsula's gold.

They had succeeded, as a matter of fact, after putting in complicated and persevering days at it. Úrsula was happy, and she even gave thanks to God for the invention of alchemy...(36).

22. "Preocupado...
Worried over his inner withdrawal, José Arcadio Buendía gave him the keys to the house and a little money, thinking that perhaps he needed a woman. But Aureliano spent the money on muriatic acid to prepare some aqua regia and he beautified the keys by plating them with gold (46).

"Con una...
With an exasperating parsimony he took down the chests, opened them, and placed on the table, one by one, seventy-two gold bricks.... The gold of the revolution...[which] was beyond all control. Colonel Aureliano Buendía had the seventy-two gold bricks included in the inventory of surrender and closed the ceremony without allowing any speeches (170f).

23. "Con su...
With her terrible practical sense she [Úrsula] could not understand the colonel's business as he exchanged little fishes for gold coins and then converted the coins into little fishes, and so on, with the result that he had to work all the harder with the more he sold in order to satisfy an exasperating vicious circle. Actually, what interested him was not the business but the work...the implacable concentration awarded him with a peace of the spirit (190).

24. "Enseñó...
He taught little Aureliano how to read and write, initiated him in the study of the parchments, and he inculcated him with such a personal interpretation of what the banana company had meant to Macondo that many years later, when Aureliano became part of the world, one would have thought that he was telling a hallucinated version, because it was radically opposed to the false one that historians had created and consecrated in the schoolbooks (322).

25. "la verdad oficial...
the official version that nothing had happened...that the historians had created and consecrated in the schoolbooks (321-22).

"Aureliano Segundo, en cambio...
Aureliano Segundo, on the other hand, recognized his twin brother's version. Actually, in spite of the fact that everyone considered him mad, José Arcadio Segundo was at that time the most lucid inhabitant of the house (321-22).

26. "El nueve de agosto...
On the ninth of August, before they received the first
letter from Brussels, José Arcadio Segundio was speaking to Aureliano in Melquíades' room and, although it
had nothing to do with what they were talking about,
he said:
    "Always remember that they were more than three
thousand and that they were thrown into the sea."
    Then he fell face down on the parchments and died
with his eyes open (326).

" ...la antigua...
...the old resemblance to his brother was becoming
accentuated again, not only because of his slim figure,
but also because of the distant air and the withdrawn
attitude (304).

27. "sentó salamónicamente...
with the wisdom of Solomon he seated Remedios the
Beauty and the intruding queen on the same dais (191).

"En la...
In the confusion of the panic José Arcadio Segundo
managed to rescue Remedios the Beauty and Aureliano
Segundo carried the intruding queen to the house in his
arms,... (192).

"Somos...
"We are immensely rich and powerful," ... "One day
you will be a queen" (195)

28. "soberana intrusa" — intruding queen [Rabassa, *et. pas-
sim*]

" ...y la bacinilla...
...and the heraldic chamberpot—which at the moment
of truth turned out to have only a little gold plating on
the crest—(341).

"El carnaval...
The carnaval had reached its highest level of madness...
when on the swamp road a parade of several people
appeared carrying in a *gilded litter* the most fascinating
woman that imagination could conceive. For a moment

the inhabitants of Macondo took off their masks in order to get a better look at the dazzling creature with a crown of emeralds and an ermine cape, who seemed invested with legitimate authority, and not merely *a sovereign of bangles and crepe paper* [my emphases] (191).

"decidió...
It was then that she decided to drown the child in the cistern as soon as the nun left...(278).

29. "Parecía...
It seemed as if some penetrating lucidity permitted her to see the reality of things beyond any formalism. That at least was the point of view of Colonel Aureliano Buendía, for whom Remedios the Beauty was in no way mentally retarded, as was generally believed, but quite the opposite. "It's as if she's come back from twenty years of war," he would say (188).

"Llegó...
She reached twenty without knowing how to read or write, unable to use the silver at the table, wandering naked through the house because her nature rejected all manner of convention (188).

"Lo asombroso...
The startling thing about her simplifying instinct was that the more she did away with fashion in a search for comfort and the more she passed over conventions as she obeyed spontaneity, the more disturbing her incredible beauty became and the more provocative she became to men (217).

30. "Hasta las...
Even Úrsula's supersitions, with origins that came more from an inspiration of the moment than from tradition, came into conflict with those of Fernanda, who had inherited them from her parents and kept them defined and catalogued for every occasion (200).

"Fernanda...
Fernanda very tactfully tried not to cross his path. Within herself she was bothered by his independent spirit, his resistance to all kinds of social rigidity. She

was exasperated by his mugs of coffee at five in the morning, the disorder of his workshop, his frayed blanket, and his custom of sitting in the street door at dusk. But she had to tolerate that one loose piece in the family machinery because she was sure that the old colonel was an animal who had been tamed by the years and by disappointment and who, in a burst of senile rebellion, was quite capable of uprooting the foundations of the house (201).[15]

"como si una ...
as if some penetrating lucidity permitted her to see the reality of things beyond any formalism (188)

"mirada asiática ...
an asiatic look that seemed to know what there was on the other side of things (15).

"la deslumbrante criatura ...
the dazzling creature with a crown of emeralds and an ermine cape, who seemed invested with legitimate authority, and not merely a sovereign of bangles and crepe paper (191).

31. "viento de luz" — wind of light

"He alcanzado la inmortalidad." — I have attained immortality.

"un Caballero del Santo Sepulcro" — a Knight of the Holy Sepulchre

33. "Se movía por ...
he passed between objects with an inexplicable fluidity, as if he were endowed with some instinct of direction based on an immediate prescience (74)

34. "Era imposible ...
It was impossible to conceive of a man more like his mother (336).

"Una noche vieron ...
One night in the room where Úrsula had slept they [José Arcadio and a friend] saw a yellow glow coming through the crumbling cement, as if an underground sun had changed the floor of the room into a pane of glass (342).

"Una noche creyó...
One night he [Melquíades] thought he had found a
prediction of the future of Macondo. It was to be a
luminous city with great glass houses where there was
no trace remaining of the race of the Buendías (59).

35. "y no tuvo...
and he did not have the calmness to bring them out into
the light, but right there, standing, without the slightest difficulty, as if they had been written in Spanish and
were read being under the dazzling splendor of high
noon, he began to decipher them aloud (381).

"*el baño* or *la alberca*" — the bath or watertank.

"Aquel...
That true brothel [The Child of Gold], with that maternal proprietress, was the world of which Aureliano had
dreamed during his prolonged captivity (364).

"Bueno niñito...
"It's all right, child,"..."Now tell me who it is (364)."

"*El Niño de Oro* — *The Child of Gold*

36. "...el instante de...
the instant of his own conception among the scorpions
and the yellow butterflies in a sunset bathroom (382)

"alambique de María la judía" — the three-armed alem-
bic of Mary the Jew (16)

40. note 12: "Tal vez...
Perhaps it was that crossing of stature, names, and
character that made Úrsula suspect that they had been
shuffled like a deck of cards since childhood (175). (For
others, see pp. 166, 175, 245, and 327).

note 13:
"los ojos árabes"—Arabian eyes

"la mirada asiática"—the asiatic look

"Era joven, cetrino...
He was young, sallow, with dark and melancholy eyes
which would not have startled her so much if she had
known the gypsies (265).

note 15:
"se sintió...
she felt more comfortable, because, after all, she was
beyond all discipline (218).

"...que, según ella entendía...
which, according to her understanding, was the only
decent way to be when at home

"un camisón...
a white nightgown that reached down to her ankles,
with long sleeves and with a large, round buttonhole,
delicately trimmed, at the level of her lower stomach.
Aureliano could not suppress an explosion of laughter.
    "That's the most obscene thing I've ever seen in my
life," he shouted with a laugh that rang through the
house. "I married a Sister of Charity" (198f.).

Chapter 2

41. "Una noche creyó...
One night he [Melquíades] thought he had found a
prediction of the future of Macondo. It was to be a
luminous city with great glass houses where there was
no trace remaining of the race of the Buendías. "It's a
mistake," thundered José Arcadio Buendía. "They won't
be houses of glass but of ice, as I dreamed, and there
will always be a Buendía, *per omnia secula seculorum*" (59).

42. "un jarabe...
See third entry for page 3.

43. "la liberación...
See second entry for page 11.

44. "Aureliano...
Aureliano would talk to him [the oldest of the Antillan
negroes]...in the tortured Papiamento that he had
learned in a few weeks and sometimes he would share
his chickenhead soup, prepared by the great-grand-
daughter, with him. She was a large black woman with
solid bones, the hips of a mare, teats like live melons,
and a round and perfect head armored with a hard
surface of wiry hair which looked like a medieval war-

rior's mail headdress. Her name was Nigromanta (354).

45. "Aureliano no abandonó...
Aureliano did not leave Melquíades' room for a long time. He learned by heart the fantastic legends of the crumbling books, the synthesis of the studies of Hermann the Cripple, the notes on the science of demonology, the keys to the philosopher's stone, the *Centuries* of Nostradamus and his research concerning the plague, *so that he reached adolescence without knowing a thing about his own time but with the basic knowledge of a medieval man* (328).

"cabeza redonda, perfecta"—round, perfect head

"cabezas de gallo"—chicken heads.

"La molestaron...
They bothered her so much to cut the rain of hair that already reached to her thighs and to make rolls with combs and braids with red ribbons that she simply shaved her head and used the hair to make wigs for the saints (217).

"cráneo pelado y perfecto"—shaved and perfect skull (217)

46. "Cuando andaba...
When he [Aureliano] was penniless, which was most of the time, he got people in the back of the market to give him the chicken heads that they were going to throw away and he would take them to Nigromanta to make her soups...(354).

"Nigromanta lo rescató...
Nigromanta rescued him from a pool of vomit and tears. She took him to her room, cleaned him up, made him drink a cup of broth (380).

47. "Nigromanta...
Nigromanta rescued him from a pool of vomit and tears. She took him to her room, cleaned him up, made him drink a cup of broth. Thinking that it would console him, she took a piece of charcoal and erased the innumerable loves that he still owed her for, and she voluntarily brought up her own most solitary sadnesses

so as not to leave him alone in his weeping. When he
awoke, after a dull and brief sleep, Aureliano recovered
the awareness of his headache. He opened his eyes and
remembered the child (380).

"llanto"—weeping
"le hizo tomar una taza de caldo"—she made him drink
a cup of broth (380)
"sabio catalán"—wise Catalonian
"pellejo hinchado y reseco"—dry and bloated bag of skin
(381)

49. "Pilar Ternera...
Pilar Ternera died in her wicker rocking chair during
one night of festivities as she watched over the entrance to her paradise (367).

"Se rompió...
He smashed his fists against the cement wall of *The
Golden Child*, calling for Pilar Ternera (380).

"Aureliano...
Aureliano and Amaranta Úrsula opened their eyes, dug
deep into their souls, looked at the letter with their
hands on their hearts, and understood that they were
so identified with each other that they preferred death
to separation.

"A medida...
As the pregnancy advanced they were becoming a single
being, they were becoming more and more integrated in
the solitude of a house that needed only one last breath
to be knocked down (376).

"activa, menuda...
active, small, and indomitable like Úrsula, and almost as
beautiful and provacative as Remedios the Beauty

"en la rudimentaria...
on Amaranta's primitive pedal machine (348).

50. "andaban por...
they walked about the house as Remedios the Beauty
had wanted to do (372)

"una tarde...
one afternoon they almost drowned as they made love in the cistern (372)

"rasgaron...
in their madness they tore to shreds the hammock that had resisted the sad bivouac loves of Colonel Aureliano Buendía (372-73)

"el animal...
the mythological animal that was to bring the line to an end (383)

51. "Se derrumbó...
This quotation is from the penultimate paragraph of the novel, and can be found on page 381 of Rabassa's translation. It begins on the seventh line down, with the words "He sank into the rocking chair, ..." and goes to the end of the paragraph.

"el peso...
the crushing weight of so much past (381).

52. "Y entonces vio al niño."—And then he saw the child (381)

"herido por las lanzas mortales"—wounded by the mortal lances (381)

"aquel instante prodigioso"—that prodigious instant (381)

"Pilar Ternera...
See first entry for page 49.

"el mismo en que se sentó...
the same one in which Rebeca had sat during the early days of the house to give embroidery lessons, and in which Amaranta had played Chinese checkers with Colonel Gerineldo Márquez, and in which Amaranta Úrsula had sewn the tiny clothing for the child (381).

"se le revelaron las claves definitivas de Melquíades"—Melquíades' final keys revealed themselves to him

"la lengua materna de Melquíades"..."en voz alta"..."de pie"
Melquíades' mother tongue...aloud...standing.

"conciencia de que...
awareness that he was unable to bear on his soul the
weight of so much past

53. "Aureliano no había sido...
Aureliano had never been more lucid in any act of his
life as when he forgot about his dead ones and the pain
of his dead ones and nailed up the doors and windows
again with Fernanda's crossed boards so as not to be
disturbed by any temptations of the world, for he knew
then that his fate was written in Melquíades' parchments (381).

"Los encontró...
He found them intact among the prehistoric plants and
steaming puddles and luminous insects that had removed all trace of man's passage on earth from the
room, and he did not have the calmness to bring them
out into the light, but right there, standing, without the
slightest difficulty, as if they had been written in Spanish and were being read under the dazzling splendor of
high noon, he began to decipher them aloud (381).

54. "impaciente por conocer...
This quotation runs from line 22 on page 382 to line 2
of page 383, beginning with "impatient to know his own
origin," and ending with the words "the mythological
animal that was to bring the line to an end."

"lleno de voces...
full of voices from the past, the murmurs of ancient
geraniums, sighs of disenchantment that preceded the
most tenacious nostalgia (382).

"entonces empezó el viento"—then the wind began

"salto"—jump or leap

55. "concepción entre...
conception among the scorpions and butterflies

"Sólo entonces"—only then

"...Aureliano saltó...
Aureliano skipped eleven pages so as not to lose time
with facts he knew only too well, and he began to

decipher the instant that he was living, deciphering it as he lived it, prophesying himself in the act of deciphering the last page of the parchments, as if he were looking into a speaking mirror (383).

"Entonces dio otro salto"—Then he skipped again (383), or, "made another leap"

"estaba previsto...
it was foreseen that the city of mirrors (or mirages) would be wiped out by the wind and exiled from the memory of men at the precise moment when Aureliano Babilonia would finish deciphering the parchments (383).

56. "otro salto"—another leap

"Una noche...
One night he thought he had found a prediction of the future of Macondo. It was to be a luminous city with great glass houses where there was no trace remaining of the race of the Buendías (59).

"hasta en sus detalles más triviales"—down to its most trivial details
"una ciudad...
a luminous city, with great glass houses

59. "empezó...
began to decipher them aloud (381)

"Sólo entonces...
Only then did he discover that Amaranta Úrsula was not his sister but his aunt, and that Sir Francis Drake had attacked Riohacha *only so that* they could seek each other through the most intricate labyrinths of blood until they would engender the mythological animal that was to bring the line to an end (382-83).

"todas las hormigas del mundo"—all the ants in the world

"madrigueras"—ant holes

"Al amanecer...
When he awoke, after a dull and brief sleep, Aureliano recovered the awareness of his headache. He opened his eyes and remembered the child (380).

60. "olvidó...
    he forgot his dead ones and the pain of his dead ones

    "Hola antropófago...
    Hello cannibal...Back in your cave again? (360).

    "Aureliano atravesó...
    Aureliano went across the porch which was saturated
    with the morning sighs of oregano and looked into the
    dining room, where the remnants of the birth still lay:
    the large pot, the bloody sheets, the jars of ashes, and
    the twisted umbilical cord of the child on an opened
    diaper on the table next to the shears and the fishline
    (380-81).

61. "el pequeño Aureliano...
    little Aureliano, at the age of three, went into the
    kitchen at the moment she was taking a pot of boiling
    soup from the stove and putting it on the table. The
    child, perplexed, said from the doorway, "It's going to
    spill." The pot was firmly placed in the center of the
    table, but just as soon as the child made his announce-
    ment, it began an unmistakable movement toward the
    edge, as if impelled by some inner dynamism, and it fell
    and broke on the floor (23).

    "Allí se quitó...
    There he took off his shirt, sat on the edge of his cot,
    and at three-fifteen in the afternoon took his pistol and
    shot himself in the iodine circle that his personal physi-
    cian had painted on his chest. At that moment in
    Macondo Úrsula took the cover off the pot of milk on
    the stove, wondering why it was taking so long to boil,
    and found it full of worms.
        "They've killed Aureliano," she exclaimed (171).

    "olla"—pot

62. "En realidad...
    Actually, in spite of the fact that everyone considered
    him mad, José Arcadio Segundo was at that time the
    most lucid inhabitant of the house. He taught little
    Aureliano how to read and write, initiated him in the
    study of the parchments, and he inculcated him with

such a personal interpretation of what the banana company had meant to Macondo that many years later, when Aureliano became part of the world, one would have thought that he was telling a hallucinated version, because it was radically opposed to the false one that historians had created and consecrated in the school-books (321f.).

"Se había...
He set about learning the art of silverwork with Aureliano, who had also taught him how to read and write (59).

63. "como si...
as if they had been written in Spanish (381).

"no tuvo...
See the first entry for page 35.

"Aureliano no había...
Aureliano had never been *more lucid* in any act of his life (381).

"En realidad...
See the first entry for page 62.

64. "Parecía como si...
It seemed as if some penetrating lucidity permitted her to see the reality of things beyond any formalism. That at least was the point of view of Colonel Aureliano Buendía, for whom Remedios the Beauty was in no way mentally retarded, as was generally believed, but quite the opposite. "It's as if she's come back from twenty years of war," he would say (188).

"alumbrando...
illuminating with his profound organ voice the most obscure territories of the imagination

"un mediodía ardiente"—a burning [or blazing, or hot] noontime

"un recuerdo hereditario"—a hereditary memory

"esfumándose...
fading away in the radiant light of noon (329)

65. "Le dio...
He gave José Arcadio Buendía a drink of a gentle color and the light went on in his memory (54f).

"se le revelaron
Melquíades' final keys revealed themselves to him

"Melquíades no había...
Melquíades had not put events in the order of man's conventional time, but had concentrated a century of daily episodes in such a way that they coexisted in one instant (382).

"una ciudad luminosa
a luminous city with great glass houses

66. "el animal
the mythological animal that was to bring the line to an end (383).

67. "Herido por...
This quotation runs from line 15 of page 381, beginning with the phrase "Wounded by the fatal lances," to the end of the paragraph.

68. "El primero...
The first of the line is tied to a tree and the last is being eaten by the ants (381) [emphasis is the author's].

"que todas las hormigas...
that all the ants in the world were dragging toward their holes (381)

70. "Macondo era ya...
Macondo was already a fearful whirlwind of dust and rubble when Aureliano skipped eleven pages so as not to lose time with facts he knew only too well, and he began to decipher the instant that he was living, deciphering it as he lived it, prophesying himself in the act of deciphering the last page of the parchemnts, as if he were looking into a speaking mirror (383).

"Entonces dio otro salto...
This quotation consists of the last two sentences of the novel, beginning with the words "Then he skipped again..."(383).

"Una noche creyó...
See second entry from page 56.

"la ciudad...
the city of mirrors (or mirages) (383)

72. "Una noche creyó...
One night in the room where Úrsula had slept they saw a yellow glow coming through the *crystalized* cement, as if an underground *sun* had changed the floor of the room into a pane of *glass*.

73. "las claves definitivas de Melquíades"—Melquíades final keys

75. "aquel viento irreparable"—that irreparable wind

"donde...
where not even the highest-flying birds of memory could reach her (223).

"estaba previsto...
See fifth entry for page 55.

"sería arrasada...
would be wiped out by the wind and exiled from the memory of men (383)

"en el instante...
at the instant in which Aureliano Babilonia would finish deciphering the manuscripts (383)

77. "baño"—bath or bathroom

"entre las plantas...
among the prehistoric plants and steaming puddles and luminous insects that had removed all trace of man's passage on earth from the room (381)

"salto"—leap

"Cuando me muera...
When I die burn mercury in my room for three days...I have attained immortality.

78. "Muchos años después...
Many years later, as he faced the firing squad, Colonel Aureliano Buendía was to remember that distant after-

noon when his father took him to acquaint him with ice (11).

"Sin embargo...
Before reaching the final line, however, he had already understood that he would never leave that room, for it was foreseen that the city of mirrors (or mirages) would be wiped out by the wind and exiled from the memory of men at the precise moment when Aureliano Babilonia would finish deciphering the parchments, and that everything written on them was unrepeatable since time immemorial and forever more, because races condemned to one hundred years of solitude did not have a second opportunity on earth (383).

79. "para siempre"—forever

"Aureliano José...
Aureliano José had been destined to find with her the happiness that Amaranta had denied him, to have seven children, and to die in her arms of old age, but the bullet that entered his back and shattered his chest had been directed by a wrong interpretation of the cards (149).

80. "No te preocupes...
Don't worry...Wherever she is right now she's waiting for you (364).

"un siglo...
a century of cards and experience (364).

83. "sombrero grande y negro...
a large black hat that looked like a raven with widespread wings (15).

"José Arcadio Buendía...
José Arcadio Buendía, whose unbridled imagination always went beyond the genius of nature and even beyond miracles and magic, thought that it would be possible to make use of that useless invention to extract gold from the bowels of the earth (11).

86. "Años después...
Years later on his deathbed Aureliano Segundo would remember the rainy afternoon in June when he went into the bedroom to meet his first son (174).

"Muchos años después...
Many years later, as he faced the firing squad, Colonel
Aureliano Buendía was to remember that distant afternoon when his father took him to acquaint him with ice
(11).

   *[The word Rabassa translates as "to meet" in the
first quotation, and as "to acquaint" in the second one,
is the same in Spanish, *conocer*. An interesting exercise,
even for one who doesn't understand Spanish, is to
examine the words and phrases in these two Spanish
quotations for similarities.]

87. "mortaja"—shroud.

    "el rey"—the king

88. "Lo colgaron...
    They hung it in an almond tree in the square by its
    ankles.

90. "en sus prolongados encierros...
    during his prolonged imprisonment as he manipulated
    the material, he begged in the depth of his heart that
    the longed-for miracle should not be the discovery of
    the philosopher's stone, or the freeing of the breath
    that makes metals live, or the faculty to convert the
    hinges and the locks of the house into gold, but what
    had just happened: Úrsula's return (42).

    "la liberación...
    the freeing of the breath that makes metals live

    "una casa...
    a house that needed only one last breath to be knocked
    down (376).

91. "olvidó sus muertos...
    forgot his dead and the pain of his dead

    "profetizándose...
    prophesying himself in the act of deciphering the last
    page of the parchments, as if he were looking into a
    speaking mirror (383).

93. "Era el final...
    It was the end. In Pilar Ternera's tomb, among the

psalms and cheap whore jewelry, the ruins of the past would rot, the little that remained after the wise Catalonian had auctioned off his bookstore and returned to the Mediterranean village where he had been born (367).

"una mujer...
a woman dressed in blue with long hair, with a sort of antiquated look, and with a certain resemblance to Pilar Ternera (259-60)

"el tiempo convencional de los hombres"—man's conventional time (382).

"Años antes...
Years before, when she had reached one hundred forty-five years of age, she had given up the pernicious custom of keeping track of her age and she went on living in *the static and marginal time of memories, in a future perfectly revealed and established,* beyond the futures disturbed by the insidious snares and suppositions of her cards (363).

95. note 1:
"Diremos que...
    "We'll tell them that we found him floating in the basket," she said smiling.
    "No one will believe it," the nun said.
    "If they believe it in the Bible," Fernanda replied, "I don't see why they shouldn't believe it of me" (277).

96. note 3: "Aureliano...
See first entry for page 53.

Chapter 3

103. "¿Cuál sería...
What would the ideal novel be? An absolutely free novel, which not only disturbs by virtue of its political and social content, but also by its power of penetration into reality; and better still if it is capable of turning reality over to show what it's like on the other side.

"La dirección...
The analogic direction inherent in man lives on in the

unconscious and surfaces in the poet, the magician of today.

105. "Esta totalidad...
This totality is manifested, above all, in the plural nature of the novel which is, simultaneously, things generally believed to be antonimic: traditional and modern, local and universal, fantastic and realistic. Another expression of this "totality" is its unlimited accessibility...

"El pavor...
The fear turned into panic when Melquíades took out his teeth, intact, encased in their gums, and showed them to the audience for an instant—a fleeting instant in which he went back to being the same decrepit man of years past—and put them back again and smiled once more with the full control of his restored youth. Even José Arcadio Buendía himself considered that Melquíades' knowledge had reached unbearable extremes, but he felt a healthy excitement when the gypsy explained to him alone the workings of his false teeth (17).

106. "empezó...
he began to decipher the instant that he was living, deciphering it as he lived it, prophesying himself in the act of deciphering the last page of the parchments, as if he were looking into a speaking mirror (383).

107. "tal vez...
perhaps the only mystery that was never cleared up in Macondo (129)

"Tan pronto...
As soon as José Arcadio closed the bedroom door the sound of a pistol shot echoed through the house. A trickle of blood came out under the door, crossed the living room, went out into the street, continued on in a straight line across the uneven terraces, went down steps and climbed over curbs, passed along the Street of the Turks, turned a corner to the right and another to the left, made a right angle at the Buendía house, went in under the closed door, crossed through the parlor, hugging the walls so as not to stain the rugs, went on to the other living room, made a wide curve to avoid the

dining-room table, went along the porch with the be-
gonias, and passed without being seen under Amaranta's chair as she gave an arithmetic lesson to Aureliano
José, and went through the pantry and came out in the
kitchen, where Úrsula was getting ready to crack thirty-
six eggs to make bread.

"Holy Mother of God!" Úrsula shouted. (129f.)

108. "atravesó la sala...
crossed through the parlor, hugging the walls so as not
to stain the rugs

"hasta muchos años después"—for many years after
(131).

"Porque la última...
Because the ultimate paradox that the analysis reveals is
this: the humor and happiness of the style, the vitality
and rapid pace of the work, its magic and fable, are built
upon the saddest, most solitary and lucid outlook.

110. "la ciudad...
the city of mirrors (or mirages) (383)

111. "cuando se vio...
when he saw himself and his whole family fastened
onto a sheet of irridescent metal for *an eternity* (55).

"Melquíades...
Melquíades had not put events in the order of man's
conventional time, but had concentrated a century of
daily episodes in such a way that they coexisted in one
instant (382).

"lo que él mismo...
what he himself called the eighth wonder of the learned
alchemists of Macedonia (11).

"fierros mágicos" — magical irons

"aun...
and even objects that had been lost for a long time
appeared from where they had been searched for most
(11).

"mirada...
asiatic look that seemed to know the other side of
things.

112. "¿Cuál sería...
See the first entry for page 103.

113. "al ser leídas...
when read aloud were like encyclicals being chanted (75).

"claves definitivas" — final keys.

114. "en aquel instante...
at that prodigious instant Melquíades' final keys were revealed to him and he saw the epigraph of the parchments perfectly placed in the order of man's time and space (381).

"Por primera vez...
For the first time in her long life Santa Sofía de la Piedad let a feeling show through, and it was a feeling of wonderment, when Aureliano asked her to bring him the book that could be found between *Jerusalem Delivered* and Milton's poems (329).

"La protección...
The final protection, which Aureliano had begun to glimpse when he let himself be confused by the love of Amaranta Úrsula, was based on the fact that Melquíades had not put events in the order of man's conventional time; but had concentrated a century of daily episodes in such a way that they coexisted in one instant (382).

115. "mediodía" — midday, noon.

"El sofocante...
On that suffocating noontime when the gypsy revealed his secrets, José Arcadio Buendía had the certainty that it was the beginning of a great friendship. The children were startled by his fantastic stories. Aureliano, who could not have been more than five at the time, would remember him for the rest of his life as he saw him that afternoon, sitting against the metallic and quivering light from the window, lighting up with his deep organ voice the darkest reaches of the imagination, while over his temples there flowed the grease that was being melted by the heat. José Arcadio, his older brother,

would pass on that wonderful image as a hereditary memory to all of his descendants (15).

"Un mediodía...
A burning noonday sun brought out a startling demonstration with the gigantic magnifying glass (12).

"Melquíades...
"Each time Melquíades was becoming more distant, fading away in the radiant light of noon (329).

"No tuvo...
See the first entry for page 35.

116. "permaneció...
he spent entire nights in the courtyard watching the course of the stars and he almost contracted sunstroke from trying to establish an exact method to ascertain noon (13).

"emancipado...
Emancipated for a moment at least from the torment of fantasy, José Arcadio Buendía in a short time set up a system of order and work which allowed for only one bit of license: the freeing of the birds, which, since the time of the founding, had made time merry with their flutes, and installing in their place musical clocks in every house. They were wondrous clocks made of carved wood, which the Arabs had traded for macaws and which José Arcadio Buendía had synchronized with such precision that every half hour the town grew merry with the progressive chords of the same song until it reached a climax of a noontime that was as exact and unanimous as a complete waltz (45).

117. "Melquíades...
Melquíades talked to him about the world, tried to infuse him with his ancient wisdom, but he refused to translate the mansucripts. "No one must know their meaning until they have reached one hundred years of age," he explained. (177)
[I have not followed Rabassa *verbatim* here, as there is one obvious mistranslation: where he translates *hayan cumplido* as "he has" I have rendered it "they have".

Hayan is plural and must refer to the manuscripts; it cannot possibly refer to "No one."]

"Melquíades le reveló...
Melquíades revealed to him that his opportunities to return to the room were limited. But he would go in peace to the meadows of the ultimate death because Aureliano would have time to learn Sanskrit during the years remaining until the parchments became one hundred years old, when they could be deciphered (329).

118. "Era...
It was Pilar Ternera. Years before, when she had reached one hundred forty-five years of age, she had given up the pernicious custom of keeping track of her age (363).

119. "En el cuarto...
In Melquíades' room...protected by the supernatural light...by the feeling of being invisible, he found the repose that he had not had for one single instant during his previous life.... Free from all fear, José Arcadio Segundo dedicated himself then to peruse the manuscripts of Melquíades many times, and with so much more pleasure when he could not understand them (289f).

"se dedicó...
he dedicated himself then to peruse the mansucripts of Melquíades many times, and with so much more pleasure when he could not understand them (289)

"El habitante más lúcido de la casa" — the most lucid inhabitant of the house.

"iluminado por un resplandor seráfico" — illuminated by a seraphic glow.

120. "con los...
with the same eyes as Colonel Aureliano Buendía (289):
"It's obvious that no one has been in that room for at least one hundred years," the officer said to the soldiers. "There must even be snakes in there" (289).

"Al cerrarse...
This quotation starts on page 289 of Rabassa's translation, at the beginning of the last paragraph of the page (with the phrase "When the door closed"), and continues to the fourth line of page 290, ending with the words "during his previous life."

121. "lo que...
what one feels in war...: in fear. In Melquíades room, *on the other hand* (289f.).

"Estaba...
She was seeing Colonel Aureliano Buendía once more as she had seen him in the light of a lamp long before the wars, long before the desolation of glory and the exile of disillusionment (363).

"El cuarto de las bacinillas" — the chamber pot room

123. "Pero se iba...
See first entry for page 19.

"El otro lado de las cosas" — the other side of things

"Las cosas...
Things have a life of their own...It's simply a matter of waking up their souls (11).

"se asemejaban...
looked more like musical notation than writing (176)

124. "Aureliano...
Aureliano made progress in his studies of Sanskrit as Melquíades' visits became less and less frequent and he was more distant, fading away in the radiant light of noon (329).

125. "estaba previsto...
See the fifth entry for page 55.

"José Arcadio Buendía...
This quotation corresponds to two excerpts, which can be found on pages 54-55 in Rabassa's translation. The first passage begins on line 6, page 54, with the words "José Arcadio Buendía then decided," and goes to the end of the paragraph, closing with the phrase "to the house of José Arcadio Buendía." The second excerpt

begins on the third line from the bottom on page 54, with the words "He opened the suitcase," and concludes at the end of the paragraph, on page 55, with the sentence: "It was Melquíades."

126. "una realidad...
a reality that was slipping away, momentarily captured by words, but which would escape irremediably when they forgot the values of the written letters (53).

"Se sintió...
He felt himself forgotten, not with the remediable forgetfulness of the heart, but with a different kind of forgetfulness, which was more cruel and irrevocable and which he knew very well because it was the forgetfulness of death (54). [Here I follow Rabassa's translation *verbatim*, except for rendering the Spanish word *remediable* as "remediable". The English "*irremediable*", given in the Avon translation, is a mistake.]

"Fue de casa...
He went from house to house dragging two metal ingots and everybody was amazed to see pots, pans, tongs, and braziers tumble down from their places and beams creak from the desperation of nails and screws trying to emerge, and even objects that had been lost for a long time appeared from where they had been searched for most and went dragging along in turbulent confusion behind Melquíades' magical irons. "Things have a life of their own," the gypsy proclaimed with a harsh accent. "It's simply a matter of waking up their souls" (11).

127. "donde más se les había buscado" — from where they had been searched for most (11)

"recuerdo hereditario" — hereditary memory

128. "Melquíades...
The two excerpts which comprise this quotation can be found on page 329 in Rabassa's translation. The first one begins at the top of the page ("Melquíades revealed to him..."), and continues for twelve lines to the phrase "if he did not hurry to buy it." The second

passage corresponds to paragraph two on page 329 (from "Aureliano" to "sawdust").

"establecer...
establish an exact method to ascertain noon (13)

129. "la luz se hizo en su memoria" — the light went on inside his memory.

"un deslumbrante resplandor de alegría—a dazzling glow of joy (55)

"el resplandor deslumbrante de mediodía— a dazzling splendor of hign noon (381)

"olvidó...
forgot about his dead ones and the pain of his dead ones (381)

"desterrada...
exiled from man's memory in the instant Aureliano Babilonia would finish deciphering the mansucripts (383)

130. "aun...
even the awareness of one's own being, until one sank into a kind of idiocy that had no past.

"sabía que...
he knew that his fate was written in Melquíades' parchments. He found them intact among the prehistoric plants and steaming puddles and luminous insects that had removed all trace of man's passage on earth from the room (381).

131. "en aquel...
at that prodigious instant Melquíades' final keys revealed themselves to him.

"estaba...
was illuminated by a seraphic glow (290).

"no tuvo...
didn't have the patience to bring them out into the light

132. "sus muertos...
his dead ones and the pain of his dead ones (381)

"La protección...
The final protection, which Aureliano had begun to glimpse when he let himself be confused by the love of Amaranta Úrsula, was based on the fact that Melquíades had not put events in the order of man's conventional time, but had concentrated a century of daily episodes in such a way that they coexisted in one instant (382).

133. "todas las hormigas del mundo" — all the ants in the world (381)

"Aureliano...
Aureliano could not move. Not because he was paralyzed by horror but because at that prodigious instant Melquíades' final keys were revealed to him and he saw the epigraph of the parchments perfectly placed in the order of man's time and space (381).

"Sólo entonces...
See second entry for page 59.

135. "entre...
among the *prehistoric* plants and steaming puddles and luminous insects *that had removed all trace of man's passage on earth from the room* (381).

"huevos prehistóricos" — prehistoric eggs (11)

140. "la novela ideal...
the ideal novel...a novel...capable of turning reality over to show what it's like on the other side.

141. "Aureliano...
Aureliano did not leave Melquíades' room for a long time. He learned by heart the fantastic legends of the crumbling books, the synthesis of the studies of Hermann the Cripple, the notes of the science of demonology, the keys to the philosopher's stone, the *Centuries* of Nostradamus and his research concerning the plague, so that he reached adolescence without knowing a thing about his own time but with the basic knowledge of a medieval man (328).

142. "para siempre" — forever

143. "ciudad...
city of mirrors (or mirages) (383)

145. note 7: "escritura musical" — musical notation

note 7: "Cuando...
When he became an expert in the use and manipulation of his instruments, he conceived a notion of space that allowed him to navigate across unknown seas, to visit uninhabited territories, and to establish relations with splendid beings without having to leave his study. That was the period in which he acquired the habit of talking to himself, of walking through the house without paying attention to anyone.... Suddenly, without warning, his feverish activity was interrupted and was replaced by a kind of fascination. He spent several days as if he were bewitched, softly repeating to himself a string of fearful conjectures without giving credit to his own understanding. Finally, one Tuesday in December, at lunchtime, all at once he released the whole weight of his torment. The children would remember for the rest of their lives the august solemnity with which their father, devastated by his prolonged vigil and by the wrath of his imagination, revealed his discovery to them:
"The earth is round, like an orange." (14)

Conclusion

150. "más allá de cualquier formalismo" — beyond any formalism

152. "aun los...
even objects that had been lost for a long time (11)

"por donde...
from where they had been searched for most (11).

153. note 2: "tarde o temprano...
sooner or later, reality ends up agreeing with the imagination, falling in line with it.